Essays on Biblical Counseling
Volume 3

THE LANGUAGE OF COUNSELING

AND OTHER ESSAYS

Jay E. Adams

Institute for Nouthetic Studies, a ministry of Mid-America Baptist Theological Seminary, 2095 Appling Road, Cordova, TN 38016 mabts.edu and nouthetic.org

Essays on Biblical Counseling, Volume 3: The Language of Counseling by Jay E. Adams
Copyright © 2025 by the Institute for Nouthetic Studies,
© 1975, 1981 Jay E. Adams

New Testament quotations are from the Christian Counselor's New Testament and Proverbs Copyright © 2019 by the Institute for Nouthetic Studies. © 1977, 1980, 1994, 2000 by Jay E. Adams

ISBN: 978-1-949737-76-9 (Print)
ISBN: 978-1-949737-77-6 (eBook)

Editor: Donn R. Arms
Design: James Wendorf | www.FaithfulLifePublishers.com

Library of Congress Cataloging-in-Publication Data
Names: Adams, Jay E., 1929 - 2020
Title: Essays on Biblical Counseling, Volume 3: The Language of Counseling
Jay E. Adams
Description: Cordova: Institute for Nouthetic Studies, 2025
Identifiers: ISBN 9781949737769 (paper)
Classification: LCC BV4012.2 .A33 | DDC 253.5

All rights reserved. No part of this publication may be reproduced, stored in a retrieval system, or transmitted in any form or by any means – electronic, mechanical, photocopy, recording, or any other – except for brief quotations in printed reviews, without prior permission of the publisher.

Published in the United States of America

Table of Contents

Foreword

The Language of Counseling	1
Your Place in the Counseling Revolution	65
The Student Pastor/Counselor Today	103
Nouthetic Counseling	117
Reflections on the History of Biblical Counseling	129
The Physician, The Pastor, Psychotherapy, and Counseling	145
Response to the Congress on Christian Counseling	161
Change Them, into What?	165
The Christian Approach to Schizophrenia	177
Biblical Interpretation and Counseling	191
Discipling, Counseling, and Church Discipline	219

Foreword

It is a joy to make more of Dr. Adams' work available in this third collection of books and essays. Included in this volume are two short books originally published in 1981 and 1975, as well as essays he contributed to books compiled by others. These two books are an especially important addition to the catalog of Dr. Adams' books that are now back in print.

The Language of Counseling has been one of our most requested books to reprint and we are thankful to finally make it available. Students of biblical counseling will be challenged to study how they communicate in the counseling room and to use language more thoughtfully.

Your Place in the Counseling Revolution is a bold invitation for others to join him in changing the counseling landscape in the church of Jesus Christ.

Look over the Table of Contents and you will find a wide range of helpful essays from Dr. Adams' pen that will challenge you to grow in your counseling ministry and encourage you in the important work you have committed yourself to.

It is my prayer that God will continue to use Jay Adams to bless you, even after his faith has been made sight, and that this volume will be the source of God's blessing in your life and ministry.

Donn R. Arms, Editor

The Language of Counseling

Preface[1]

This is a small book, but I'm convinced it is a vital one. There is nothing else like it in the field of counseling. Is that because few people are eager to read something on this subject? I won't deny that just yet. But assuming, for a moment, that few care enough to study the role of language in counseling, *that in itself* would offer plenty of reason to write a book like this. If there is a lack of interest in this topic, then by all means, interest needs to be stimulated, just as it was necessary to rouse concern over the neglected task of biblical counseling not long ago.

I suspect, though, that there is more ground-level interest in this topic than some people think. When the substance of this book was presented in a course at the Christian Counseling and Educational Foundation's Institution of Pastoral Studies during the spring of 1980, the response was deep interest and appreciation.

Was that audience peculiar? I doubt it. More likely, they typify a hunger for something that is not readily available in counseling literature. While secular (and much so-called "Christian") counseling has engrossed itself in so much sociological and pseudo-scientific verbiage void of substance or truth, Christians (who, of all people, possess the truth) have not been attentive to the full potential of language in counseling.

Even void of truth, language has power. And therein lies its potential for good or ill. Freud is a case in point. He gained his reputation *not* as a competent scientist. In fact, he couldn't be called a scientist by today's standards. But he was able to win a large following because of his persuasive use of *language*.

Unlike Freud, Christian counselors have every reason to make themselves clear. As people of The Book, their appreciation for language is

---

[1] This essay was first published as a short stand-alone book in 1981.

inseparable from their understanding of Scripture and their ability to communicate its message. That means knowing how language functions—in the Old and New Testaments, and in counseling today. *Christian* counseling depends on a *Christian* use of language. We must not neglect this great gift and responsibility from God.

I fully expect, therefore, those who wish to be as biblical as possible in their counseling to catch the vision I try to impart here. It is my prayer that this book will encourage many to enter this study with joy and that in their ministries they will be able to use what they learn to the honor of God and the blessing of their counselees.

Jay E. Adams
The Millhouse
Juliette, Georgia, 1981

Introduction

I have been concerned about language for a long time. Every writer must make a careful study of language; after all, it is his stock in trade. But I have also been interested in language as a language major in college, as a preacher, as a teacher of speech and of homiletics, as a translator, as a counselor, as an editor, and as a teacher of counseling. Indeed, one of the major unifying themes in my rather zigzag career has been the central place language holds in all the activities in which I have been involved.

My concern for a serious consideration of the language of counseling has grown over the years as I have been reading and editing materials in the field, as I have been involved in counseling, as I have observed counseling, and as I have taught it. Again and again, these endeavors have pointed up the fact that many problems, especially complicating problems, stem from faulty language usage and the fact that, so far as I can see, no Christian is adequately addressing himself to the language question. The prejudicial language of psychotherapeutic labeling is perhaps the most glaring example of language abuse that we must consider. And yet there are others, not quite so apparent, that, by reason of their subtlety, are all the more dangerous.

Among biblical counselors, ineffectiveness resulting from a failure to weigh, develop, and employ proper terminology has had its disastrous effects on counseling. And there has been much confusion in the Christian church because of language manipulation and inaccuracy in counseling. All in all, a more needy area for thought and discussion could hardly be imagined.

But there is another important reason for my concern to elevate language interest among Christian counselors. If any group of counselors should consider language significant, one would think Christians would be that group. You'd expect to see them in the forefront of every discussion of language, constantly monitoring what is happening, pioneering in the field, ready to discuss language matters on the slightest pretext, contributing much, setting the pace for others, since—as the Koran calls them—they are "the people of the Book." That is the way it used to be among Christians two or three generations ago—language was of vital concern to them in every endeavor in which it was used. But all that has changed. Because of the "mania" among self-styled Christian "professionals" to be thought scholarly and respectable by their counterparts in the world, they have followed the trends of the times, which, interestingly enough, manifest a shift away from many of the truly scholarly pursuits of past generations to pseudo-scientific studies and to the theories of those bent on glorifying human experience. Consequently, language study among Christian counselors is nearly extinct.

The Importance of Language

From the beginning of history, language has been a prominent and crucial part of human life; indeed, one may say that true, propositional language distinguishes human life from purely animal life. It was by His Word to Adam and Eve in the garden that God established an intelligent, moral relationship with them. The central place of God's words of command, of explanation, of promise and warning, and of fellowship may be noted in that pre-fall relationship. It was language that bound God and man together. Language enabled Adam to interpret the universe, and it was by language that God expressed His will. Language, more than any other factor, is *conspicuous* in the paradise account. Without language, there could have been no moral responsibility, no obedience, no worship, no test of fidelity, no promise or acceptance of salvation. Language was an absolutely indispensable element in the makeup of the man whom God created. It is not going too far to say that without language, man could not exist.

But precisely because of this central place of language in the divine/human relationship, it was *at that very point* that Satan insidiously chose to make his first inroads into the human race. For the first time in human history, language—the great gift of God to man—was used to deceive by distorting and denying God's Word. Prior to that, language conveyed true information and brought nothing but blessing to man. But with Satan's first question, language took on a new and sinister dimension. That question ("Has God said …?") represented a challenge to the factuality and truth of God's statements. Significantly, questioning was shortly followed by history's first words of denial.

The successful Satanic approach in the garden was not physical; it constituted a verbal attack on God and on the human race. The issue was strictly ideological. But, again, ideological communication depends wholly on language. Adam's allegiance to God had been cemented by language, and it had to be undermined by language. In the Scriptures, Satan is called the "deceiver" (Rev. 12:9) and the "father of lies" (John 8:44). In Hebrew terminology, the word "father" in such contexts means "originator." Thus the lie, and entirely new and different use of human language, had its beginning. Since then, in his most successful efforts, in every avenue of life, the devil has continued to use questioning, misrepresentation, and denial of the truth. Preeminently, he is a destroyer and manipulator of language. Because he is after men's minds, he uses language as his tool to captivate and ensnare. Ideological attack, rather than physical attack, has been Satan's most successful ploy. As Tertullian said, "the blood of the martyrs is the seed of the church." We might paraphrase Tertullian and say that the belief of the unwary has been the destruction of the church. Like Adam, the church has fallen into Satan's traps whenever she has listened to and believed his seductive words.

It is important, then, for us to become well acquainted with the fact that Satan's supreme strategy is a language tactic that employs questioning, distortion, and denial. Paul speaks of the importance of understanding the devil's wiles. In the study on which we have set sail, we shall encounter that strategy at work in every port. While we shall not be able to exhaustively unmask the many ways in which this strategy has been used to dupe unwary Christians, we shall discover quite enough instances to expose both its prevalence and its basic patterns.

Although I shall not always be able to identify it for you as such, you should keep in mind at all times that behind the scenes a battle is being fought for men's minds. It is a battle that uses language and ideas as the principal weapons.

But, for a moment, let us consider Genesis 3 once more. Careful examination of the language of the Genesis account (Gen. 3:1-7) reveals that Satan used words that were similar to God's words when he began to tempt Eve. But he took from, added to, and twisted what God had said. That is one reason for the stern warnings found in Deuteronomy 4:2 and in Revelation 22:18, 19. God gave Adam permission to eat from every tree of the garden, with the exception of the tree of the knowledge of good and evil. Satan asked whether God had forbidden the same. Eve was sharper than some modern-day eclectics who have much greater difficulty in distinguishing what God has said from error and untruth. She readily recognized the discontinuity between the two statements. But she fell into the error of adding to God's words when she appended the statement, "neither shall you touch it." God had said no such thing. Eve's claim that He had was the first sign of her defection from the truth: she was being led into something other than a *strict adherence* to God's word. God had given Adam and her all that was necessary; but Eve seems to have thought it wise to add to what He had said.

Whenever we think we must add to God's words, we show that we doubt their sufficiency and efficacy as they stand. And then, we are open to questioning the truth of what He *has* said. Eve's greatest error was in allowing Satan to question God's Word in the first place without reproving him for his sin. Because she failed to resist the devil with language, she too began to distort truth through language. Similarly today, some Christians delight in "dialog" with those who express doubts about, or who deny the truth and sufficiency of the Scriptures. This is done, of course, in the hallowed name of "scholarship" (which is the Christian's sacred cow in modern times). But that language dodge should make the activity no more respectable than when Eve engaged in dialogue with the devil about the same subject. People who willingly deny and distort God's Word do not need dialogue; they need to be rebuked and convicted of their sin. The carefully chosen words "scholarship" and "dialogue" must not be allowed to cover the facts; when we get involved in allowing someone to question God's Word, we are doing nothing more or less than what Eve was doing. Notice, if you will, that the cover for such activities (once again) is a language cover. Interestingly, but sadly, those who become seriously involved with such scoffers (the biblical word exposing them for what they are) in the end usually find themselves adding to the Bible.

When tempting Christ (Matt. 4), Satan did not misquote God's Word: he had to be even more subtle. He simply quoted the Scriptures out of context and misapplied them. Instances of both contextual misquotation and misapplication of Old Testament passages abound in the sayings of the Jewish elders. It is about these that Christ straightened us out in the Sermon on the Mount. Both problems are found in profusion also in the circles of eclectic Christians who speak and write about counseling.

Those eclectic counselors who spot language similarities between the Scriptures and the counsel of the ungodly (again, notice how scriptural language tells it like it is) are quick to make easy (but erroneous) identifications between the two. Thus, many of the unwary and uninformed are taken in, not knowing that much of what passes for Christian is not Christian at all. How vital then, is language study and language awareness to Christian counselors! How necessary for both pastors and Christian workers to make the ordinary members of the church aware of the language problems connected to counseling.

Language is *the* fundamental tool of counseling; it is used by both counselor and counselee in every phase of counseling. That is why no conscientious counselor may avoid the study of language. He recognizes that *nouthesia* is *verbal* confrontation. He wants to guard against error and ineffectiveness. He realizes that if he fails to give proper attention to language, as a preacher or counselor, he exposes himself and those to whom he ministers to grave peril.

In Proverbs 15:14, the healing properties of language (*marpe* in the Hebrew text and *iasis* in the Septuagint, roughly equivalent to our word "therapy") are contrasted with its post-fall destructive possibilities. Here the destructive language of the smooth talker, who can "put it over on you" by means of his language, is in view. Since the corruption of language and language usage by Satan and by fallen human beings, its potential for good has been accompanied and rivaled by a potential for doing evil. According to this verse, the healing tongue revives the listener; the smooth tongue of the one who uses language for his own sinful purposes "breaks" or, as the word frequently means, "disables" him. The tongue of the counselor likewise either helps or hurts those to whom he speaks in counseling. What one says, and how he says it (i.e., form and content—cf Proverbs 15:1) are important.

Language usage is never neutral: Proverbs 15:14 knows nothing of a third alternative; language is true or false, it helps or hurts. Therefore, it is the task of every biblical counselor to concern himself with language so that he knows what he is doing when he speaks to his counselees; otherwise, unwittingly, he may hurt when he wants to help.

A counselor must concern himself with both the selection of language tools that he makes and the way in which he uses them in his work. Yet, many biblical counselors, not to mention eclectics, are far less concerned with the tools of their trade than a plumber or automobile mechanic. That is the sad commentary on a dangerous situation. You will not be able to plead ignorance of the matter when you stand before God some day and give an account of your ministry. You may not dismiss the whole question by saying the study and the use of language were of no special interest to you (as if language could be a specialty for some limited number of counselors only!). Indeed, you will be able to plead your case on such grounds only when mechanics no longer take an interest in screwdrivers and wrenches. Language is so basic to the counseling enterprise that it *must* be the concern of all biblical counselors.

But the Christian counselor's concern for language extends not only to its misuse; he is interested in how to use language effectively to bless counselees. It is true that language has been manipulated smoothly to deceive many counselees (and their counselors), but by giving His Word to man in propositional form in the Bible, God Himself demonstrated the powerful impact for good that language can have. Because the Christian counselor is deeply committed to the study and use of the Scriptures, it is inevitable that he should develop an insatiable interest in language. The slight interest that is currently evidenced among Christians who are doing counseling, therefore, is indicative of the dearth of genuinely *biblical* counseling that is actually going on.

But language, as I have pointed out, is the basic tool by which a counselor confronts others and ministers the Word to them. Moreover, the counselee thinks in language, expresses his problems in language, interprets his difficulties in language, and often justifies and makes excuses for himself in language. All of the ill effects of Satan's distortion of language become apparent to a counselor who is aware of the language problem. He encounters deceit, self-deceit, anger, lying, sarcasm, stinging criticism, whining, and a host of other evils regularly in his counseling ministry, and they are all expressed and propagated by language.[2]

Can there be any wonder then, that Paul represents the field of language as the very battleground on which spiritual war is waged against the enemy? Because our warfare is not physical, but ideological, it is a struggle that is carried on in words and thoughts that are a part of our language. This clash of ideologies is vividly portrayed by Paul when he writes:

> *Of course we do walk in the flesh, but we certainly don't fight according to the flesh. The weapons that we use to fight aren't fleshly; rather, they are divinely powerful to tear down strongholds. By them we tear down arguments and every high barrier that is raised against the knowledge of God, and take every thought captive and bring it into obedience to Christ, being prepared also to deal justly with every act of disobedience, after your submission is complete* (2 Cor. 10:3-6).

The divinely powerful weapons that Paul used were *arguments* based on the Scriptures. We see him *reasoning* daily in the synagogues and in the marketplaces of various Mediterranean cities (e.g., Acts 17:7). His message was *verbal*; it was based on the Old Testament *writings*. His arguments, marshaled from the inspired prophecies and teachings of these books, were also *verbal*. Writings, arguments, reasonings, etc.—all of these activities are language-related. The preaching of the gospel and the teaching of the believing bodies of the saints that were formed into congregations were done in language. It is with the sword of His *mouth*

---

2   Often, he will have to point out to counselees how they are using language and what its effects are on others. He may even have to say, "I may not permit you to talk like that here; please stop."

that Jesus Christ rides forth to battle in Revelation 19:15. Christian warfare involves language.

Language! What would the church have done without it? She began her outward expansion on the day of Pentecost in a verbal explosion, as an effusion of languages enabled her to proclaim the gospel to persons from all sorts of backgrounds. The very curse of Babel was reversed at Pentecost! Instead of confounding languages, at Pentecost God enabled His people to declare the good news in *all* tongues so that men who had been dispersed abroad on the face of the whole earth might instead be joined together in one great empire under God consisting of believers from every nation and tribe and people and *tongue* (i.e., language; cf. Rev. 7:9). Language! Can you think of *anything* more central to the work of the Christian church?

It is for these reasons, as well as for others that will appear before we are finished, that I have *begun* to consider language in relationship to counseling in general and to Christian counseling in particular. Notice, I make no greater claim for what I am about to do. The work here is preliminary. I am concerned about raising the issue during a period in which almost no one else seems willing to do so.

It will take many others, perhaps picking up on what I have begun here, to enter into the task with the sort of fullness it deserves. I hope, however, that I can point the way in this book. An in-depth study on every aspect of the question of language in counseling is needed. But it will never be done until others become concerned about it. Therefore, it is also my desire to challenge others to get involved in this altogether vital task.

For now, however, let us be content to survey the problem in a suggestive, but admittedly incomplete, way. To do more in this context is impossible. When you have read this book, doubtless you will be aware of the fact that the task has not yet been completed, but if you also have been convinced of the great importance of the subject and of the need for every Christian counselor to pursue his personal study of language, then the purpose of the present volume will in large measure be fulfilled. I say "in large measure" because there is more to this book. I have included a personal improvement program, made many specific suggestions, and have alerted the reader to a number of concrete problems.

Chapter 1
The Origin and Function of Language

As we have seen, language is not of human origin. Prior to the creation of man, God spoke. We see this, for instance, when we read the words, "Let there be light!" Both the power and the source of all language are exhibited in those remarkable words. Language, then, is not merely the creation of God; it is also an attribute of God.

Jesus Christ told us that there is some sort of language communication between the persons of the Trinity (John 8:38; 3:32). And of course, God constantly spoke to man verbally and deposited His revelation with us in the form of written books. God's living revelation to us He called the Word (John 1:1ff.) because, like a word, Jesus Christ revealed to us what we could not know otherwise.

When we rightly concern ourselves with language, therefore, we involve ourselves in a high and holy task. Created in God's image, man is the only creature that reflects this important divine activity. Teachers of freshman English classes in Christian colleges would do well to consider this fact and take the time to introduce their students to it in full rather than laboring over the artificial and inaccurate "rules" of grammar (actually, Latin grammar ineptly applied to the English language despite the fact that the two do not fit) that in so many places are still the rage. So far as I am able to discover, no one has yet given us a genuinely *English* grammar—i.e., one that describes what we actually do when we speak English. But enough of that; back to the origin of language.

We know that Adam was *created* with the capacity both to speak and to understand speech. But the question arises, did he come prepackaged with a vocabulary and a system of syntax—in short, with language? Or did he *develop* a language out of his capacity for language?

Of course, we can't be sure of everything, but there are very strong indications that from the beginning, Adam had a full-blown, though rudimentary, language. We do not read anything about God teaching Adam how to speak or about Adam teaching Eve. Yet their ability to communicate with God and the serpent, as well as with one another, is most clearly set forth. Indeed, that ability is assumed. There is no gradual, step-by-step process of gaining language capability or even language proficiency.

To believe that Adam was prepackaged with a language is in accord with the other facts of creation. For instance, it is clear that Adam and Eve were created *adults*. Just as trees were created trees, not seeds, so too Adam and Eve were the first adults; they were never babies, children, or adolescents. The biblical record of creation solves the old problem: the chicken came before the egg.

So too, Adam, at creation, also possessed a basic language that had structure and vocabulary. Doubtless, this vocabulary was limited and, in time, was to be enriched and amplified as he would explore and subdue the earth. New structures would also be developed to express new discoveries, insights, experiences, shades of meaning, etc. But Adam's language was plainly a working language, though it was not complete. (No language is yet complete!) We know that his language would grow because Adam had not yet named the animals, though he knew the word for animal and probably had to determine names for specific plants and much else. But there can be no question at all that man spoke and understood language from the beginning, because language was used in communicating with God and in naming the animals.

Moreover, for Adam and Eve, language meant the ability to think uniquely. They could reason, worship, remember propositions, promises, and warnings, and in general bear a moral relationship to God. They could receive, interpret, and discuss God's word, as well as classify the particulars in the creation, and (doubtless) they could do many other things because they were language-capable. What a priceless treasure language was!

In all of this, man reflected God and demonstrated the great advantages that language gave him over the animals. Yet, while retaining all of these advantages to some extent, Adam's sin ruined the image of God. And with that, sin cast its ugly blight upon all of man's functions, including language. Nothing in his experience and make-up escaped; he became totally depraved so that every part of his life was adversely affected by sin.

It is useless to speculate about the wonderful possibilities man lost in the fall, and about the possibilities language would have afforded a perfect, sinless race. In this life, there is no way to know all that was forfeited. But we may await even greater opportunities in the redeemed, glorified state into which every true believer will enter at death. Only then will we begin to see the enormous potential of perfect persons using a perfect language in perfect ways to achieve perfect results. When we read of the "tongues of angels," we are reminded of these possibilities; but the language potential of man, once he has been redeemed in Christ, Who is seated at the right hand of the Father in the heavens, is even greater.

We have seen how the devil distorted and misused the great gift of language and how sinful man has followed him in doing so. Here are a few of the sad results of this apostasy of which we should be aware:

1. Man's ability to use language properly to think, reason, worship, and communicate has been seriously impaired.
2. Communication with God was cut off, and accurate, helpful communication with other human beings has been greatly diminished.
3. The creation has been categorized, interpreted, and classified in improper and inaccurate ways. Language constructions, terms, phrases, etc., have been formed to excuse man's sin, to keep him from God, and to explain away his miserable state as an unredeemed sinner.
4. Language has been perverted to mislead, to propagate and defend sinful concepts, attitudes, and actions, and to further error.
5. There is an inability to understand the right meaning and application of God's Word (apart from the illumination of the Holy Spirit), while on the other hand, there is a sinful, inborn tendency to see all of life Satan's way. Language plays a significant role in this phenomenon.

All of these facts are of the utmost importance to Christian counselors. The particular problems of counselees are often the direct result of defects in language usage. Not only must the counselor use language to locate and correct sinful patterns, but there is the added difficulty of having to rely largely on the language of the counselee (affected as it is by sin) to discover what his problems are. Clearly, counselors have a large investment in language, and unless they study it and understand it thoroughly, they will constantly be tripped up by language difficulties in both the analysis of and the solution to problems.

Leonard Bloomfield wrote, "… psychologists generally treat language as a side issue" (in Mowrer, "A Psychologist Looks at Language"). Though more concern has been evidenced since those words were written, they are, doubtless, still an accurate description of the situation today. Others may consider language a side issue, but Christian counselors must not. It is at the very core of all they do. In order to understand this better, let's try to discover some of the functions of language.

Language Functions

What does language do for us? Why did God share this amazing attribute of His when He created us in His image?

First, language unifies or separates.

The word *communication* and the words *communion* and *community* all have a common root. Language was given to allow the communion of persons to occur on a deep level that involves sharing, participating in, and directly influencing another's thinking. Such sharing binds and unites in ways that the mere presence of persons does not. Jesus' description of a friend (John 15:14,15) is instructive in this regard. Two elements are involved in friendship:

1. Obedience to commands (action growing out of God's verbal, written communication to us, v. 14).
2. Willingness to share with another what one is doing (sharing one's thinking through language, v. 15).

It would be instructive for someone to analyze thoroughly and develop fully an essay, or even a book, on the concept of friendship presented here by Christ.

But back to the main point: language was designed to *bind*; it bound man to God, Adam to Eve. The animals provided no counterpart to Adam; they were unlike him in many ways, but especially in terms of the means of communication. He simply could not communicate with them by language, the vehicle of thought that sets man apart from the rest of the creation in this world. As Genesis 2:18, 20 points out, that is why Adam was lonely before the creation of Eve. When God made Eve, Adam called her bone of his bone and flesh of his flesh, i.e., *someone exactly like him*.

But there was a risk in language; man could also become bound to another creature that had language capability. And he did. Listening to the false, damning counsel of Satan, he united himself to the father of lies. Along with that bond came sin, misery, death, and all the evils of the curse.

The very purpose of language was perverted. It was designed to bind, but in cementing this forbidden bond, man discovered that language also could separate. It separated man from God, and human being from human being. The separation of man from God was total; the separation of man from man was partial. Though language remained the principal means of intellectual communication between human beings, communication became faulty. Individuals misunderstood and misled one another as language began to be used for all sorts of wrong purposes. Man discovered ways of using language to exalt himself rather than God. Through this cooperation in evil, the human race began to build a tower to heaven, substituted false gods for the true Creator and, as the result, brought upon itself yet another devastating judgment that was aimed at the very uniting power of language.

God was infuriated by man's proud attempt to usurp His power and position. So He struck mankind at the point of cohesion: He confounded our language! Ever since, the unity of the human race has been an impossibility. A common language binds together while (as we have discovered to our continuing sorrow) distinct languages divide. Indeed, many of the misunderstandings among the races of mankind, including wars, can be traced, at least in part, to language differences.

Today, even among those who have a common language, it is easy to see how language makes or breaks relationships. We read of people wanting to propagate "black English," while others, seeing that this will

further divide, fight any such attempt to set it apart as a distinct, recognized language of its own. But, even within the same dialects, where there is no confounding of the understanding, it is still principally by language that persons are united or divided. Listen to the following two exchanges:
1. "Hi!" "Hi!"
2. "Hi!" "Get lost!"

We must conclude that the biblical evidence clearly describes the origin of what we all experience day by day—language binds or, in this world of sin, separates. That is one of its principal functions.

A **second** function of language is to share information. Slamming a door in another's face says something to him, but it also leaves a lot unsaid that only language can communicate: *why* the person reacted that way is never made clear in the act itself. It takes language to share that kind of information.

Moreover, man is not only a social creature but a moral-reasoning creature as well. His relationships with God and his neighbors involve intellectual and responsible elements, regardless of what Skinnerians and the existentialists may say. He cannot, indeed, does not want to, avoid these elements in his relationships with others. Man's nature demands language; language is not simply a tool that man originated and developed later on in history. No, from the outset, his nature cried out for the kinds of relationships that could be brought about and maintained by nothing less than language.

Language was a valuable, moral force that enabled man to become a moral creature. There is no morality among the creatures that do not have a propositional language; similarly, man could not have sustained moral relationships without language. This relationship depended upon shared information: commands, covenantal relationships, etc.—all of which are language-dependent activities. But, because this is so, as I said, human language capacity made man potentially able to relate to Satan on an immoral basis. He too, is a language-capable being who sustains responsible, moral relationships. The fact is that, without language, man could not have sinned! But neither could he have been saved. Language, then, is a powerful force for good or evil because language makes it possible to share information, whether true or false.

A **third** function of language is to talk to oneself, or as that implies, to think, reason, plan, meditate, and decide inwardly. Psalm 14:1 makes it clear that the atheist is a fool, because without evidence, he has allowed no greater authority than himself to talk himself into disbelief: "The fool has said in his heart,[3] 'there is no God.'" Look who he is listening to—a fool!

Not only are good plans and resolutions devised and determined in the heart by talking them over with oneself, but sinners concoct every sort of evil and self-deception in the same way. When we speak audibly, the process is still at work: we may not be able to convince others, but we are very likely to believe what we say ourselves. We are very susceptible to our own arguments, especially when articulated. The repetition of what Margaret Meade once called "pickled cliches" is an element for which every counselor searches diligently in the speech of his counselees. This is a good example of self-persuasion. We tend to believe what we have heard others say often, but especially what we have heard ourselves frequently repeat. Examples of this are the old saws, "You'll never teach an old dog new tricks" and "You'll never understand a woman." The counselor looks for statements like these because he knows that when a counselee says them often enough, he soon believes them and lives by them. More often than not, as in the two cases cited above, these cliches are quite contrary to biblical fact.

Moreover, the counselor looks for inaccurate and biased words and language constructions that, when repeatedly spoken by him, may influence the counselee's thinking and behavior. Some counselees live by these maxims. If he keeps hearing the counselee speak of his "need" to do this and his "need" for that (a somewhat newer excuse that is spreading rapidly because of its inherently self-justifying character), the counselor will soon find it necessary to explain to him that what he persists in calling a "need," God actually calls a "desire," or, sometimes, "lust."[4]

But now, on the brighter side of things, in the Bible, God shows us how to use self-talk productively when He commands us to meditate.

---

[3] On the heart as the inner life that one lives before God and himself, see my book, *More than Redemption*.

[4] For more on this idea of needs, see "Who Needs It?," an article in my book, *Matters of Concern to Christian Counselors*.

This human capacity for self-talk, like every other God-given capacity, has a positive use. Meditation is one good example of such a positive use. In my book, *Ready to Restore*, I have said this about meditation:

> If meditation is useful for [counselees or Christians in general], then the pastor ought to take the time to explain
> 1. What meditation is:
> 2. How it relates to the problem (depression or whatever);
> 3. *How* to meditate (in detail).

Since this is rarely done, it might be important to sketch an idea or two on the subject. Moreover, meditation itself, as we shall see, is intimately connected with the "how to" about which I have been speaking.

To begin with, he would want to distinguish biblical meditation from T.M. (transcendental meditation) and other similar forms of meditation practiced today. These focus one's attention on himself. The Christian, in contrast, meditates on biblical truth. He focuses his attention on Christ and His teaching. Christian meditation is not a trance; it is thought—deep thought—about truth, its implications, and its implementation. Christian meditation involves rational thinking about content.

The two principal words for *meditation* in the Bible mean "to murmur or mutter" and "to speak to oneself." Meditation is a process of thinking (not feeling) through language that takes place in the heart (or inner life). In meditation, a Christian discusses various biblical facts with himself *in an intensive way*. The italicized words at the end of the previous sentence are significant. Sometimes we talk things over with ourselves and quickly come to a decision. That isn't meditation. Meditation is careful, detailed thought that gives the fullest possible consideration to what one is thinking about. And, as I have noted, this all goes on in the heart (Ps. 19:14; 49:3; Isa. 33:18), which is the inner person (1 Pet. 3:4) who lives, thinks, and speaks (Ps. 14:1) to himself before God (1 Sam. 16:7).

Moreover, as one of the Hebrew terms for meditation (the OT was written in Hebrew) indicates, meditation refers to productive self-talk. This inner meditation on the Scriptures is like a tree with inner resources that cause it to bud, and at length to blossom. So the purpose of meditation is to produce various outer life responses (Josh. 1:8; Prov. 15:28). A Christian meditates, not to attain peace, calmness, or a sense of tranquility, as so many wrongly seem to think. Indeed, meditation may at times be quite upsetting (Isa. 33:18). Meditation is not feeling-oriented; it is a process of focused, concentrated inner reasoning that leads to outer action. As God told Joshua (Josh. 1:8), success in fulfilling God's law depends upon it. The process itself is of no merit or value, nor does it seek to accomplish something subjective for the person meditating. No, it is an inner experience, but one that is designed to achieve objective results. What are these results?

The meditator, as Joshua 1:8 makes clear, wants to understand how to relate biblical truth to life. He will not settle for mere Bible reading, rote memorizing, or filing away facts. His burning desire is to turn a truth over and over, and over again, until he knows all he can possibly know about it. He examines it intently from every vantage point as one views the many-hued refractions of light that glance off every facet of a diamond. He will not let a truth go until it blesses him! He wants to know that truth in all its length and breadth in his own life. He is not satisfied merely with intellectualizing scriptural data; he thinks through all of its implications and studies ways to implement it. He takes time to plan out ways and means of gearing it into daily living. Meditation is a process of deepening the understanding and planning.[5]

So, as you see, language has an important function in the thinking and planning process as one literally talks himself through a matter to its conclusion.

A **fourth** function of language is to interpret. As I noted earlier, the slammed door in a salesman's face does not carry its own interpretation. But if, at the same time, one shouts, "You're the tenth salesman to appear this morning!" he knows a lot more about the act. There is

---

5   Jay E. Adams, *Ready to Restore: The Layman's Guide to Christian Counseling.*

no other way to know the motives, desires, and internal thoughts of another person.

Without language, our salesman is likely to misinterpret the reason behind the action: "She is afraid of me," "She didn't like my face," or "I guess she doesn't want to buy any magazines," etc. Because language interprets what cannot be interpreted otherwise, it is an essential factor in helping us to understand God and one another. Actions alone give you some of the *what* but rarely any of the *why* in a situation, unless the action is performed in a previously language-conditioned setting.

Language, then, helps us to understand persons as well as actions. There is no other way to understand God. If He had not revealed Himself to us, we would not have known His will. Nor would we have been able to do more than guess at His character and attributes. Chances are that we would have ended up like the polytheists of Greece and Rome who created their gods in their own images. That might have gotten them somewhere (though not far enough) in a perfect world of perfect people, but in a world where God's image in man has been ruined by sin, man could conceive of nothing better than sinful, erring, weak, jealous, fighting gods who reflected the worst of human sin. When Jesus Christ Himself came, along with the *written* Word, to interpret God to man, He was called *the Word* (John 1:1ff.). John Calvin called Christ God's "speech." Jesus was called *the Word* because, like a word, He interprets:

> *Nobody has ever seen God at any time; it is the unique God Who is closest of all to the Father Who has explained Him* (John 1:18).

The term *explain* in this verse is, in the Greek original, "exegete." God could not be understood apart from the Word.

Language also helps us interpret the environment. When Adam named the animals he was engaged both in a scientific classifying act that made communication about animals possible through labels that declared, "This is like that," and in an interpretive act in which he said, "They are not like me and serve a different function in God's world, and they will not satisfy my need for companionship" (a genuine need, by the way). He understood this as he began to name them according to their characteristics and functions. That act of interpretation is implied by the explanation given in Genesis 2:20b, "but for the man himself there was found no suitable helper." The same principle is used in naming the woman *Eve*: "She is the mother of all living." Both are functional explanations.

Language also interprets problems and interprets other language that is not immediately clear. As counselors know, it allows us to ask questions and to gather and interpret the data that we glean from the responses to those questions. Because I shall say more about this later on, I shall go no further with it here.

A **fifth** function of language is to help us remember. Recorded history, a uniquely human product, has made the heritage of truth and the discoveries of previous generations available to subsequent ones. This allows for progress. The animal world makes no such progress because there is no propositional language capability among the various species. Propositional memory made possible the writing and the transmission of God's Word in the Bible. God's commands, promises, warnings, and instructions thus became available to all generations. All technological advancement depends on language capability. But propositional memory also combines with conscience (the human capacity that God built into us to enable us to make self-judgments) to create the important and necessary sense of guilt that modern psychotherapy is so bent on erasing in the wrong way.

A **sixth** function of language (the last I shall mention, though not necessarily the final word on the subject) is its ability to get things done. Language is a powerful means of accomplishing what we wish to do. The great phrase of the general semanticists, which we tire of hearing, is "The word is not the thing." I cannot altogether agree with that dictum, however. The biblical word *dabar* is a Hebrew term that means both word and thing. Clearly, the Hebrews saw a closer affinity between the two. They believed that there is power in words; they knew, for instance, that God said, "Let there be light," and there *was* light. We know that the world was created through the Word (John 1). So, it is plain that in the Scriptures, word and fact are closely intertwined.

Because man was created in God's image, his words have power too. They are not creative, of course, in the way that God's words were, but they do bear a very close relationship to things. For instance, we have seen how powerful the effects of talking to oneself can be. By convincing oneself that something is true, one's lifestyle is significantly influenced. Words contain ideas which, in turn, are the substance of action.

But words can have powerful effects on others as well. Shout "Fire!" and, if taken seriously, the word itself will have the same effect as the thing. In its *effect*, in all such instances, then, we can see how the word and the thing are the same. This is an important fact for counselors to understand. A person, in reality, may have nothing to fear; yet the fear may be present just as surely and just as debilitatingly as if the thing he fears were a reality. All he must do is *believe* that the dreaded situation exists to arouse within himself the very same emotional response as if it did. Very frequently, counselees labor under misinterpretations of fact that, in one way or another, influence their lives. When you analyze what they are grappling with, often it is a wrong concept that is encapsulated in a wrong word, e.g., "I *can't*," "It is *hopeless*." Wrong words must be countered with the freeing, life-giving Word of God; God says "You can."

I could mention how words put a handle on problems to allow us to take hold of them and deal with them scripturally, but I shall come to that at a later point when I shall discuss labeling. Likewise, the precision-making power of words and their ability to fix ideas and concepts for good or ill are subjects of discussion in other places. So, with one final comment I shall conclude this chapter.

The function of language is great, and the importance of language in all of life (not only in counseling) is obvious. We all use language for these purposes and others, all of the time, all day long. We cannot avoid doing so. The only question is whether we use language properly—God's way—or whether we go along stumbling over our own feet as well as stepping on the feet of others by our sinfully harmful use of this great and wonderful gift of God. That is what counselors are deeply involved in analyzing as they listen to the words and thoughts of their counselees. In the redemptive renewal of the mind, so vital to successful counseling, language plays a most prominent role. How, then, can a Christian counselor say, "Oh, language? That's not my interest"? It is at the very heart and core of what he is doing all of the time.

Chapter 2
Some Guiding Principles

Once again, what I shall say here will be far from complete; hence the wording, "*Some* Guiding Principles." But because it is necessary to begin somewhere, stop somewhere, and in between treat some important implications of language study for counseling, I have chosen several principles concerning counseling that, in my opinion, every counselor ought to understand and to which he should refer often in his day-by-day work of helping others.[6]

What is language? Of course, it has been defined, redefined, and defined once again. Many of the definitions (which, incidentally, are examples of language used to interpret language) amount to something like this:

Language is communication through signs or symbols in a meaningful arrangement.

Whether that definition is accurate or inaccurate, or, perhaps better, *how* it is inadequate or inaccurate, I shall not stop to debate, but the *one* factor that is of importance for us in it is that language gets the job done by means of signs. And that fact is universally accepted. This leads us to our first principle.

Language Uses Signs

Words are signs (in this sense, it is true that they are *not* the thing). I shall develop one aspect of this fact later when I discuss labeling, but for now, I wish to make only one other point: Words are not only signs that

---
6 Perhaps he will want to list them on one of the blank pages at the end of *The Christian Counselor's New Testament*.

identify but also signs that *direct*. That is to say, words are not only *labels*, but they are also signposts.

This sign-as-sign*post* function of words becomes very important in counseling. If, for instance, a problem is described in medical terms, using clinical language ("sickness, illness, disease, therapy, health," etc.) according to the medical model that is so widely accepted in counseling circles, that medical language consists of innumerable signposts, all of which point to a physician (or someone purporting to do medical work) as the one who holds the solutions to that problem. If, on the other hand, a Christian counselor consistently avoids erecting any such misleading signposts, but instead of words like "mental illness" and "therapy" uses biblical terms like "sin" and "biblical counseling," by his signposts he clearly marks the way to Jesus Christ as the One who can solve the counselee's problem.[7] One set of signs points to the physician; the other, to Christ. That is how important the difference that a right or wrong choice of words can make.

You should have no difficulty recognizing that the effect of each contrasting set of terms is significant. It troubles me greatly, then, to hear men, who ought to know better, carelessly using words that can only confuse counselees and hinder their best efforts to help them. While all of us will slip from time to time in our use of language, there is no excuse for the constant, almost cavalier lack of concern about language that is so characteristically found even among many of the otherwise best conservative, Bible-believing counselors today. It is time, therefore, for you to make a conscious and conscientious effort to change all of this if you are guilty of the offense.

But perhaps you aren't sure. Usage is habitual and so unconscious. Then I suggest that you begin to record your counseling sessions and ask your wife to monitor your daily conversation. Play back the recordings and listen carefully to your own use of terminology. Have your wife point out the terms that you want to eliminate or change whenever you use them. We are all affected greatly by what we have heard, read, and

---

7   Of course, I am speaking here of problems in living not occasioned by organic difficulties. Organically generated problems are rightly labeled in medical terms, and physicians (not psychiatrists) should be involved.

repeated. Since so few have been saying or writing or repeating anything approximating the biblical terms, the likelihood is that your counseling vocabulary and word usage are, at best, scrambled and inconsistent. For the sake of your counselees and for the honor of Christ, study your language usage. I shall say more in a later chapter about how to alter your usage of language, but for now, let me simply observe that it is necessary to discover, if you do not already know, what your current usage is. That will be the basis for every change that you seek to effect later on.

Let's now take a look at a sample of what I have been talking about. In *Ready to Restore*, I have analyzed one of the cases in the *Casebook* this way:

"MY LIFE IS A BIG FAT ZERO"

Midge is a 23-year-old, single working girl. She is a graduate of a Bible college and now works as a secretary at the same school.

On the Personal Data Inventory, she describes herself as being often "blue," "shy," and "lonely." She also adds: "I'm a nothing," and "I feel inferior." She says that she prays often but reads her Bible only occasionally.

As she sees it, this is the main problem: "My self-concept is just absolutely zero. That may surprise you, but it is. My whole life has been a big, fat zero. Nobody notices me, nobody likes me, and nobody cares about me. I may as well be dead. I feel so inadequate. Even when I pray, I can't find any relief. Probably the Lord doesn't even like me. But He is the one who made me this way, so maybe He does."

Most modern counselors would say that Midge has a problem with "self-image." Her "self-concept," they would hasten to add, is poor, and she needs "ego-enhancing." She must be helped to acquire a sense of "self-worth"; that sort of thing then becomes the major task of counseling. If we were to analyze her past, we'd probably discover that in one way or another, she has been put down continually. That will be thought to be the cause of her problem. That is the assessment of the case that you'd hear from many today. But the analysis is faulty and will point in the wrong direction. The fact that others who have been demeaned by parents or peers did *not* develop similar problems will be ignored.

And that Midge's attitude may have involved much of this will not be considered.

The words in quotation marks in the last paragraph actually structure a non-biblical analysis of Midge's problem for us. They do not really help; instead they limit and direct one's thinking into the wrong channels. Nor are these channels hopeful. We know there is no way to bolster or pump up her image of herself. Some, following Adler, would focus on her comments, "I feel inferior, I feel so inadequate," and say that she has an inferiority complex.

But as a biblical counselor, you will avoid all such analyses. Midge herself has already bought the Maslow-Adler line (especially the former) and analyzes herself *in terms* of self-image and inferiority. Her own thinking and responses to life have been shaped, limited, and conditioned by the construct this eclectic view of things presupposes and, indeed, demands. That means that as her counselor, you will have to help her see the problem differently. You must help her open her thinking to new, biblical concepts.

Notice, also, that with Maslow (who provides the excuse), Midge explains that since others have not satisfied her basic needs by loving, liking, and caring for her, she is incapable of making it in life. The categories that one accepts will structure his analysis of the problem. Midge depends largely on self-image notions in analyzing her situation, and it is clear that the acceptance of the categories leading to that analysis has done her little good. She may not know much about Maslow or self-image views, but, like so many, she has picked up ideas here and there which are generally abroad in the culture.

Now, how would a Christian view Midge's problem? Since the Bible nowhere tells us that we cannot obey God or solve problems unless our needs have been met by others, and because in the Bible God treats all of His children alike, giving them the same commands and holding before them the same standards, regardless of whether they were raised in a pious Hebrew family, knowing the Scriptures from childhood and worshiping the true God

Jehovah, or they were pagan Corinthians who were involved in idolatry, temple prostitution, lying, etc., we will analyze Midge's problem quite differently. Our Christian categories demand a different outcome; one that is more hopeful because it is God's.

First, we must take her seriously when she says, "I'm a nothing" and "My whole life has been a big fat zero." We will want to respond with words something like this: "That's serious; to waste a life that God has given that way is a tragedy. You must have some pretty good reasons for reaching such a drastic conclusion. Tell me some of the ways in which you have failed." Those statements, in accordance with 1 Corinthians 13:7, "Love ... believes all things," place the responsibility for her problems just where it belongs—on her. We must take her seriously about her negative evaluation of herself.

But there are some other statements of hers that we must counter. They are not statements of fact, such as those that we have accepted, but statements of value, particularly those that demonstrate by language and orientation an incorrect, unbiblical interpretation of these facts. The string of Maslow/Adler interpretations of her plight must be rejected. To do so is crucial; there is no other way to (1) rightly analyze the situation, (2) honor God, and (3) give her hope and direction that will enable her to do something about her problem.

Moreover, we shall want to correct her statements about *feeling* inferior and inadequate, pointing out to her that neither inferiority nor inadequacy is a feeling. One simply doesn't *feel* inferior or inadequate. Doubtless she feels lousy, but that isn't because either of these factors is a feeling. She feels *bad* because she has *judged* herself *to be* inferior and inadequate. The bad feelings she has were occasioned by her judgment about the facts.

Viewing the matter this way, we may ask, "Is her judgment about herself correct or incorrect?" We can help her reexamine and reassess the facts on which that judgment is based. If inferiority or inadequacy were feelings, we could do nothing about them. There is no way that a counselor could get her to change such "feelings." Let me take one of her judgments and run it through such an analysis:

Judgment: "I am inadequate."

If a careful reassessment of the evidence does not support this conclusion, she must admit that she is wrong. Such an analysis will eliminate the bad feelings that the false judgment triggered.

If a careful reassessment of the evidence supports Midge's conclusion, she must then decide what to do about it. Her next step is to ask, "Is it or isn't it right before God for me to be inadequate in the ways that I am?"

If it is right not to be inadequate in some way or other (it would be right to be inadequate in the ring with Muhammad Ali), then, on acceptance of this fact, bad feelings from guilt should disappear. Other bad feelings from disappointment, regret, etc., may linger for a brief time but should not debilitate unless they grow out of anger and pride that make her want to be able to do anyway what God has not gifted her to do.

If it is wrong (for instance, she may have gifts she ought to be using but isn't), then the counselor may help her to lay out a plan for developing and deploying these gifts. As she begins to do so out of a commitment to God, her bad feelings will lift.

Moreover, when we read her language of exaggeration ("nobody ... nobody"), her blame-shifting (even expressing it toward God), her resentment toward others, and her self-pity and self-centeredness, we discover where some of her real problems lie. She doesn't have problems because of a bad self-concept; she has a poor self-concept because of her sinful, unrepentant patterns of life and the unresolved difficulties they have occasioned. Her problem is neither a bad self-concept nor bad treatment by others. Rather, it is a bad self (that she knows is bad) and bad treatment of others (that is clear from her resentful attitudes toward them) that is her major difficulty. She has the biblical principle turned around: instead of losing herself for Christ and His gospel, she is seeking self-gratification. It will never come that way; satisfaction is a by-product and cannot be sought and found directly. No wonder she is miserable—she has never learned that "it is more blessed to give than to receive." She thinks, "If people would only be better to me, then I'd be better." She is wrong. Doubtless, many people may have wronged her, but that isn't her problem. Her difficulty lies in the wrong way that she has responded to the wrong done to her.

Possibly also, she is concerned that she is still single, though a graduate of a Christian college. She may be angry with God for not providing a husband. But her whole approach to problems is calculated to drive men away rather than to attract them. She needs to be told to stop blaming others and look at herself—that's where the responsibility for change really lies. Why would she consider herself (as she now is) a good risk for marriage?

The Christian analysis is honest, forthright, and hard (one might even think severe). But it is accurate, and that is why it is calculated to give hope, to produce change through repentance, and to lead to a new lifestyle. The present Maslow/Adler self-concept stance that Midge has taken, though in line with many pagan analyses, will do just the opposite. Midge's problem is sin, and she must be told so. Words like "self-concept," etc., only cloud the issues, create excuses for sin, and orient one's thinking in the wrong direction. Midge needs truth.[8]

Perhaps this much is sufficient to alert you to this first guiding principle. Now, let's look at a second principle, which is a corollary to the first.

Whenever possible, use biblical terms

Of course, some biblical concepts do not have specialized terms, or any single term that is associated with them. In such cases, it may be important to coin a term that expresses the biblical concept or to follow the Bible's lead in not developing any term whatsoever; but it is always wrong to use a term that is commonly used by others who teach something that is unscriptural (unless that term is qualified in some way) because it will carry freight that inevitably will be imported into and intermixed with the biblical concept, thus diluting, polluting or otherwise distorting it.

---

8 Jay E. Adams. *Ready to Restore: The Layman's Guide to Biblical Counseling*

An example of a biblical concept for which an identifying term may be usefully coined is what I have called the "holding principle."[9] It is more than a matter of convenience to refer to the concept—which is not named but clearly described in the Bible—under a descriptive title like this. There is also teaching value in doing so, in that the label helps to interpret and fix the concept. If accurate, as I believe it to be, the label is a good one because it is a coined term that teaches truth and carries no freight, left over from other associations, that might lead us astray.

As we shall see later, such labeling is essential to human welfare and useful as long as the labels are accurate and convey the truth both denotatively and connotatively. A good example of a freighted term is the word *acceptance*, which was used by Bill Gothard. In psychotherapeutic and psychological literature, the word refers to behavior, attitudes, values, etc., and connotes (if not also denotes) the idea of non-judgmentally accepting these regardless of whether they are sinful or righteous. Gothard, however, uses the term to refer to inherited physical characteristics (red hair, big noses, etc.). So, when he says, "accept yourself," he really means accept God's sovereign determination of such characteristics—a perfectly proper exhortation. But I have met a number of people who confuse his words with the idea that it is unnecessary or impossible to change various sinful life patterns. It is possible, of course, that they may be purposely distorting his meaning by such a misinterpretation of his teaching, but, even so, why give them the handle to do so? The freight is too bulky; the phrase must be abandoned and another substituted for it. Perhaps it would be better to speak of willing *acquiescence* in God's will rather than acceptance of oneself. The emphasis, at any rate, ought to focus on *God*, not on *self*, in the matter, since that is really what Gothard wants to say.

There is no way to avoid the use of some terminology in counseling; you must say something about the problem and its solution. People rightly will want to know what is wrong and what must be done about it. Moreover, in order to identify for them something to avoid in the future, their problems must be described and labeled. That involves terminology. To be inaccurate or fuzzy is to set the counselee up for a fall.

---

9   For more on the principle itself see *More Than Redemption*, p. 31.

It is important, therefore, to use accurate biblical or biblically derived terms for instruction, for structuring viewpoints, for giving accurate direction, etc. Otherwise, a counselor cannot speak about the counselee, the problem, the solution, or even various aspects of counseling.

It is time for all biblical counselors to become aware of the great importance of this matter and to endeavor to make the changes that will purge out the old leaven. If you have never done so before, I urge to you to examine your vocabulary and sentence structure ("Your husband made you angry"—he didn't. She made herself angry. He could only tempt or provoke her) to make sure that you communicate God's truth, and nothing but God's truth. Here too, the holding principle ("whatever is not of faith is sin"—or, in modern terms, "if it's doubtful, it's dirty") is applicable: If you aren't sure that a term or expression accurately conveys the biblical truth, then don't use it. On a strict application of this principle alone, most of the wrong vocabulary of the pagan systems would be eliminated from your vocabulary. Anything that even possibly might conflict with the Scriptures must be washed out of your usage. Anything that confuses, that is vague, or that is questionable must go. Use only those words that you can use confidently.

You have already developed some sort of terminology, so what I am suggesting is not a matter of adopting something for the first time. You will find it necessary, therefore, to *replace* wrong terms with proper ones. I suggest that as often as you think about the matter, starting right now, you enter, on a growing list, every faulty or questionable word and word usage. Then later, using the put off/put on principle,[10] next to each write a term or phrase that truly exhibits the biblical truth. Having selected an alternative term or word construction in which you can have confidence (and this may take you some time to do), begin to use it over and over again in daily conversation. Don't try to do so in counseling itself—the attempt will distract you from the work that you are doing. But through daily practice, you will discover from the examination of your counseling tapes that you have begun to substitute the newer usage for the older. From regular daily use, when you consciously try to knead it into the

---

10 See *The Christian Counselor's Manual*.

dough of your speech, you will find that it has bled over unconsciously into your speech during counseling sessions. But don't expect this to happen unless a daily, conscious effort is made to use the proper word in the place of the faulty one. If you make this alteration of vocabulary a matter of concerned prayer, you will learn how God will bless you in transforming your language so that you may be a greater blessing to those to whom you minister.

Nouthetic counselors have developed extensive biblical and biblically derived terminology. Among the words used by them in counseling, you may find a considerable number that you may wish to adopt; one way to begin to amass such a vocabulary is to consult the indexes of various volumes published by the writers who belong to this movement. Also, there is a book designed specifically for the purpose of giving counselors this very kind of help: *The Practical Encyclopedia of Christian Counseling*. In it, most of the principal terms used by nouthetic counselors are listed alphabetically together with explanations, observations, and cross-references to the volumes in which they are discussed in greater detail. Today, therefore, there is no compelling reason for the continued use of misleading language. Even if one doesn't have the time or the capacity to develop such a terminology on his own, he has ready access to more than enough help. Even if he doesn't adopt all of the terms in the *Practical Encyclopedia*, he will find it a stimulus to his thinking about the matter. So, the second guiding principle is: Be biblical, even in terminology, by using biblical or biblically derived terms.

Synonyms have a place

The use of synonymous parallelism in Hebrew poetry and other wisdom literature makes that abundantly clear. There is more than one way to say the same thing, and it is often very helpful to say it in more than one way. Every teacher worth his salary knows that fact. The repetition, the approach from different angles, the comparison, and the contrast of things similar and different, all contribute to understanding and tend to close the doors on possible misinterpretations. So then—and I hope that this is very clear—I am not trying to say that there is one and only one language that is acceptable. (Watch the reviews; someone will accuse me of that.) What I *am* saying is that, *however* a counselor says what he is saying, he must say what the Bible says, and there may be more than one way of doing so. He must say what he says in a well-thought-through set of terms and expressions that he has consciously adopted as a part of his working vocabulary of counseling. These terms and expressions must have been adopted because, in his opinion, they convey most clearly what God wants the counselee to know. So, while there is great value in the widespread usage of a uniform terminology among biblical counselors (and if something has been said well, why not adopt that terminology?—There is no virtue in simply being different, especially if doing so produces a fuzzier result), it is certainly not necessary to adhere to any one line of terminology. The Bible gives plain evidence of both a uniform and a diverse use of terminology. Flexibility is a part of the biblical approach and must never be lost in whatever system of terminology one adopts. Indeed, for particular purposes, with specific counselees, he must be free to depart even from his own normal usage if that will convey God's truth more clearly.

Flexibility is the biblical rule, but it is always a flexibility that serves a purpose. You never discover flexibility merely for the sake of being different. As I have pointed out in *More than Redemption*, there are 17 synonyms for sin in the Bible. But in the discussion of each, by comparing and contrasting them, I tried to show that each contributes something to our understanding of the subject that otherwise would have been lost, and that each is appropriate to its own situation. Sometimes, more than one of these is used in Hebrew parallelism in order to make clear what the total intent of the author is. So, there can be no question about it, synonyms and variations in terminology and language constructions are necessary to good counseling.

It is always a concern to me whenever I hear someone who, through reading my books, has picked up the terminology that I employ and is using it in a frozen, stereotyped manner as I listen to him. It is often true of such persons that they have learned the terms, could even pass a test on the system, but have missed the spirit of what is happening by a wide margin. I am not opposed to others using the terminology that I have coined and systematized; that isn't the point, and it would be foolish.

But it must be used intelligently, sensitively, and flexibly. Otherwise, its use, in the eyes of those who oppose nouthetic counseling, will be seized upon and made a laughing stock—as indeed it should, if that is all that there is to it—and counselees will not be helped.

Language affects life

Language is so wrapped up in human life that what one says and how he says it make a significant difference. Change one's language and, at length, you will change his life. The change in Peter's name (John 1:42) plays a part in the subsequent change in his life. It was not the only factor, nor was it the prime factor in that change, but it was a factor. The very fact that he knew that Jesus planned to turn him into a rock must have had an impact from the time that he understood the significance of that name change. Every time someone addressed him, he was reminded anew.

Similarly, when a counselor wants to help a counselee overcome lust or violence, one factor in achieving that change is to help him replace the language of lust with the language of love, and the language of violence with the language of gentleness. The use of the new language in those circumstances in which he previously used sinful language will vividly point the way toward different thinking and different actions as well.

In part, it is this dynamic that is in view in Colossians 4:6,

> *Let your speech at all times be gracious, seasoned with salt, so that you may know how to answer everyone.*

If you consciously work on your language *at all times* (not just in the crunch), you will tend to respond properly when the critical situation arrives. And it will not be merely a matter of manner, but of how you *think* and *act* under those circumstances. Use of biblical language day by day in every situation will stand you in good stead when you are confronted by others to whom you must give a Christian response under pressure. The choice and practice of gracious language in regular, everyday activities provides the proving ground for the weaponry used in the battle.

In part, that is also the dynamic in Proverbs 15:1, although the proverb also points out the *effect* of seasoned language:

A pleasant answer turns away wrath, but a harsh word arouses anger.

Here, one's language, used in responding to wrath, affects another's life and influences his response to your response. Both ways, then, we can see how language affects life—someone's life—either the counselee's or the life of another.

Language structures life

The *form* of a language, for example, structures one's way of looking at things. It provides a grid for thinking and talking about reality, determines largely what one sees, helps to interpret meaning, and screens out those things that do not fit the language structure. Language is a framework by which we structure and order the reality in which we live. The Eskimos have several words for snow that distinguish between falling snow, wet snow, dry snow, etc. As a result, they are able to think and speak more precisely about this aspect of reality than we are. Until recently, there was no word in English for biblical counseling; consequently, there was no way of thinking or talking about it. It was difficult to propagate biblical counseling or even to communicate with others about it. By introducing the words "nouthetic confrontation" into English, I was attempting to remedy that deficiency. Whether or not in time that term will stick and have an effect on the English-speaking church remains to be seen. But one thing is certain—whatever term may finally be adopted for biblical counseling, it will have its effect. Inherent in the term, and the meaning that is packed into it, is a concept for structuring thinking, speaking, and acting. It will affect the church in this way by virtue of the impact that it bears as a carrier of meaning and structure. But it will also have another effect: the very presence of a term for biblical counseling is itself significant. Its presence *alone* says that Christians (1) are in the business of counseling, (2) have a viewpoint of their own to offer, etc. Even if the title "nouthetic counseling" fades, it will have already done its job because it has already made these two facts clear.

In observing that God gave much of His revelation in Hebrew and in Greek (written largely in a Hebraic Greek by Greek-speaking Jews), it is worth noting that parallelism is one of the most important structures of the Hebrew language. This parallelism, among other things, lends itself to antithetical expression and thought (see, for example, the book of Proverbs). The world is described, and consequently viewed, in either/or terms. This choice was providential, deliberate. A language was prepared for a message. The Hebrew language background helped writers like John, even when writing Greek, to develop and present a world view in which reality is seen rightly as twofold: light versus darkness, truth versus error, good versus bad, life versus death. The clean versus the unclean structure of life for the Jew of the Old Testament era taught the same thing. At bottom, there is not a variety of positions that one can adopt about the world—there are only two: God's and all others. Modern thinkers, whose languages do not structure their thinking in such either/or categories, but who think along a continuum, suppose that there are not only two ways of life but many. They are wrong, and their thinking leads to all sorts of wrong ideas, like the concept of neutrality toward God, but in their language, there is no built-in corrective to alert them to the problem.

But those who regularly read the Bible, even in English, encounter this antithetical structure over and over again, and are influenced in their thinking by it. And this has a salutary effect on their thinking and living, regardless of the structure of their own language. Like the Greek-speaking New Testament writers who Hebraized their Greek, the more biblical they are, the more they tend to Hebraize their English, German, etc.

But those whose language and literature do not emphasize antithetical elements, and who, while ignoring the Bible, read and write only in this modern tongue, tend to develop quite a different view of reality, to which their own sinfully structured language forms give support. The proverb, on the other hand, which was so important in the life of every young Hebrew, surely must have had a great formative influence on his future life and world view. There, in the majority of the couplets, the antithetical structure into which life is set consciously or unconsciously must have molded his thinking. He developed a view of reality that saw everything in life either for or against God. The lack of this basic view of reality among so many eclectic counselors accounts for their readiness to eclectically adopt views that are antithetical to biblical truth.

Surely, it was not by chance that the Hebrew language, with its love for antithesis, was the vehicle of God's revelation. It *fit*, *emphasized*, and helped to *construct* a concept of the true God over against all the gods of the nations, of Israel as His people over against the Gentiles, and of righteousness in life over against unrighteous ways of the unsaved.

One factor that ought to be noted about the present struggle for biblical counseling is that biblical counselors must constantly read the Bible and, as a result, absorb the antithesis of its form and message, while eclectic counselors do not spend so much time in the Book and are deprived of this influence. Their structures of reality (and therefore of counseling) are instead formed by other sources they read and study. That means they are continually exposed to a different view of life set forth in the relativistic writings that abound in the counseling field. These two contrasting influences—even in terms of the language structures that they employ—lead to two widely different effects. The biblically informed (and formed) counselor sees life and sees his counselees one way, while the eclectic counselor sees them both from quite a different perspective. As a result, each will view problems and their solutions differently. We can only be thankful that some eclectic counselors have not abandoned the Bible altogether. And we may hope that in time some of the influence of its form and content will break through the insipid views of those who see the world in other than God's black and white terms.[11]

Language itself has been affected by sin

Obviously, error has crept into human thinking, and it is both the faulty information and the sinfully constructed language structures that are a part of our languages that continue to spread error. There is even vocabulary that would not exist had there been no sin (e.g., "luck," the names of the false gods that appear in the Bible and elsewhere, and the 17 scriptural synonyms for sin themselves). Plaintive, contrary-to-fact

---

11   Of course, there are shades *within* the two categories as the Bible consistently maintains.

statements ("If only I had ...") and blame-shifting constructions ("You made me sad when you ...") are examples of language constructs that not only have resulted from sin but also encourage wrong thinking and living.

The effects of sin on language is a very important subject that I shall leave for now because of the many intricate issues involved. I hope at some time to be able to investigate this intriguing labyrinth in depth in another writing, but if I try to do so here, I recognize that it will take me too far afield. I would be delighted, however, to find that someone else has taken up the task and has preempted my efforts.

Now let us note a final principle:

Words aren't always used in the same sense

Not only is language constantly changing so that in the King James Bible, "to let" means "to hinder" and "to prevent the dawn" means "to get up before dawn," but the same word may have multiple meanings and shades of meaning in different contexts. Words like blackboard and black board also present problems (even more so now that blackboards may be green!), and connotation is of great importance. The word "fundamentalist" refers to one sort of person in the mind of a Bible-believing Christian of a particular ecclesiastical background, something else to another Christian, a third thing to a liberal theologian, and still another to a person totally uninterested in religion in any form whatsoever.

Similarly, the word "counseling" today has no agreed-upon denotation. There was a time when it invariably meant *to give direction*. But since Carl Rogers, a great number of people think of counseling as exactly the opposite. The impact of Rogers' non-directive counseling has been so great that, in his own lifetime, he has been able to reverse the longstanding definition of a word so that, in the popular mind, it now means the opposite! Think of it! How the power of a false concept can bring about the sudden mutation of a word, which in turn influences the thinking of many others.

When dealing with words that may convey quite different meaning to different persons because of their background, bias, or whatever, the counselor must avoid the temptation to allow the listener to fill the word with his own ideas and images. If this is permitted, the likelihood is that he will import concepts that are foreign to the intention of the counselor and thus destroy or greatly pervert the communication. He must not even allow the listener to color the word with the wrong hues connotatively if that will distort meaning.

In order to obviate any such misunderstanding, it is often necessary to append qualifying adjectives, like *biblical* counseling, *Christian* counseling, or *nouthetic* counseling. From time to time, and from person to person (or group to group), any one of the three qualifiers just mentioned might be preferable. There is no one *correct* or *best* qualifier. The correct and the best one is the one that best conveys the message intended to the particular listener or listeners at any given time.

These three terms themselves are not precise. *Christian* is, perhaps, the vaguest (but that too, will depend on the context). The reason this good term has been so sadly thinned out that in many respects it has become all but meaningless is that non-Christian counseling is being done by Christians, who *call* it Christian. To do this, as one person aptly put it, is like speaking of *Christian robbery*! Just because Christians do it, that doesn't make an activity Christian.

The title *biblical counseling* is a bit more precise, but more and more problems are becoming connected with that term ever since it has become popular in Christian circles to call one's counseling, biblical. People have begun to refer to their counseling as biblical, even when it is based largely on Freud, Adler, and Ellis. I predict that it will become an increasingly common problem that we will have to deal with in the immediate future. Consequently, the word biblical will become less and less useful.

That leaves us at the present time with the most precise term, *nouthetic counseling*. I am afraid we are stuck with it unless someone can come up with a better alternative. But even this title is beginning to denote more than one thing in some areas, as persons who have little or no acquaintance with nouthetic counseling have begun to do counseling under that rubric. All of which goes to show that no matter how precise one tries to be, in a world of sin, there will always be misunderstanding and distortion. So, the best that one can do is to attempt prayerfully to be as precise as possible. And that will call for sensitivity to contexts and persons. It will require constant vigilance and an ability to remain flexible.

One must be willing to fight for some terms and not let them go (like important biblical or theological terms), while at the same time he must know when to abandon a term to the enemy as too polluted to be used any longer ("divinity" has had to be replaced by "deity" just as "inspired" has had to be coupled with "inerrant").

Christian counselors must become aware of these problems, stay current in their understanding of language shifts, and determine to use words as carefully as possible. This is of great importance in educating the Christian public. Bad things unavoidably result from failure to do so. Confusion brings ruined lives. It is so difficult at times to make oneself clear. At such times, I have found myself resorting to all sorts of circumlocutions. One of those awkward trips around Robin's barn that I frequently take is, "He is a Christian who is also a counselor." To call such a person a Christian counselor would be inaccurate and misleading.

In counseling itself, it is important for the counselor to be sure that he is understood by the counselee. Whenever there is a possible confusion of meaning, it is worthwhile to spell out what one has in mind. The counselor also will find himself saying things like, "Now what I understand you to be saying is…"

Terms are often misunderstood. When a grade school teacher simply says, "Clean your desks," and doesn't spell out the specific results she is looking for, the frilly-dressed girls will take the word "clean" to mean one thing, and the boys with frogs in their pockets will take it to mean something quite different. It is inexcusable, for instance, for a counselor to speak about love in a counseling session without ever defining it according to its biblical categories. The word itself has been so twisted, warped, stretched, battered, and manhandled that, in and of itself, it hardly has any specific meaning left at all.

With these guiding principles in mind, let us now look more closely at various areas in which the language of counseling is of significance.

Chapter 3
Labeling

In my introductory words I mentioned labeling as an area in which abuses particularly have created problems for biblical counselors. Because that is true, I propose to devote a separate chapter to the subject.

Actually, there are two extremes that must be considered. On the one hand, there are those who, fed up with abuses, reject labeling outright. Karl Menninger is a good example. Much of what he has said against abuses is informative and correct. But when Wallace Hamilton writes, "... we know that the name of a thing doesn't matter,"[12] I must dissent. My reasons for dissent will appear later. On the other hand, there are those who think that they have achieved the acme of counseling when, as Erik Erikson put it, they engage in "diagnostic name-calling."[13] Both extremes are wrong. Names and labels for persons, things, situations, problems, and conditions are absolutely necessary not only for biblical counseling, but also for carrying on everyday conversation with God and one's neighbor.

Labeling is inevitable. God *required* Adam to give labels to the animals by which he classified them and made meaningful communication concerning them possible. Apart from commonly accepted labels, all one can do is imprecisely point and grunt. God Himself calls some of us saints, others unbelievers; He speaks of drunkards, homosexuals, gossips,

---

12 Wallace Hamilton, *Ride the Wild Horses* (Nashville: Abingdon, 1980), p. 16. Because the reality remains constant, he thinks the name doesn't matter, but if followed to its conclusion, this logic would destroy all communication: the name communicates a lie when it doesn't tell the truth about the reality.

13 In Paul Roazan's *Erik Erikson* (New York: Macmillan, 1976), p. 66. Erikson puts down labeling, but his comments must be taken seriously only about those *abuses* of labeling that we so often encounter.

the slothful, etc. (see 1 Cor. 6:9ff.). *God* labels. What we want, then, is not to eliminate labels; instead, we want appropriate and accurate labels, labels that help because they tell the truth. The fundamental problem with labels is that, as sinners use them, labels often tell lies.

Labeling that is accurate helps the counselee to get a handle on his problems so that he can begin to *do* something about them. I can remember one counselee who was describing a problem, and he said he somehow couldn't put his finger on it. After listening for a while I said, "Why, what you've been describing to me is just plain, old-fashioned pride!" Instantly, his eyes lit up and he shouted, "Ah! That's it! Now that I have a name for it, I know what I must do about it." The label enabled him to get a grasp of the problem and pointed to its solution.

The difficulty with labeling isn't that diagnosticians call names; all of us must call names. The trouble comes (1) when they carelessly gum the wrong label on someone's file, (2) when they don't warn about the fact that labels often refer to temporary, changeable states of being, and (3) when they substitute labeling for genuine help as though a label were an end in and of itself rather than a means to an end. What we must protest and guard against is the distortion of a good thing, not the thing itself. Labels identify, direct, classify, and enable us to understand and communicate. Labeling began in the Garden of Eden, before the fall, as a good activity in which man was required to participate for his welfare and for the honor and glory of God. That it has been abused and done harm is a consequence of human perversity since the fall.

Why has there been such a ready acceptance of false labels? Because of man's basic nature, his thirst for knowledge and order, he must have labels. But because of his sin, he will settle for wrong ones. A wrong view of life leads to false classification. The combination of these two factors spells trouble.

God Himself put into men the impulse to speak, but without labels, one can say very little. Freud was a great writer (largely of fiction). He was *not* a scientist. Actually, above all else, he was a master inventor of labels. This ability was what sold Freudianism; he appealed to and satisfied the natural tendency to label at a time when old labels were being readily rejected. But his labels were lies; they distorted the facts, communicated untruths, and thereby caused great confusion and much harm. Yet, if anyone doubts the power of language in general or of labels in particular, let him study the influence that Freudian labels have had on Western society ever since.

Abuses

Because poor labeling is so dangerous, it is important for us to know ahead of time some of its misuses and abuses that arise in counseling. We must also be able to point out the insidious influence of poor labeling in the lives of our counselees and to avoid all such usage in our own counseling.

First, there is always the danger that some persons who have been inaccurately labeled will try to live up to the label.[14] This can happen when one is looking for an excuse to get out of work or to justify sinful behavior; or, as we so often tragically discover, the label shapes the person's life as he closes out options that the label doesn't allow him to enter. In all such cases, counselees must be shown that the label doesn't really fit. A label may add a complicating problem to those that already exist.

Second, to some, labels imply a permanence that does not actually exist. When applying a label, don't do it as though you were articulating the laws of the Medes and the Persians. Otherwise, you may rob the counselee of hope. Rather, always apply a label in a hope-giving way: "Thank God that you are a 'drunkard,' John, and not a so-called diseased 'alcoholic.' Christ didn't come to deal with the fictional disease of alcoholism, but He *did* come to deal with the sin of drunkenness."

Third, often labels are given to cover ignorance and disagreement. When one doesn't understand something, he may save face by appending a vague or wrong label. Labels so used are sometimes also substituted for investigation, work, or careful analysis of a person's problem. In some cases, they are used merely to enhance the ethos of the one who pins them on another. It is always necessary therefore, to probe deeply enough to discover exactly what the labeler means by the label he gives, unless you

---

14   Or, what is equally bad, they may try to live it down (spend unnecessary time and energy denying it). Or they may lose hope attempting to solve problems that don't exist.

are already absolutely sure. Be wary of one who will not explain a label; he may be trying to put something over on you. In the field of counseling, this precaution is doubly apropos because of the widespread ignorance among practitioners, many of whom are very proud of their status. Such sinners, rather than admit ignorance, will sometimes resort to labeling.

But a similar thing can happen among Christians, even pastors, who get caught up in label usage that really doesn't grow out of understanding but out of ignorance. The next time you hear a Christian say someone has a "guilt complex," ask him what he means by that. Chances are he means no more than a sense of guilt. But that isn't what a so-called "guilt-complex" is supposed to be. Yet, many pastors and others use such words, seemingly because they sound more profound than simpler (but clearer) terms. The question, "What do you mean by that?" can rarely be overworked when you are discussing labels. More often than you might like to think, when you press the question, you will get a vague, unintelligible response from the one who, a minute or so before, was affixing labels with a flourish. Doubtless, ignorance is one of the principal reasons for the labeling craze among psychotherapists.

Fourth, watch out for umbrella labels like "schizophrenia," "neuroses" (a label recently dumped by the A.P.A., but still used by many), and "psychosis." These labels are bad because many different problems are categorized under each of them. Take "schizophrenia," for example. The same effect (bizarre behavior) can be generated by organic or inorganic causes. To use the common label schizophrenia to cover all varieties of both, therefore, is foolish and certainly not helpful. One word to cover problems stemming from sleep loss, hallucinogenic drugs, brain tumors, chemical imbalances of various sorts, camouflaging, fear, inappropriate habits, etc., is, to say the least, confusing. Certainly, it is not helpful. And it can be quite misleading both to the counselee and to those who are treating him (especially in the mental institutions of this country, which are notorious for their diagnostic errors and slipshod treatments).

In a book on schizophrenia, *The Construction of Madness*, there are no two chapters that are in agreement.[15] The term schizophrenia disguises

---

15 Peter A. Magaro, *The Construction of Madness*.

these differences of opinion and the ignorance involved, so that a counselee has little or no idea of the vast range of problems that may be the possible cause of his difficulty and the large variety of interpretations of these held by those who practice counseling. Terms, covering up differences of opinion, then, can induce a counselee to submit himself for treatment when he ought not to do so without a thorough investigation of what the counselor means by the terms he uses and what the particular practitioner intends to do about it. Moreover, the common umbrella term tends to keep the practitioner from making a complete investigation of the problem himself. It locks him into his theory and tends to close out other options, when it is essential to investigate what, in each particular case, is behind such an instance of behavior.

Fifth, note that labels limit. It is possible to use a label in such a way that one blinds himself to other factors. Often, a problem is multi-caused; there is no one cause, but a combination of several features lies at the bottom of the difficulty. A label can eliminate these far too easily. The simple statement, "John is a farmer," for instance, limits. One tends to think of him as a farmer *only*, and not as a husband, a father, and an elder in the church. The label brings *one* feature into such prominence that others are lost sight of. Of course, the same thing can happen when a biblical counselor says, "John is an adulterer." Some are repentant adulterers, some are not. You know little about John's farming or his adultery by that sentence alone. You must remember to deal with each case as John Smith, farmer, or John Smith, adulterer. John's farming or adultery may not be like Bill's. The category word is not useless; it teaches you something. But it must not be allowed to limit you so that you do not investigate all the facts of each case individually.

Take the phrase, "out of touch with reality," that is so readily attached to people in cases that are labeled "catatonic schizophrenia." This label, in conjunction with that phrase, can keep a counselor from pursuing communication with the counselee ("If he's out of touch, why bother?"). It structures the relationship and limits counseling. You get from a counselee no more than what you expect, and what you expect is what you look for.[16] But, if, on the contrary, you believe that a person like this, so long as he has suffered no physical damage, is indeed fully in touch with reality, and yet chooses to behave as though he were not, that in turn structures quite a different relationship and dictates counseling of the most intensive communicative sort.

A case in point is found on page 202 of my book, *The Christian Counselor's Casebook*. In that case, the label "hereditary" and the heavy use of deterministic psychiatric jargon ("accept myself," etc.) close down all action by the counselee and will continue to do so until the situation can be rectified by the adoption of new labels.

For these and other similar reasons, the Christian counselor will be careful about his acceptance and use of labels. Whenever possible, He will use biblical labels or labels that clearly express biblical concepts. And he will be careful to use them as the Bible does.

---

16   How important it is, therefore, to have proper biblical expectations.

Chapter 4
The Counselor's Language

To set an example of appropriate language usage, to make counselees aware of the situation as it is biblically, to be accurate and truthful, and to point counselees to God's solutions to their problems, Christian counselors must learn to use language properly. This takes time and effort and some measure of regularity and discipline; it is not an optional matter. Language study is an essential part of one's counseling activities.

To learn how to use language properly, as I have already indicated, the Christian counselor must study his own language patterns. It is not as though his mind is a clean slate; on it, he will find all sorts of scrawling in his own handwriting and in the handwriting of others. He must learn how to scrub down this language in order to remove the graffiti of the many eclectic influences that have competed for space in his mind. He must deliberately adopt new words and constructions that more aptly express the biblical facts in each counseling situation. He must consciously work hard to make these new approaches a viable part of his working language. Some initial help in doing all of this will come from some injunctions from Paul that may serve as a positive guide and influence for good language use in counseling.

In helping us to think more carefully about the language of counseling, it will be valuable to examine Paul's discussion of the preacher's language in Colossians 4:3-8:

> ... praying at the same time also about us, that God may open for us a door for the Word, to speak about the secret of Christ, because of which I am in bonds, so that I may proclaim it clearly, as I ought to.

> *Walk in wisdom before those who are outside, making the most of opportunities. Let your speech at all times be gracious, seasoned with salt, so that you may know how to answer everyone.*
>
> *Tychicus, our dear brother and faithful servant and fellow slave in the Lord, will give you all the facts about me. I sent him to you for this very purpose, so that you may know all about us and that he may encourage your hearts.*

While it is true that the immediate application of the principles set forth in this passage has to do with the use of the Scriptures in missionary evangelism, nevertheless, those principles are brushed in by Paul with a brush large enough to extend to any phase of the pastoral ministry as well. We shall, therefore, try to understand each principle and then apply it concretely to counseling (which, I should remind you, is a pastoral function).

Speak biblically (Col. 4:3)

It is a "door for the Word" about which Paul is concerned and about which he asked the Colossians to pray. It was not for his own, or someone else's ideas that he wanted to get a hearing, but for God's Word. He did not even see the possibility of some sort of eclectic mix; Paul was oriented toward *one* thing—the ministry of the Word. In every sense, that is what counseling ought to be. I do not have the space here to justify that statement, but in *Competent to Counsel, The Christian Counselor's Manual, The Big Umbrella, Lectures on Counseling*, and *More Than Redemption* I have substantiated that claim in depth.

That ministry of the Word, of course, meant proclaiming the "secret about Christ"—that He would come to die in the place of guilty sinners to save them from the guilt and the power of their sins. That is what counseling is all about—helping converted sinners to grow more like Christ as they defeat their problems God's way and are thereby freed to serve Him and to wait for His Son to come from the heavens.

Paul made it clear earlier in this same letter (1:28) that announcing or proclaiming Christ involved not only "*teaching* every person" (an evangelistic ministry) but also "counseling every person." Thus it is clear that, in part, what Paul had in mind even in Colossians 4:3 included the counsel that he gave to young converts (cf. the chapter, "Counseling New Converts" in *More Than Redemption*).

I have already made it clear that the use of biblical language and biblically derived language is important, and I have given several reasons for making that statement. Here, I wish to mention one additional factor to support that contention and urge you to be aware of and actively concerned about it. That factor is *authority*. To motivate counselees, it is imperative, especially when they resist good counsel, to be able to assert God's authority. Apart from an objective, revealed authority from God, there is no way to counsel effectively. All other authority is specious. With a counseling ministry that depends on the Scriptures for all of its teaching, however, that authority becomes a powerful, vital force that may be used for good.

Of course, authority may be misused. I shall not discuss that matter here, however, or the distinction between authority and authoritarianism, because I have dealt with these matters elsewhere.[17]

But here I would like to observe that *how* the Scriptures are used in counseling makes a big difference. It is a matter of first importance. If they are used, as so often they are in most so-called Christian counseling, to support and to illustrate non-Christian counseling principles and practices, they soon lose their authority. If on the other hand, they are used properly, if they are carefully exegeted and explained in detail to the counselee so that he understands (1) what the Scriptures say, (2) that this teaching really does come from the Bible, and (3) how to apply and implement it in his own life, then—and then only—will the Scriptures lend their full authority to the counsel that is given.

No flip-and-point system of Scripture use or "take this verse three times daily with prayer" approach will do. Biblical language and concepts are not magical formulae by which one says "open sesame" and all is well with the counselee; no, they are to be presented for what they are: God's

---

17 See *The Christian Counselor's Manual*, pp. 15–19; *More than Redemption*, pp. 18ff.

Word to the counselee. If a counselee doesn't understand what is taught and doesn't understand that it comes from the Scriptures, then he will not accept it for what it is. Indeed, he shouldn't. He must be certain that it is God who is telling him what to do, not merely some other sinful, fallible human being. Biblical concepts, in biblical language, without such explanatory backing, even when correct, lose their authority for the counselee.

Speak clearly (Col. 4:4)

Paul wanted to proclaim Christ clearly. When we proclaim Christ, we must set forth His attributes and His requirements plainly. To be unclear is to misrepresent *Him*. Clarity is the first cousin to honesty, while obscurity is kin to lying. When one reads Tillich's book of sermons, *The New Being*, and then plods through his two-volume *Theology*, he is struck by the dissimilarity of language. Could the same man have written both? The first is lucid; words flow and surge. The second is tedious; one lumbers his way along. If he is inclined to be of a suspicious or skeptical bent, he will ask himself, "Why did Tillich choose to write so differently in these two places?" If he could write so clearly in *The New Being*, why does he change his style in the *Theology*? Was it that he sought to disguise his basic atheism and unbelief beneath an avalanche of obtuse language? Or does what Jack Horn so aptly calls "bafflegab" better explain what was going on? We don't know what motivated him, of course. But it is interesting to notice the marked difference and to think about the kind of reasons that might lie behind that phenomenon.

J. Scott Armstrong, professor of the Wharton School of the University of Pennsylvania, tells us that controlled experiments demonstrated that

> an unintelligible communication from a legitimate source in the recipient's area of expertise will increase the recipient's rating of the author's competence.[18]

That means that once you make a name for yourself, people in your field will rate you higher if you write nonsense. That is a rather humbling fact for us writers who attempt to be clear to swallow. But I do not

---

18 Psychology Today (May, 1980), p. 12.

doubt that it is often true in this sinful world, where so many things are turned bottom side up. Of course, it makes us wonder whether Tillich was laughing up his sleeve about putting one over on his fellow theologians with his theologically bafflegab. I don't know, but one thing is certain: he didn't have to write that way—the language in *The New Being* makes that sure. He deliberately chose—for some reason or other—to write obscurely. The Christian counselor will make every attempt to be clear in spite of human perversity and its bent toward the obscure. This is what Paul was concerned about doing. It is the task of the minister of the Word. And counselees, confused and hurting, are not recipients in one's area of expertise, but persons in desperate need of help.

Speak graciously (Col. 4:6)

I have already said something about this earlier. Gracious speech may be frank, but it may not be insulting, demeaning, harsh, or inconsiderate. To speak of human beings deterministically is not to speak graciously. Gracious speech, in ministering the Word, focuses on the counselee and shows a definite sensitivity to his or her genuine concerns. Grace here probably refers to speech that is both appropriate to the person and to the occasion, and is helpful. Gracious speech in counseling is speech that edifies the one to whom it is spoken. But it is more than that; to speak graciously also means to

Speak persuasively, attractively

Or, as Paul says, with speech that is seasoned with salt. Such speech is tangy, tasty; it is never bland, dull, or uninteresting. It is not enough to tell the truth or to rehearse facts. Nor is it enough to read the Bible to people. The biblical truth must be presented in language that is persuasive.

Counseling is not merely cognitive, educational. There are plenty of counselees who know what God wants them to do, and many of these even have a good idea of how to go about getting it done, but they don't do it. Often they *won't*. Paul, therefore, speaks elsewhere of encouragement and rebuke. To facts must be added warning and promise, and these must be spelled out with a salty tongue.

Then there is the *manner* in which the truth is presented—that too comes under Paul's purview in these words. All counseling should be appealing both in the array of data assembled by the counselor and in the hopeful, enthusiastic way in which he uses these data. There is no subject, no matter how hard it is to hear or do, that cannot be presented in a light that makes it shine if the counselor will only pay attention to manner as well as to matter. And what he says must have a barb on it to hook the counselee and the biblical truth together in a way that makes it very difficult for him to shake it loose.

Often, illustrative material will help. Any counselor who does not use illustrations in his counseling is serving unsalted food to his counselees. Illustrations can be overdone, but they can also be powerful assets in communicating a point and in hooking the counselee on the truth. The thoughtful timing, according to which the counselor presents what he has to say, will also often be of great importance. And the very choice of vocabulary, coupled with the attitude of the counselor and the expression on his face, can be of major significance.

These four factors are of great importance in all biblical counseling. But how can they be achieved? Let me suggest two aids.

First, develop a biblical style (style means language usage). A good counseling style is always current, appropriate, and conversational.

To be *current* in style is to be up-to-date. That means that you must wash out all the King James vocabulary and constructions, the so-called "preachy" language that has turned off so many young people as well as others. If you don't normally say "thou" or "thee," then why say "unto" or "beloved"? It would be more appropriate in our day simply to say "to" and "friend." Don't say "trust the person of Christ" (a pseudo-Elizabethan construction) when what you mean is "trust Christ." The words "the person of" don't add anything helpful. They just confuse—and make you sound silly. The New Testament writers used the current, popular language of their day, not the more formal Greek.

To become *appropriate*, learn to shift your choice of vocabulary according to the person you are addressing and according to the situation. In counseling a garbage collector, you will use a different vocabulary and style than when counseling an English professor. I am not speaking of making a shift from intelligibility toward unintelligibility as Tillich did. What I am referring to is a shift that is required in each situation in order to achieve the maximum intelligibility and persuasiveness. What I mean is that in talking to a counselee about the recent death of a loved one and in speaking to a teenager about his dirt bike, the styles used will necessarily differ, if you want to reach each person for Christ. Once one has developed the ability to shift styles according to persons and circumstances, he need not *consciously* do so. It is a lot like shifting gears in an automobile: once you have become familiar with the gear shift, you use it unconsciously at the proper time. One whose concern for counselees allows him, with Paul, to weep with those who weep and to rejoice with those who rejoice, will also shift language styles effortlessly. It is important, then, to develop more than one style and to know how to adapt as the need arises. The use of many styles, rather than one uniform style, demands flexibility. Any man who cannot change styles, once he has prayerfully attempted to do so in the right way, ought to reconsider his call to the ministry. Flexibility grows by constant, conscious effort and use combined with proper concern, sensitivity, and know-how. It will rarely appear on its own.

The ability to become all things to all men, as Paul put it when speaking of this adaptability, is demonstrated most vividly in the preaching and in the speeches of Paul in the book of Acts. For more on this whole subject, see my book, *Audience Adaptation in the Sermons and Speeches of Paul*.

To become *conversational* means to do in counseling what you do in other conversations. You will not always sound the way you do in the pulpit. You must learn to be more relaxed (not sloppy), more tentative at times, more casual, more personal, more soft-spoken. Again, this will come only by determined, conscious effort.

Second, develop wholesome language.

In Titus 2:8 we read of healthy or wholesome speech that "cannot be censored." Here, Paul's concern is to shut the mouth of an opponent and bring him to shame (note the powerful influence of language on another). But in a counseling session, this wholesome speech has an even more positive purpose. As Titus 1:9 and 2:2 indicate, healthy teaching leads to the acquisition of a healthy, wholesome faith. The right sort of speech leads to the right sort of belief and life in those who are taught by it. This wholesome speech, Paul tells Timothy, agrees with the wholesome words of Jesus (1 Tim. 6:3) and is the opposite of "an unhealthy desire for discussions and controversies over words." Counselors must stay free from wrangling with counselees, debating inconsequential issues, etc. (cf. 1 Tim. 6:4; 2 Tim. 2:14). Instead, they must use words that "build up."

How does one learn to speak in a wholesome manner that will please his Lord? Certainly not by reading E.S.T. materials or by immersing himself day after day in the ideologies and the language of Fritz Perls. Ellis won't help either. No, Paul gives us the answer to this question in 2 Timothy 1:13.

Hold on to the pattern of healthy words that you heard from me.

These healthy words are found in the Scriptures and include the gospel and the counsel subsequently given to new converts, about which Paul was speaking in these pastoral letters.

But in order to speak what Paul spoke and to speak as he spoke, we must know the pattern that he used, and we must hold on to it. That we are exhorted to hold on to it indicates that it is possible to lose it and that there are forces at work that would like to take it away from us. In our day, the biblical pattern has been lost by those who substitute worldly ideas for it and by those who try to mix them with it.

But what of the pattern? Calvin rightly says,

> Paul commands Timothy to hold fast the doctrine which he learned, not only as to substance, but as to the very form of expression.

So, if we would use wholesome language, i.e., language that honors God and leads to the welfare of the counselee, we will see to it that our language, as well as our teaching, accords with the apostolic pattern in the Scriptures. Only then can we be sure that *what* we say and *how* we say it is nourishing and life-giving. That means that a diligent counselor will spend hours each week studying biblical teaching and counseling in an attempt to learn all he can about both. It will be his desire to reproduce in his ministry the pattern by which Paul counseled.

Chapter 5
The Counselee's Language

You can learn a lot about a counselee, his views, and his problems from his language. Counselors, therefore, must study language in order to be able to gather data in counseling. It would be a shame to miss so much valuable data. Evaluating the language of a counselee requires skill in carefully noticing both the language used and the way in which it is used. It is also important to note who it is that is using a particular sort of language. (If a Christian leader starts swearing or using language not characteristic of his previous vocabulary, this itself could be a most significant clue that, properly investigated, would lead to the heart of the problem more quickly than anything else.)

When listening to a counselee, ask yourself, "Do his words ['can't,' 'impossible,' 'ruined'] reflect a Christian viewpoint on calamity?" You'd have to conclude, "No, rather they give evidence of a basically pagan outlook." You recognize from his words that his working view of God (not the theoretically articulated one that he would give you if you asked, but the one that emerges in a crisis) at best is deistic. No wonder, then, he has caved in under the stresses and strains of the problems he is confronting. On the other hand, if his words gave evidence of a day-by-day faith in the sovereign power of God at work even in this trial, you would probably put the emphasis in your counseling on different matters.

Or, take another situation. Suppose you notice that the counselee's language is stilted, stuffy, abstract, and impersonal. You then will be asking a different sort of question: "Could he be trying to impress me or someone else by his [often wrong] use of technical terms? Could there be a frightened or possibly a hypocritical person hiding behind this language? Is it stiff because it has all been rehearsed and recited this way many times before? Is he in some way trying to excuse some behavior or attitude that will presently emerge?"

In another instance, a counselee's language may exhibit a tendency to shift blame to someone else. In still another, the jargon he uses indicates the influence of a psychiatric viewpoint that is being used to structure and to interpret the data that you are receiving. You will want to know how far his thinking has gone in this direction and how greatly his perception has been clouded by this influence. You will want to learn whether it is a continuing, pervasive influence, or whether it was merely a passing phase adopted by him in his endeavor to understand his situation. These and dozens of other considerations like them make a difference to the perceptive biblical counselor. And these answers, so important to counseling, in one way or another, depend upon the counselor's awareness and knowledge of what is present in the counselee's language. All through counseling sessions, the biblical counselor will be carefully analyzing the language of the counselee—what he says and how he says it.

From this kind of information, not only from the verbal content itself, a counselor may reach any number of tentative and (ultimately) firm conclusions. For instance, he may wish to probe more fully into how a counselee views his problem: "You spoke of your '*sickness*,' if I am not mistaken. Tell me, do you really view it as an organic illness, or did you have something different in mind?" Or, he may determine that he will get nowhere until he has countered the attitude that is so evident in the language of despair to which he has been listening. Biblical hope may not be accepted until the counselee has been brought to repentance over someone's working deism that we mentioned above. He must be confronted with his worship of another god. Until the counselee recognizes that God is in the problem, working all things together for His children, there is no possibility of moving on to other things. But, N. B., language analysis brought this deism to light.

The biblical counselor will be concerned about the counselee's language. He knows the influence that language can have on a person's thinking and life. So, at times, he may have to step in and challenge it. ("What you really mean is that it would be very difficult; it isn't impossible, as you said.") If he believes that language changes life, he will be alive to the fact that the counselee's wrong structure of reality governs his life for ill and will want to help him to put on new ways of thinking and speaking that are in accord with biblical truth. He knows that if the counselee persists in saying the wrong things, or trying to say the right things in the wrong way, this will defeat his efforts. So, he will help the counselee express his thoughts and structure his thinking in the proper language. Instead of allowing a counselee to go on saying, "Well, it happened to me again," when that isn't the way it really was, he will urge the counselee to say, "Well, I've done it to myself again." In that way, he can gain an accurate perception of the situation, and the words point to a solution to the problem rather than confirm his resignation in a deterministic despair.

As I have observed, the *way* in which the counselee says what he says is significant. Is he tense, angry, fearful? Emotion is revealed in tone of voice and rate of speech. But it is also revealed in the counselee's choice of words or in his inability to find the right words to express the overwhelming emotion.

Unedifying language exchanged by two or more counselees will be stopped with a statement to the effect that "I'm not going to allow you to talk to one another like that in counseling. This cutting each other to ribbons is one of the reasons you're here, and for your own sakes, as well as because God says it is sin, you will have to learn to speak differently. I'll stop you on every occasion from now on to make you aware of what has become a destructive habit. And each time, I'll help you say what you have to say in a manner pleasing to God, which is calculated, therefore, to get better results from one another as well."

I have mentioned pickled cliches. These too, must be challenged and replaced. In addition, listen for

Language of exaggeration: "Impossible! Nobody cares."
Language of helplessness: "I can't; I don't know how."
Language of hopelessness: "What's the use?"
Language of blame-shifting: "I would have if only he had ..."
Language of sickness: "He's sick/ill/mentally ill."
Language of self-pity: "Why? Why me? Why not? Why this?"
Language of excuse: "I know, but you see ..."

All of this reveals a lot about the counselee, his basic working orientation toward life, his view of God, his perspective on the problem, and his estimate of himself.

You will hear most of the language that I have described in the counselee's presentation and explanation of the problem before he has become aware of your concern for language. Counselors must not allow themselves to be so caught up in the data content during this period that they fail to note such things. Frequently, the language in which the data are given is every bit as enlightening as the data themselves. This is especially true when the language and the data contradict one another.

Jot down notes about language on your Weekly Record. Note exactly all potentially revealing terms and constructions for later use. Exact quotations bring conviction when read back to a counselee later at the appropriate time. When you have enough notes to discover a pattern, get ready to discuss it with the counselee. Don't guess; have the evidence. You will find yourself noting and quoting it frequently in counseling.

Revelation 3:17 powerfully demonstrates how Jesus used this approach:

> *Because you say, "I am rich," and "I have become rich and have need of nothing," and don't know that you are miserable and pitiable and poor and blind and naked ...*

His evidence of the wrong attitudes and understandings of the Laodiceans was gathered from their own words (notice his quotation of their assertions): "Because you say ..." Having quoted them, He continues, "... I counsel you ..." His counsel was backed up by their very own language. He analyzed their sinful error: "You don't know [that is, your words indicate that you don't] that you are ..." Their proud language revealed their totally wrong approach to everything. And, it was by quoting their own words back to them that he silenced all objections. Counselors will do well to learn to counsel like their Lord.

There are times, however, when you must not wait; rather, you must jump in immediately with both feet when some statement, or the language in which it is phrased, reveals the very heart of the problem; and you must do just what Jesus did when He said to the rich young ruler, "Don't call me good."

Much more could be said about the counselee's language, but this will suffice to alert the concerned counselor to the possibilities that such language analysis holds for biblical counseling.

Chapter 6
A Personal Improvement Plan

Throughout, I have mentioned the possibility of changing your current language usage. It is absolutely necessary to adopt language that fits into the counseling system you use rather than language borrowed from another that clashes with it. The latter distorts your best intentions and leads you and the counselee toward ends that are contrary to those you have in view. It is my hope that by now you are aware of this problem and would like to make a change in your present language patterns. How can you do so?

A simple, effective program is needed. Busy pastors and Christian workers do not have the time to establish elaborate programs, and even if they try to do so, the pressures usually get to them before the program has an opportunity to work, and they abandon it. Moreover, if it can be done simply and fairly painlessly, then why enter into any elaborate program? So, for what it is worth, here is a program that has grown out of much experience in helping students of all sorts to change their language patterns.

Review

A. Become thoroughly acquainted with your present practices. Because we do what we do by habit unconsciously, easily, and automatically, you should record your sermons, your counseling sessions, and some of your casual conversations to see what the consistent patterns are that run throughout your speech and what your patterns are in counseling itself. Do this for a period of time under different circumstances to obtain a fairly representative sample of what you are actually doing. Better still, if you have some recordings from the recent past, use them. They will give you a less biased sample. (You were not then aware that you were recording for this purpose, as you now are.) Knowing that you will be recording will make you somewhat wary, and you will find that, as a result, problems will occur less frequently. While that messes up your sample a bit, it nevertheless is the beginning of the structure by which you will effect change. So it's not so bad after all. If you have older samples, include these in your review of what you are doing, but don't rely on old recordings alone. Make some new ones too.

I stress the use of recordings because it is not usually wise to depend on your memory or to determine how you speak from an armchair position. Get some actual samples; otherwise, you will miss items that you will pick up on a careful perusal of recordings. It will eliminate the guesswork.

B. From these recordings, make a list of all of the words that must be washed out of your language and all of the phrases and constructions that you must eliminate. Be brutal. Include everything that seems questionable. Then rank these in order of importance. You will not be able to work on them all at once.

Revise

Go over your list carefully; add or subtract material as you think you ought to. But do not remove any item for less than a *good* reason. Next to each item on the list, write out why you think it ought to be removed. This is important. It will get you thinking through language usage in a new and more thorough manner. Don't skip this step.

Then, next to each wrong word or construction, carefully write down a biblical, or biblically derived, alternative that says it correctly. This may take time. You may have difficulty finding the exact substitute for some items. That is OK. Take your time. Fill in the alternatives where you can. Continue to pray, study, and think about the rest; in time, they will come. Consult the indexes of books by nouthetic counselors; check *The Practical Encyclopedia of Christian Counseling*. There is no rush; work on those that you have alternatives to first, and while you are doing that, you may find the alternatives for the rest. Keep your list. Revise it until you are sure that you have the best possible alternatives. You can do all of this at your leisure, but I would suggest that you take about a half-hour each day for a week or so to do this.

Redo

A. Use these new words and constructions in practice sessions with a recording, and go over them often enough to make yourself completely familiar with them until they sound right to you on playback. You want to become comfortable with them.

B. Consciously include the words and phrases you are currently working on in daily conversations to get the feel of them under actual combat conditions. Continue to do this until you think you have them down pat.

C. Make some more recordings of sermons and sessions. Play these and note improvements and the areas in which you have failed to make any progress. Note also any new words or phrases that you should include on your list.

D. Continue steps B and C until you are satisfied. Then repeat the whole process for the remainder of the items on the list as often as necessary. All of this must be done as a prayerful commitment to God. You must want to change in order to please God and to be a greater blessing to your neighbor.

Conclusion

What can I say in conclusion? There is little more to add. I have exhorted throughout, and I don't intend to do so again at this point. I have outlined a simple but effective program that you may follow if you wish to; nothing more needs to be said about that either.

Let me conclude, then, with one additional observation. It is not possible or necessary to design a program to teach you how to become aware of and to interpret the language problems of your counselees. This cannot be done very well in a book. But there are two things that can be done to improve your ability to do so. First, if you can take supervised work with a certified member of the National Association of Nouthetic Counselors, it is possible that he can arrange to work with you on this problem. Second, when you have followed the Personal Improvement Program that I outlined in the previous chapter, you will have become so fully aware of the sort of thing to look for that you should have no great difficulty in discovering the language problems of others. It is always harder to be self-critical. If you have achieved that, there should be little trouble in generalizing what you have learned to others.

Best wishes as you set out on your program. May God bless you greatly and make you a blessing, too.

Your Place in the Counseling Revolution

Foreword[1]

Because I was deeply concerned about the matters included in this book, I chose the subject for my Staley lectureship of January 1975, which I delivered to the student body of Cedarville College, Cedarville, Ohio. And because the subject matter is pertinent to those who belong to a larger audience, I am sending these lectures forth to the Christian public in general, hoping that in some measure, God will use this humble effort as one small contribution to bringing about the revolution in counseling that may in time spark a new revival of the Christian faith in this country.

The book has been released with two sorts of target audiences in mind. First, this includes the large number of Christian men considering a ministry of Christian counseling. Secondly, I have in mind the average church member who must determine to support efforts made in this direction, or the coming revolution in counseling will not materialize. I want to convince the former that they should consider the work of the pastoral ministry, and I wish to inform the latter about what is happening in the Church of Christ and enlist not only their support but their participation as well.

If, at first, the word revolution sounds too sweeping and belligerent, let me urge you to reserve your judgment about this until you have finished reading. By then, I hope that you will see the necessity for nothing less. I like the definition of a revolt (or revolution, as we now call it) in Crabb's English synonyms. He writes:

> *Revolt...* signifies originally a warring or turning against the power to which one has been subject; but revolt is mostly

---

1 This essay was first published as a short stand-alone book in 1975,

taken either in an indifferent or a good sense for resisting a foreign dominion which has been imposed by force of arms.

That definition, in every way, is appropriate to the situation that has prevailed until recently. If "force of arms" may be considered figuratively referring to the warnings by which pastors and Christians have been intimidated, the picture is complete. A power, foreign to the Christian Church, has held her tightly in its grips for a long while. There have been many collaborators. But, at long last, tired of the failure, convinced that within the Church itself there are resources that have been virtually untapped, many are awakening to the need and to the opportunities and are beginning to throw off the yoke of oppression. The collaborators, understandably, are not happy. Hopefully, some of them can be won to the cause. But largely, the revolution—as indeed most revolutions are—has begun as a grass-roots struggle. To better alert and inform those at the grassroots level who sense its importance, I am sending forth this book.

Chapter 1
Don't Be Short-Changed

I thought at first of entitling this address, "Anyone who goes to a psychiatrist ought to have his head examined," but I thought better of it and settled for "Don't Be Short-Changed."

Counselees, or those who urge them to receive counseling, are interested in change. In one way or another, the uppermost concern is to change their lives.

- Perhaps they have had it with wives/husbands/parents/children. They want a change.
- Possibly, they seek relief from depression, worry, or fear, or mysterious voices speaking out of nowhere.
- Or, they are anxious to learn how to get along with others, how to control tempers, how to communicate with persons they love, how to keep a job, and how to rope and tie a runaway sex drive.

Any one of these, or dozens of other problems, impel people everywhere to seek counsel from others, hoping they will provide the change that will bring peace and joy.

Counselors are people who try to help them affect that change. Many of these people who counsel are well-meaning and enter the field from altruistic motives; others are themselves confused, seeking answers; some are in the work for the prestige, the power, or the money, and some for the gratification of baser desires.

But in this attempt to effect change, profound and urgent questions arise, such as: Who sets the standard for change? The counselee? The counselor? Someone else? Does the counselee know enough? May the counselor's values be accepted? And—who answers the question about who sets the standard? Who effects the change? Counselee? Counselor?

Both? Another? What means will be used to bring about the change? All those that work? Then is brainwashing acceptable? Surely, there must be *some* limitations in *some* directions—but that's just the problem: where shall the lines be drawn?—and who shall draw them? These and many other similar questions inevitably arise in the minds of all thoughtful counselors.

The trouble is—there isn't one in a thousand who can begin to answer them. Yet, without answers, where are we, what shall counselors do, and what of the counselee?

Counselors read, experiment, debate, and write, yet they are no nearer to agreement on these questions than when they first began. Seated in his plush, expensive study, lined with learned tomes, the typical counselor, seemingly serene and secure, is nothing of the sort if he is a man of integrity and a diligent student of his profession. Daily, he is harassed by the silent but strong protests over every action he takes and every word that he speaks, which come from the authors who observe him from their perches on his shelves. "Too directive," cry some. "Why don't you reflect his feelings?" shout others. "Get rid of all that nonsense about value; focus on the behavior," demands a third. From all sides, competing 'isms and 'erapies woo and warn.

In his better moments he tells himself: "Toss the whole business overboard. After all, who can know what is right? I don't even have time to learn all of the systems, with their presuppositions, principles, and practices, let alone try them out! Why, there are classical Freudians, Dynamic Freudians, Neo-Freudians, Adlerians and Jungians, Logotherapists, Integrity Therapists, Reality Therapists, Radical Therapists, Rational-emotive Therapists, Gestalt Therapists, Contract Therapists, Primal Screamers, Laingians, Transactional Analysts, Skinnerians, Behaviorists by the buckets, Rogerians, Group Therapists, Family Therapists, etc., etc., etc. Why in the world should I suppose that what I am doing is right?"

And think of the poor counselee—in confusion, meandering from one counselor to another—looking for someone who can help him. In the process he is diagnosed, misdiagnosed, and re-diagnosed. He may be told that he is sick, or that he has been poorly socialized by parents and peers, or that he has been wrongly conditioned, or that his difficulty is genetic, or that he has failed to live up to his full potential. He may be assured that the problem is illness, or bad training, or learned behavior, or emotional immaturity, or chemical, or interpersonal, or constitutional, or existential, or whatever in origin. Appropriately, he will be treated, trained, encouraged, taught, or medicated in widely varying ways. "Let it all hang out," says one. "You need to get it all together," says the next. "Tell me about your childhood, your sex life, and your dreams," says another. "Take these pills four times a day and see me in six weeks," or "Renegotiate all of your personal contracts," or "Get rid of those inhibitions—find a man with whom you can have successful sexual relations," or "You must have a series of E.S.T. treatments (i.e., electroshock therapy—or, to put it more realistically, grand mal seizures, artificially induced)," or "We shall recondition your behavior," or "Hypnotism will help," or "Get a frontal lobotomy," or "Talk it out," or "Scream," or well, that's just about what one feels like doing when he hears even so small a portion of the whole as this.

In the process, people have been advised to urinate upon their father's graves, punch pillows until the feathers fly, file for a divorce if they don't get along with a spouse, and just about anything else one could imagine. Before he is through, a counselee may run the gamut, being assured that all will be well if only he medicates, or copulates, or urinates, or meditates, or ventilates!

What is he to do? Who should he believe? Where is he to turn?

And, in the face of all of this uncertainty, don't fail to notice what it is all about. Remember, all of these views, all of these persons, all of these methods are concerned about *changing people's lives*! If physicians were so divided and uncertain, would we entrust our bodies to them? If airlines and airline pilots differed so widely about flying principles and practices, who would fly? Yet, think, people by the millions turn to such counselors to *change their LIVES*! That means—to change their values, to change their attitudes, to change their beliefs, to change their behavior, and to change their relationships to the significant persons in their lives! DARE we allow anyone to meddle in such matters when all is in flux?

Think about the trick a psychiatrist played upon his fellow practitioners—he sent twelve persons—sane as you or I—into twelve of the nation's leading mental institutions for the expressed purpose of discovering how accurate psychotherapeutic diagnosis is. What do you think happened? You guessed it; some of them were wrongly diagnosed as having a serious mental illness. How many do you think? Would you believe half? Wrong. Would you believe three-fourths? Still wrong. Would you believe all twelve? Right! *All Twelve!* A one hundred percent failure!! And listen to this: of the twelve diagnoses, eleven were diagnoses of schizophrenia! Moreover, these "patients" made no attempt to deceive but acted normally during the entire period of diagnostic evaluation! No wonder Karl Menninger, commenting on the farce, said: "Schizophrenia is just a nice Greek word."

Surely, by now, we should be asking not only where counselees can find help but also how they can be protected in their gullibility and vulnerability from misguided (even though well-intentioned), incompetent, foolish, and unscrupulous persons. Who (or what) will prevent them from making changes of thought and action that can only disappoint and that may lead to ill consequences equally as bad or worse than those previously experienced?

And, surely, all of this confusion, contradiction, and chaos not only must give us pause before approaching or sending someone to the self-styled experts or professionals, but it should also make us ask an even more basic question: What is behind the disorder or (as Zillborg called it) the "disarray?" Other fields, while having healthy disagreements, seem to make progress and seem to be able to tack down many areas of common agreement. Yet, in counseling, there is a consensus about nothing. Is there not something radically wrong in the discipline of counseling? *What could it be?*

As I gather it, coming here today necessitates an answer to that question. As you might suppose from what I have said, giving that answer is no small task. Indeed, after hearing something of the various opinions and ideologies to which I have alluded, you may wonder why I came—how I could accept the invitation in good faith, and what brings me here anyway. Certainly, I could not be arrogant enough to imagine that I had the final word. Could I come to make another vain thrust and thus stir up more sediment to foul the pool further? Dare I even think that I could introduce the idea that would clarify the situation and point toward a pathway that emerges from the fog? No, if I came with another such word, I should not only be a fool but also a charlatan. I do not so come.

"Then, what brings you here?" you ask. Answer:

To point to the path leading to the clear light and sunshine, to explain what is behind the confusion and how it may be swept aside, to herald a new day of counseling that has already begun to dawn— and about which you may possibly hear much more in the not-too-distant future; to challenge you to join the ranks, and to hope that this meager effort may bear some fruit toward these ends!

"Wait a minute," you reply.

First, you said that you were not bringing in another opinion or ideology, yet now you seem to say just the opposite. You'd better explain—and make it plain; I've heard just about all I want to take of confusion and contradiction for one day!

OK, OK—I'll give it to you straight. I have not come to offer one more opinion, system, or ideology. I would not dare; as a matter of fact, I wonder continually at the audacity of those who do. Instead, I have come with good news. There is hope in the midst of the chaos, but it is not found in *my way*.

Remember the question I asked earlier but did not answer? It went something like this: since other disciplines (engineering, business, medicine, and even non-clinical and non-counseling psychology) seem to be able to arrive at some measure of order and cohesion—enough at least to produce some concrete results—must not something be radically wrong with counseling? The answer to that question is "yes." Something *is* radically wrong with counseling, and *this is it:* almost to a man, counselors have rejected the only true standard of human values, beliefs, attitudes, and behavior. Yet those matters comprise the stuff of which counseling is made. They have *looked* everywhere else and tried everything else, but have totally *ignored* the one Book that can bring order out of chaos. Only a word from God Himself can properly tell us how to change. In the Bible alone can be found the true description of man, his plight, and God's solution in Christ. Only the Scriptures can tell us what kind of persons we must become. Only God can command, direct, and give the power to effect the proper changes that will enable men He redeems to renew the image corrupted by the fall. Two Skinnerians in a room with their latest sausage grinder, by which they claim to be able to grind any sort of sausage one wishes, cannot agree about what kind of sausage they want, i.e., what sort of man to produce. Each wants sausage that thinks like himself. God has not only *told us* what man must become, but has *shown* us in Christ! In short, counselors are in their present state of confusion, swayed by every new fad precisely because they have rejected the one and only perfect and lasting textbook on counseling.

Textbook did you say? The Bible a *textbook* for counseling?' Yes, the Bible is God's basic text for living. It contains "all things pertaining to life and godliness" (II Peter 1:3). In it is all that a counselor or counselee needs to know in order to honor God by loving Him with all that he has, and by loving his neighbor as himself. As a matter of fact, on those two commandments—and in the scriptural explanations of how to fulfill them—hangs all of the work of counseling.

In counseling—per se—we do not find many persons presenting problems about the troubles they are having with *things*. ("You see Doc, there is this chair that I have been having difficulty with... " or "I came here to discuss the state of the carburetor on my Toyota.") When those with organic difficulties have been eliminated by sending such persons to physicians, what is left is that large number of people who are in trouble in one way or another with other *persons*—with God and their neighbors.

"But," I can almost *hear* the objection, "you don't use the Bible as a textbook for engineering or architecture or medicine, do you?" Of course not. "Well, then, why do you use it as a textbook for counseling?" Because, while the Bible was never *intended* to be a textbook about business or engineering, God Himself, in the passages cited, as elsewhere, tells us that it *is* a textbook concerned precisely with the problems encountered in counseling. And from the confusion seen uniquely in that field, it should be evident that just such a text is what is desperately needed.

How extraordinary, indeed, it is for Christians, those who claim to believe in the inerrancy and authority of the Scriptures, and who have been saved through faith in Jesus Christ, whose death for their sins is recorded therein, to doubt the fact that the Bible is the textbook for living—and, of course, for effecting every change in living! How could it be otherwise? God alone can tell man what values to espouse. No one else originated the Ten Commandments! God alone can disclose the chief goal of man, explain the core of his problems, and offer the fundamental solutions to them. Indeed, if counselors, apart from the Scriptures, could do so, the Bible—and, to be sure, Christ Himself—would have been given in vain! But counselors *cannot*. That is precisely why we are presently in this thick soup.

Well, then, what is the alternative? "There is hope, you say? Then tell me about it—I shall listen cautiously."

To begin with, God everywhere in the Scriptures commands change:

> *As obedient children, do not be conformed to former lusts ... but like the Holy One who called you, be holy yourselves also in all your behavior (I Peter l:14,15).*
> *You must walk no longer as the heathen walk (Ephesians 4:17).*
> *Grow by grace, even by the knowledge of our Lord Jesus Christ (II Peter 3:18).*

I could go on and on, but you know already that this is true. What you may not have realized, however, is that every biblical exhortation, every insistence upon change, implies hope. God never demands of His children that which He has not provided for them. We are not only saved by grace, but our sanctification (i.e., our continued growth and change from sin toward righteousness) as Christians is also the result of God's grace. As Paul told the Galatians, we did not begin the Christian life by grace ... only to complete it by our own efforts (Galatians 3:3). No, all is of grace. That means, therefore, that God Himself has provided the instructions and the power to live and grow according to them. The instructions—the goals, values, presuppositions, principles, and practices—are found in the Scriptures. The power for Christians to live by them is provided by His Spirit. That is the good news about counseling that I bring today. And everywhere—throughout the country—and even elsewhere in this world, Christian ministers are awakening to the fact. The same Book that says that God has provided what is needed for counseling also says that it has been provided for the equipping of ministers for the work of changing lives: that the "man of God" (a term picked up from the Old Testament and used in the pastoral letters to refer to the pastor/teacher) may be adequate, thoroughly equipped. While every Christian should do counseling, it is to the minister that He has assigned the task as a life work.

No wonder there has been confusion! The wrong persons, using the wrong standards, have tried to do all sorts of wrong things without power.

But what of the Christian "professionals," most of whom espouse an eclectic view ("Something from Freud, something from Rogers, something from Skinner... and a little from the Bible")? Hal Brooks once said, "If you don't know where you are going, any road will do." *That* is the problem with eclecticism. It is good only for those who do not know where they are going. Skinner does not eclectically use Rogerian methodology, nor does Rogers use Skinnerian. Why not? Both see man's problem differently and therefore have different objectives in view. Each is committed to the different methodologies that will take them most surely to those destinations. Christians have an entirely different objective than all the rest—to change men so that they may become like Christ. Only God's road leads to that. It is time for Christians to stop riding on the world's bandwagons—they are headed in the wrong direction! The Bible, and the Bible alone, points the way. Therefore, as in salvation, so too in counseling—no other road will do.

But to be more specific, just what *does* the Bible provide? Let us look a *bit* more closely at II Timothy 3 to see.

In this fundamental passage concerning the Scriptures, it is important first to note that their twofold "*use*" or "*purpose*" is described *in terms of change:*

- Salvation: they are able to make one "wise unto salvation" and
- For those who *are* saved, they provide four things:
1. **Teaching**—they become the standard for faith and life; they show us all that God requires of us.
2. **Conviction**—they show us how we have failed to measure up to those requirements in our lives. The word used is a legal term meaning more than to "rebuke" or "accuse," but speaks

of pursuing the case to its end *successfully*. The Scriptures show us our sin; they flatten us in repentance.
3. **Correction**—the word means (literally) "to stand up straight again." While it is true that the Bible knocks us down, cuts and bruises, rips up and tears down, it is equally true that this is done only to prepare us for its work of picking us up again and heading us in God's proper direction. The Scriptures also bind up and heal; they plant and build. By God's Spirit, who works in and through them, they not only help us put off sin, but also enable us to put on righteousness.
4. **Training in Righteousness**—It is not enough to quit the past ways, break old habits, and stop sinning. If that is all that occurs, one will find himself soon reverting to past ways. He must not only do so, but learn *as a way of life to* walk in the new ways (Ephesians 4).

And what does all of this amount to? Change. We have just been describing the process of *change*. Change in depth. Change as profound as one could imagine. Eternal change. And it is all found in God's Book, the counselor's textbook on human change, the Bible.

I urge you—consider the facts and make the decision. Perhaps God is calling some of you to such a ministry of vital change. If so, answer in faith. With such powerful resources available, why should you or your counselees be *short-changed?*

Chapter 2
The Picture On Your Wall

All right. So we have located the fundamental failure in modern counseling—God and His revealed Word have been omitted from the counseling picture. In discussions among counseling people, including Christians, the names of Mowrer, Glasser, Perls, Harris, Rogers, Skinner, Lazarus, and Erickson are more frequently heard, and their views are better known than the names of Paul, Peter, David, Solomon, and even Jesus Christ. God and His viewpoint, for most, are not a viable option. *That* is the problem. Now what? How can we rectify that situation?

"Isn't that simple enough to answer?" you may ask. "After all, if God is missing from the picture, what we need to do is to bring Him into it."

Well, that reply can be either right or wrong, depending entirely upon what you mean by "bringing God into the picture." The suggestion, of course, is not revolutionary or new. For years, people have been writing books with titles like *Psychiatry and the Church, Freud and Christ,* etc. But when you begin to explore the ways and means that have been used to achieve this end, and even how some Christians have conceived of that end itself, you soon begin to recognize that there are problems connected with "bringing God into the counseling picture." The matter is more complex than it might seem at first. And, in my opinion, that is precisely why so many Christians have unwittingly fallen into the sin of accommodationism, which consists of accommodating Christianity to some other view. I find it necessary to define this sin because it seems so few say anything about it. Moreover, there is more than one way in which Christian counselors have attempted to include God in their counseling, and as a result, more than one way that accommodationism can take place. And finally, I think that further study of the problem will convince you that these attempts to bring God into the picture mainly have been unsuccessful.

But, before we turn to the discussion itself, let me go one step further and state categorically that this issue is not merely an academic matter. It is not something that we can leave to the counselors to squabble over as an intradepartmental feud. Instead, it is nothing less than a question fraught with large practical consequences for both the counselor and those whom he counsels. The wrong answer to the question involves grave dangers to both, and grave dangers to the Christian Church. Counselor and counselee alike stand in personal jeopardy.

"*That* is *strong* language. Are you sure that you are not overstating the hazard? Why do you make such an extreme statement? Wouldn't it be better merely to say that the matter is of *some* moment to all of us because it has practical consequences?"

No, I am *not* overstating the case. Indeed, I will go so far as to say that if God is not brought into the picture properly—i.e., if He is not included in counseling in a manner that accords with what He Himself has required in the Scriptures, it is worse to introduce Him than to leave Him out altogether.

"*Wait* a minute. How can you *say* that? How could leaving God out of the counseling room be less dangerous than including Him—wrongly perhaps—but including Him? Aren't you the one who is always complaining about people leaving God out of counseling? I don't think that I *understand* you. Have I caught you in an inconsistency, or can you clarify what you are saying? I should think that even a little consideration for the place of God in counseling is to be preferred to none."

Well, your question is fair enough, and it surely represents the thinking of many persons today, one of whom may have influenced you by their writings. But I must stand by what I have said. And, by the way, let me make it clear to begin with, that I do *not* wish to reproach anyone for his good intentions; that clearly is not the issue. There is nothing personal involved in my disagreement with the persons who have attempted to bring God into the counseling context. So there is no inconsistency in what I am saying. The real issue is whether, indeed, the wrong way of bringing God into the picture (to which I have alluded) does anything of the sort. That is to say, the issue is whether He will allow Himself to be brought into the picture that way. And, there is *one* personal matter, I confess, that I cannot avoid: *God is a Person* who does make this sort of thing more than an academic issue with reference to Himself. He takes it personally!

In this brief consideration of the matter, I want you to understand that I can do no more than scratch the surface of the problem; its implications are numerous. I certainly would not claim even to know how many there are. But as I peel off a few bits here and there, I think that you shall see plainly enough from those samples the depths of the subject that we have chosen to discuss. I shall focus on only one or two of these implications then, and try to give you at least some inkling of what I am talking about through them.

First, one way to bring God into the counseling picture *wrongly* is to introduce Him as an *additive*. This adjunctive use of God and His Name dishonors Him as God, denies His sovereignty, and deceives and discourages counselees.

"Wow! That's quite a charge. Can you substantiate it?"

Without a doubt. Ask yourself this question: When God is *added* to an already existing picture, to *what* (precisely) is He added? Well, the very fact that He is needed as an addition tells you, doesn't it?

"What do you mean?"

Just this. If there was a need to bring God into a picture in which He had no place before, the fact is that the picture to which He is added is an *ungodly* one. But I think that you can see that the very idea of associating God with such a picture by attaching God's name to a godless system is repugnant. To attempt to put Him into a system that was designed with no thought of Him, and in the final analysis, is (therefore) bent upon leaving Him out, is to dishonor Him. God refuses to be thus associated. He will not be identified with the golden calf. He rejects every idolatrous system created by men. Indeed, He declares: "I will not give my glory to another" (Isaiah 42:8). Do you think then that He will allow you to add His Name and that He will give His blessing to any system that was conceived in a proud autonomous spirit—a system, that by its structure finds no need for the living God?

"Well..."

There are no wells about it. God will not allow us to add Him to a system that, by its basic presuppositions, by its principles, and by its practices, excludes Him. The result would lead to God's participation in that unequal yoke that He Himself condemns. Christ simply does not associate with Belial!

Therefore, to baptize counseling systems like Freudian Psychoanalysis, Skinnerian Behaviorism, the Rogerian Human Potential Movement, or the Berne/Harris/Steiner views of Transactional analysis into the Christian fold unconverted by adding on God's Holy Name and sprinkling in a few assorted scriptural proof texts, ultimately amounts to taking His Name in vain. It means to represent God as in favor of ungodliness. To say the very least, the attempt to bring God into a picture in which there is no place for Him and into which He will not come can only be futile.

"Well, I can see your point, but are you talking about what people actually do, or are you fighting a straw man that wears clothes that *you* bought for him, then stuffed yourself?"

I can assure you that this is no straw man that I have been describing. As I have shown in my books, he is alive and all too healthy, and his practice is widespread. But before I give you a concrete example of what I am talking about, let me at least mention one other implication of the God-as-additive approach.

While the most serious error has been mentioned—i.e., misrepresenting God by saying that He is in favor of godless systems—there is another aspect of that fact: counselees thereby are seriously deceived. By labeling a system *Christian* when, in fact, it has no place for God, the counselor leads his counselees to believe that they are receiving *Christian* counseling (that is to say, counseling that, from the ground up, is from God—straight from His Word). Affixing a smattering of Christian activities or symbols to that system may give it a Christian appearance, particularly to an uncritical, hurting Christian who is confused and perhaps overly anxious to obtain help. In fact, although the additive counselor himself may be a Christian, and may think and speak of his counseling as Christian, in truth it is not. What is hard for counselees to understand is that the mere fact that a counselor is a Christian is no assurance that the counsel that he gives is Christian. Yet, the addition of a Christian counselor and Christian trappings to an ungodly system does not make it more godly. It simply makes it more dangerous. Thereby, the true content of the system is disguised. As a result, the trusting counselee stands in greater danger because he lets down his guard. If the system had been plainly labeled for what it was, he might have been able to protect himself.

"Then that is what you meant when you said that bringing God into the picture wrongly is worse than leaving Him out altogether!"

Exactly. There is no vital change in the picture itself when God's words and God's symbols are added to it. The picture has been *retitled*. The new title only *misrepresents* the facts; it does not *change* them. The fact that a painting depicts Whistler's mother cannot be altered by renaming her portrait "Whistler's Mother-in-law."

This deception, in which godless systems are depicted as godly ones, has many grave effects upon counselees. Let me mention just two.

On the one hand, this retitling of the picture leads to a false assurance in counselees (and perhaps also in self-deceived counselors). They think that the blessing of God is upon what they are doing when it is likely that it is not. (Of course, it is possible for God to work sovereignly even in such a context if He so wills. But then He will work against the system, in spite of it, and not because of it.) The deception leads counselees to trust in an unscriptural system as if it were biblical, thus according to it an authority and giving it a kind of submission that it does not deserve. The presence of a counselor, whose personal Christianity cannot be doubted, the use of prayer, and the sprinkling of a sufficient number of Bible verses often is all that it takes to make the deception complete. But these Christian additives, no matter how good they are in and of themselves, will not sanctify systems that (at their core) are godless and therefore, anti-Christian. To put it another way, even when employed by Christians, together with Christian additives, the effect of any anti-Christian system must always be harmful rather than helpful. And because God may choose to bless in spite of the sinful circumstances, that does not justify those circumstances for either the Christian counselor or counselee. Nor may either *expect* such help from God in that situation.

And not only is there a false assurance, but on the other hand, when the system at length fails to produce godly living (and that is something that no ungodly system *can* produce; the fruit of the Spirit grows and is harvested nowhere but in His field), the failure contributes to doubt and despair about God ("God's counsel didn't work," says the counselee).

OK, I've tried to tell you what it is like to attempt to *add* God to counseling, and I appreciate the fact that you have been waiting patiently for my answer to your earlier question. You've been wondering whether anyone really does such a thing or whether I'm beating a stuffed mule. Well, you realize, of course, that people don't *speak* about *adding God* to ungodly systems as I have, but they *do* it. The most recent example of this that I can cite appeared in a widely circulated Christian magazine. In an article on counseling, surveying what Christians are doing today, Vernon Grounds quotes Quentin Hyder as saying,

> The actual psychotherapy I had given him was not significantly different from that which he would have gotten from a non-Christian psychiatrist. However, there were three factors which were different. First, he felt more easily able to express his problems in biblical terms and knew that I understood what he was trying to say. Second, being reassured that I was myself a committed believer, he was much more readily able to accept my explanations and respond to my suggestions. Third, I was able to read a few relevant passages of Scripture to him and we often concluded our sessions with prayer together.[2]

Significantly, Grounds comments: "It is this stance and spirit that most Christian counselors appear to identify with today."[3] Notice several things about Hyder's description of his counseling. First, he considers neither the Scriptures nor prayer to be part of the psychotherapy as such. Secondly, notice what Hyder added to the pagan system of psychiatry that he uses: biblical terms, a few passages of Scripture, and occasional

---

2 *Eternity* Magazine, January 1975, p. 19.
3 *Ibid.*

use of prayer. But thirdly, and probably most importantly, notice how the counselee let down his guard. Hyder says that because he was assured that the counselor was a Christian, he more readily accepted the non-Christian explanations and suggestions that were offered. The great danger of such a misrepresentation of the facts is that the willing counselee gullibly will accept as Christian what is not, because of its Christian packaging.

Just let me mention another example. John Drakeford, Director of the Marriage and Counseling Center at Southwestern Baptist Theological Seminary in Fort Worth, Texas, has identified himself so closely with O. Hobart Mowrer that, in fact, the main dish on his menu is little more than Mowrer warmed over. Recently, Mowrer wrote this concerning Drakeford: "… when he returned to his seminary, he reorganized his whole program along Integrity Group lines." Integrity Groups is the name that Mowrer uses for his humanistic group counseling system. He also mentions a booklet that 'Drakeford compiled… called The Little Red Booklet,' which" (says Mowrer) "is an encapsulated version of Integrity Groups."[4] This booklet is a perfect example of the additive syndrome. After setting forth unadulterated Mowrerian dogma from start to finish, pagan and humanistic as it is, Drakeford added eight scriptural passages on the last page! Mowrer does not believe in the existence of God (he told me personally that the Bible could be improved by eliminating the vertical element in it), and his system is, from start to finish, ungodly. Yet Drakeford baptized it unaltered into the faith.

So, you see, I am not tilting at windmills. The problem of using God as an additive to sweeten all sorts of bitter psychiatric potions is a very real one.

Closely related to the additive view (and sometimes linked with it) is what I call the Eureka view. This way of trying to introduce God into the counseling picture differs slightly, but significantly, from the first. This difference makes it all the more subtle and, therefore, all the more dangerous. The advocates of the Eureka view differ from those who follow the first because, instead of attempting to bring God in from the outside in order to tack Him on as an adjunct to a godless system,

---

4 Unpublished mimeographed ms., 1974.

they purport to discover that He was in the picture all the time. The zeal and growing ability of some of these advocates of the view to find all sorts of parallels and similarities, as well as outright identifications of Christian truth with pagan theory, at times, is truly remarkable. As they comb the writings of the framers of the unbelieving systems, they may be heard to cry continually, Eureka! as they supposedly discover one after another. Some maintain that there is a positive identification while others, or even the originator of the system, think otherwise. Accordingly, Freud's Id has been identified with the biblical view of original sin, Rogerian listening with the Christian concept of listening, Glasser's idea of responsibility with biblical responsibility and even Skinnerian reward and aversive control with the scriptural reward/punishment dynamic.

In actuality, there is no discovery of anything that was there in the picture; instead, the desire is the father of the fact—God is first projected into the picture and then found. This is accomplished by reinterpreting the contents of the picture to conform to Christian vocabulary. Tragically, in the end, one is left with the same picture, but the Bible has been bent to fit it.

"I'm not about to ask you whether you can cite any examples of this trend because I suppose that you can. But tell me this—how can they get away with it? Can't people see that this is going on?'

Well, I'll give you some examples later anyway, but first, let me answer the immediate question that you have raised. Remember from the previous discussion how gullible and disarmed a Christian can be when he is anxious to get relief from a pressing problem, and he finds a Christian "professional" who claims to be using Christian counseling. Add to that the psychotherapeutic jargon and the ethos that the medical model lends to the *psychiatrist*, and you have the basic ingredients for easy acceptance. The poor counselee may think, "I don't see it," but then he remembers that Dr. so-and-so says that it is so, and he acquiesces. "After all," he reasons, "the good Dr. said that the problem was too deep for me anyway." Moreover, many things that unbelievers suggest do resemble Christian methodology. But careful investigation of similarities always reveals fundamental differences.

The problem of the Eureka mentality is a serious one; the practice of crying Eureka is nearly universal. In an almost ludicrous statement, Marion Nelson wrote: "I have never found any command or exhortation in the Bible which, properly translated, interpreted and applied, contradicts any psychological principle."[5] I say that this is almost ludicrous, because at first it brings a chuckle as one thinks of Nelson trying to retranslate and reinterpret hundreds of biblical passages in order to square them with thousands of conflicting psychological principles made by the advocates of scores of conflicting systems. But upon further reflection, the smile must give way, for it is because of the acceptance of this palpable nonsense that many lives will be ruined. The only way for Nelson to support his thesis, so far as I can see, is for him to judge which principles are the true psychological principles. He could only do this, of course, by using a standard, and if that standard is the Bible, then the statement is nonsense since the Bible would eliminate all principles that conflicted with it.

Gary Collins is perhaps typical of the tendency to cry Eureka. In his book[6] *Effective Counseling,* he not only equates Fromm's view of love with I Corinthians 13, but even finds Freud in favor of religion.[5] Without saying more, let me finally mention the astounding statement of L. I. Granberg, who had the temerity to write: "The Christian who thoughtfully considers the findings of the psychotherapist sees many of the processes associated with the Christian's rebirth and sanctification operating in another context and described in a different vocabulary."[7] How blind men can be, to identify what psychiatrists do with that which the Bible teaches may be done by the Holy Spirit *alone*. Paul plainly states, in I Corinthians 2, that the natural man neither understands the Spirit's work, nor what has happened to men who have been transformed by His work.

Usually, the pious label that is gummed on the Eureka process is "common grace." But common grace is another thing. It does not mean that pagan dogma can be taught as Christian truth by translating it into

---

5   Marion Nelson, Why Christians Crack Up (Moody Press, Chicago: 1960), p. 16.
6   Gary Collins, *Effective Counseling* (Creation House: 1972), p. 59.
7   L. I. Granberg, "Counseling," *Baker's Dictionary of Practical Theology* (Baker Book House, Grand Rapids: 1967), p. 194.

Christian terms. The goodness of God is manifested in common grace as He makes the sun shine upon both believers and unbelievers alike. He restrains evil in unbelieving men so that they do not totally destroy one another, and He allows them to excel in many of the arts and crafts of society. But, as Calvin so well put it, "many monstrous falsehoods intermingle with those minute particles of truth scattered up and down their writings . . . To the great truths, what God is in Himself, and what He is in relation to us, human reason makes not the least approach."[8] And, as we saw in the previous lecture, it is with those truths that counseling deals.

In short, every Christian must become wary of the sort of confused thinking that leads both counselors and counselees alike to conclude that any slight alteration of the prevalent pictures of counseling will do. No such tinkering with ungodly systems will ever make them Christian. We can settle for nothing of the sort. Nor can we merely hang another picture in their midst. No, indeed; all of the pictures must be removed from the wall. In their place, a new one must be hung. It is a picture into which God and His Word are neither intruded as an extraneous appendage, nor is it one in which He is projected and then discovered. Rather, God is in the *background* of the picture at every point. *He* is its theme and its subject, and certainly not of the least importance is the fact that He Himself is the artist who painted it. When we hang that picture on the wall of every Christian counseling room, the world will begin to cry EUREKA—at last we've found it!

---

8   John Calvin, *Institutes* III, IV, 4

Chapter 3
Turning The Tide By Counseling

"We see the problem as you have presented it. You've helped us to understand how some Christians have wrongly tried to solve it. But now, don't you think it's time to say something about what can be done to turn this sad situation around? After all, we are looking toward our futures in the Lord's vineyard. And many of us do not yet know how our gifts ought to be used there. Perhaps you can say something that will be of help."

This is an extremely reasonable request. And I am so entirely caught up with it that I plan to spend the time talking about it in both today's and tomorrow's lectures. What I hope to show you today is that counseling is tied far more closely to your future than you may realize.

To begin with, I want you to understand that the opportunities for serving Christ were never greater than they are today. You will take your place in the church and in society at a remarkable time. The decline of the liberal churches, the political and moral confusion on every hand, and the self-confessed failure of psychiatry and psychology to really help men with their problems have combined to make people everywhere examine again the basic issues of life. People everywhere are beginning to recognize the need for what you have. To meet that need, God has been blessing His faithful churches with numbers, finances, resources, and increasing influence. The time is ripe for a sweeping proclamation of the saving gospel of Jesus Christ, with its impact for good in every area of our culture. All is ready. All but *one* thing.

There is one major obstacle: Christians. Christians by the thousands, just like their non-Christian neighbors, are suffering from unresolved personal problems. They are turning in droves to counselors of all sorts.

Pastors are overburdened by husbands or wives threatening to dissolve their marriages, by parent/teen struggles, and by interpersonal conflicts among various members of their flocks. There is immense power abroad in the church today, but much, if not *most* of it is being drained off by these energy-wasting difficulties. If even a small proportion of the energy of God's people that is now consumed in anxiety, worry, guilt, tension, anger, and resentment were able to be released into productive activity for the kingdom of God, the world would soon know that Jesus Christ is at work today. Sadly, instead, the world still searches for the answer to its problems, seeing little or no difference in the lives of professed Christians.

Yet, the potential for untold change now exists; God has enmassed in the church an enormous amount of resources that are virtually untapped. Were the holes in the barrel, through which so much power is being lost, repaired, the effect for good could be overwhelming. In a vital sense, then, a necessary preliminary to any real impact upon those around us who do not know Christ, is for us to become the sort of Christians whose lives, in the midst of confusion and chaos, nevertheless shine. But shining lives today are rare. The church is shot through with the same attitudes toward life that may be found in any other place. There is little distinctive living. Christians look too much like the world. God has told us that usually, it is not our distinctive teaching or belief that first makes an impression, but rather, as Peter explained to Christian wives, they would have to win their unsaved husbands without a lot of talk by *demonstrating* their faith in daily living (I Peter 3:1,2ff.). What Peter told wives holds true elsewhere: when others *see* Christianity in action, they will be ready to *hear* about it in words.

That's where counseling comes in. Not only is there the need for the kind of counseling that always was and always will be essential to the welfare of the church and to the evangelization of those unsaved persons who come to Christians for help, but if I am not entirely mistaken, in this period of national breakdown, there is a special need for Christian—truly Christian—counseling. If the church can be repaired, the holes plugged, and the power preserved and harnessed, the effect upon the surrounding society might even occasion another Great Awakening. Surely, the need is apparent. The opportunity appears to be present, too.

But will we seize it? That is the question that I come here to put to you. All of the evangelism programs that may be conceived, no matter how true and how biblical, will not bring about the desired results if, on two fronts, weakened lives stand in the way.

First, as I have indicated already, Christians must be strengthened in the witness of their lives, demonstrating in their personal decisions, in their practical actions, and in their expressed attitudes and comments that Jesus Christ enables them to weather the economic, political, and social storms that are raging uncontrolled. Indeed, others need to see in us that peculiar combination of realistic joy and peace that comes from righteous living empowered by the Holy Spirit (cf. Rom. 14:17).

Secondly, Christians whose lives are weakened by unending strife and turmoil make poor recruits for evangelism. They are too embroiled in their own problems to be of much help to others. So, in one sense, it does not seem to be going too far to say that today, proper counseling is a prerequisite for evangelism.

But be that as it may, how shall we reach the goals that we have described? What sort of strategy must be followed in order to plug so many holes soon? Where will the counselors come from, and how shall they be trained? How shall we alert the church to the solution and convince Christians that there is hope even in the midst of the present disorder? Those are large questions that require more detailed answers than I could offer here. Yet, they are not abstract issues; they are deeply practical, and you will be involved in their answer because you belong to the generation that will constitute the emerging leadership that can either carry the day or lose the battle. The outcome will largely depend upon how well you enter into, energize, more sharply define, and bring to its fullest flower the counseling movement that some from our generation have conceived and have gotten underway. We have begun, and I hope begun well (that will be for your generation finally to determine). But, at any rate, the real task we must bequeath to you. We stand near the close of a transition period, most of us will die in the wilderness. It is up to you to lead the church into the promised land.

So, if you are going to take up the challenge, you will need to know something of the history of what has happened so far, as well as what is expected of you in the future. You need perspective. It is hard to know where to begin, but perhaps it would be best to go back to the situation that existed when some of us entered the ministry about twenty-five years ago. Liberals were riding high; they had nearly all of the ecclesiastical clout that did not belong to the Roman Catholic Church. Conservative churches were in the minority: weak in finances and nil in national influence. Great blows had been struck at the church successively. Evolution had all but successfully destroyed belief in creation and in the fall of man. Adam had come to be considered a mythical character. That meant that the whole question of man's sin in Adam and the consequences of the fall were up for grabs. Moving from questions about the origins of man and his fall into sin to doubts about the second Adam and His death for guilty sinners was but a short journey. None, however, except the most extreme, wanted to eliminate Christ from the picture; after all, His life and many of His words could be used (or misused) to support some of the idealist values and programs of the new humanism. So, through the advent of a so-called higher criticism of the Bible that purported to be *scientific,* Jesus was stripped of His deity and made instead to be the first and best Christian. His role became that of an example and a teacher who taught self-sacrifice and good deeds. By following in His steps, we could bring about a new and better world in which to live. The portions of the Scriptures that so obviously taught the miraculous and the redemptive, and that contradicted the views of the liberals, were no problem to them since the Scriptures were no longer considered to be *God's* revelation to man, but *man's* best endeavor (to date) to reveal God. They were conditioned by their times (as indeed was Jesus Himself), and they were caricatured as filled with local and dated elements. Belief in the Supernatural (to which now "Science" had given the gate) posed no problem, since it could be discarded as a form of magic. After the layers of such accretions had been scraped away, and after the mythology had been reinterpreted in scientific terms, presumably one could find the true historical Jesus and his teaching lurking behind. It was simple enough for each one to remove what was not wanted at any point by this highly subjective process.

Well, the attacks were relentless, and the gains were substantial. Everywhere, denominations, institutions of learning, and organizations that had been developed by Bible-believing Christians and dedicated to the service of the Lord Jesus Christ fell into the hands of unbelievers. Funds, resources, programs, and institutions that had been given to further the teaching of the gospel were now used to destroy faith. Those few who did not capitulate, those men and women who under trial, loss, and even persecution held true to the Word of God, were thrown on the defensive. Energies that previously could have been used for the positive work of evangelism and edification were now spent in fighting battles, most of which took place within the borders of the church itself. Many of these battles were lost. For the badly outnumbered, battle-worn troops, that meant retrenching. With supplies, personnel, resources, and strategic positions all in the enemies' hands, they found themselves faced with the mammoth task of rebuilding again what had crumbled, but this time not in virgin territory; it had to be done in the midst of the Samaritans who did all that they could to hinder. Vast amounts of energy were consumed in these battles and in the rebuilding of the church in America. The critics jeered, the opposition sneered, and even capitulating Christians (of which the woods were full) heaped discouragement upon the faithful few who, from their several denominational and ecclesiastical backgrounds, tried once more to build on a sure foundation. The infighting had been exhausting; the opposition had been bold and ruthless, but the current situation shows plainly enough that in spite of all, God has blessed those who persevered.

But there were losses even in the ultimate gains. With energy consumed in waging war within and without, with resources and manpower poured into rebuilding, there was little energy and little time left over to spend cultivating one's personal and family faith. Few books and few efforts were forthcoming in these areas. Consequently, the Church, the family, and the individual suffered greatly. Some Christians, indeed, forsook the battles and the rebuilding and went off to the caves. There they developed subjective mystical and deeper life concepts based upon individual communion with God and personal experience. But far from helping the situation, this factor brought more division and confusion.

Then too, there were those who saw in the defeats and the growing apostasy the end at hand and, in the spirit of eleventh-hour thinking, gave up all hope of restoring the faith. Their energies also were diverted and dissipated as they turned to the study of prophecy with *such* a vengeance that little else mattered.

In all this, concerns about Christian living were largely missing. In the confusion, church discipline evaporated. Personal ministry of Christian to Christian was mostly unknown. Young people were raised with little or no instruction about marriage or the home. They were taught the doctrine that they needed to withstand the foe— and that was good—but rarely were they taught either the implications of biblical truths for daily living or how to study the Bible in such a way that one can discover those implications. My generation, therefore, has grown up knowing little or nothing about these matters. Consequently, our homes and our lives have suffered. We have made some terrible mistakes. Nor have we taught our children what they need to know—that is why some of you find yourselves in some of the dilemmas that you face right now. Currently, evidence of that need is apparent in the size of the crowds that seek help from those who give such basic instruction.

Some of us who have begun our Christian lives and have entered into our ministries during this period of tumultuous upheaval have found ourselves veering from one of these emphases to another. But, as a consequence, we have come to see the great need for balance. We fought and were ourselves, at times consumed with fighting. We built and often became so weary in the work that at times we became weary *of* the work. We argued prophetic viewpoints until we were able to divide and subdivide not only the times and the seasons, but ourselves. We lived at church and found no time to live before the world and in our homes. Now we have come full circle. We want to hand you a better and more balanced approach, one that, while neglecting none of these emphases, nevertheless knows how to put each in its proper place according to biblical priorities. That is one reason why I have tried to paste together this historical/personal collage for you. It would be wrong for me to entreat you to put an emphasis on counseling, which is unquestionably *needed* at present, if by doing so I were to cause you to neglect the other factors that are essential to maintaining the faith collectively and individually. That is also one reason why I have tried to point out what I think is a valid connection between counseling and evangelism. In other words, I am trying to get you to see that a strong emphasis on counseling is the strategy for today. But at the same time, I want to warn you that if we are to enter into the opportunities that lie just ahead, we must not reject the emphases of the past, imbalanced as they may have been at times, and we must not become so caught up in counseling and biblical truth about Christian living that we forget other vital matters. While the practical must not be sacrificed for the doctrinal, neither is it right to move in the opposite direction. We must not lose the true gains that have been won so dearly by creating a *different,* but nonetheless, *another* unhealthy imbalance.

There is a need for continued doctrinal warfare with the forces of the evil one. The building of the church must have our continued efforts. Zeal for evangelism and missions must not flag. Prophetic study is important. But, while doing these things, we must also restore the home and the quality of relationships that we sustain with one another and with God. Otherwise, all of these other efforts will be in vain. Yet, we may not allow this concern to water down our theology like those who have been teaching what is called the new Relational Theology. Those who have taken more than a *taste* of Keith Miller's *New Wine* have become *intoxicated with* it and have found their ability to walk in the straight paths of biblical orthodoxy seriously impaired. Theology does not come from experience; it must always issue from the Scriptures. Experience must be judged by the Bible. What we need, then, is not a new theology, but a concern for personal living that grows out of a solid theology and that at every point is conditioned by it.

So, Christian young people, I call you to get involved in the need of the hour. Get involved by beginning to square off your own life with God and with your neighbor. Examine each area of your life to discover how anger and resentment, fear and worry, envy and personal ambition, laziness and lack of discipline, guilt, and depression have been hindering the development of your gifts for ministry and service to one another and to the world that so desperately needs to hear of a Savior. Take an inventory of your relationships, beginning with your relationship with God. Are you in proper fellowship with Him and with your parents and peers? You cannot begin to counsel others until you have begun to learn how to receive God's counsel for *your* life.

When you have sufficiently attended to these matters, and when you have learned how to maintain loving relationships with God and your neighbor, get involved in helping others. There are so many who need your help. Some of you will be called to counseling as a life calling in the ministry. Others will not. Nevertheless, you must recognize that God has called every Christian to a ministry of counseling someone at some time. In a number of passages, every Christian is called to become competent to counsel someone.[9] But, in closing, let me just read one other passage to you that says it so clearly:

> *Brothers, if a man is caught in any trespass, you who are spiritual should restore him in a spirit of gentleness, looking to yourself, lest you too be tempted. Bear one another's burdens, and so fulfill the law of Christ* (Galatians 6:1-2).

That is what we need—and by the grace of God, that is what we shall have if you respond in obedient faith!

---

9   Cf. esp. Romans 15:14; Colossians 3:16; these verses strongly attest to the fact.

Chapter 4
Your Part In The
Counseling Revolution

Today we come to the concluding lecture in this series. It is last, but in many ways it is the most important of all. I could not present what I have to say until first I took time to set the stage for it. That, either adequately or poorly, I have done. Let me summarize what I have said. The current despair and disorder, both within and without the church, create the need. Combined with that, the growing resources accumulated by the faithful churches of Christ, newly emerging as the victors in the century-long struggle with liberalism, provide the opportunity. The roadblock to seizing the opportunity and thus meeting the need is the weakness of Christians themselves, and the resultant weakness of a church that, otherwise, might be powerful. An outstanding and strategic answer to this problem, that will plug the holes and conserve energy, that will repair the disunity, and bring about the release of the strength of love working in concerted effort, is biblical counseling. But godly counseling will not be forthcoming if we incorporate the world's failures into the church, baptizing them as Christian when, in fact, they are not; rather, it is only to be attained by digging deeply into the mine of scriptural truth to discover those presuppositions, principles, and practices that God so graciously has provided, and that we so ungratefully have neglected. God's power in the church is going to be released widely, with great impact both within and without, only when Christians everywhere begin to straighten out their lives and their homes before Him and before one another. Then, in the spirit of gentleness, they may begin to minister both formally and informally to one another. That, as I say, is the background that I have tried to sketch out. Now, against that background, let me explore the last statement in some depth. We shall bring it into the foreground. It is this: God has obligated Christians to minister to one another both formally and informally as each other's counselors.

Counseling, as you already know from the quotation with which I ended the last chapter, as well as from other sources, is not unknown in the Bible, nor was it unknown to the churches of the New Testament. Galatians 6:1,2 is explicit: each individual, as God gave him occasion, was to restore his brother whenever the need for such restoration was necessary. He could not remain disengaged. Whenever, in the providence of God, he discovered a brother caught in any sin from which that brother was unable to extricate himself, he was obligated to move in and help. That, in contrast, is rarely done today. But, it is clear from the large number of passages that have to do with mutual ministry in the New Testament that this practice was universally taught by the apostles and was followed widely. Many of the scriptural passages that require this sort of activity contain the keywords "one another," and many of the "one another" verses refer to exhortation, encouragement, restoration, admonition, rebuke, and the giving of other sorts of counsel.[10] What is of greatest importance to note is that all of them are concerned not with the ministry of someone who is called to counseling as a life calling, but with the ministry of individual, everyday man-in-the-pew Christians to one another.

While it is impossible to provide the training or know-how for counseling that you, as a Christian, may need in a lecture series like this, it is proper to urge you to consider your responsibility to find such help. Much of what you lack can be obtained by personal study of the subject as it is taught in the Word of God. God will bless you with increasing wisdom and finesse if you prayerfully and earnestly search the Scriptures and faithfully attempt to put into practice what you find there. But remember, you must show the spirit of gentleness in it all. The biblical encouragement to engage in counseling of one another is given with that clear qualification. Increasingly, other helps to understanding and applying the Scriptures are becoming available. Books, short cours-

---

10 Cf. Galatians 6:2 to begin with.

es, counseling materials, and courses on cassettes have been prepared for such purposes.[11] Moreover, and of the greatest importance, many pastors who themselves have been studying their obligations anew and who also have become concerned about mobilizing their congregations for mutual ministry, are preaching about these matters and conducting courses to supply what is needed. It may well be that with some slight encouragement on your part, your pastor would be willing to organize a course of study in your church. Many pastors, as a first step, are already working with their elders and deacons to prepare them to join in the work of counseling.

But mutual ministry means more than merely helping others; it also means a willingness to ask for and to receive help from others when needed. There is not one of us who at some time or another does not need the counsel of his brother. We must not become too proud or too embarrassed (which is only another way of saying the same thing) to seek help when we recognize that we are at the end of our own resources. We dare not turn down what God has provided through brotherly counsel. It is not always easy to accept help from another. But whenever a brother approaches us to resolve some problem between him and ourselves, or to restore us when he thinks that we are caught in a trespass, we must learn to humble ourselves and receive him with thanksgiving. It helps to remember that in so doing, he is being obedient to God. His effort honors God because he honors God's Word by following it (cf. Matthew 18:15ff.). We must be thankful for that, no matter how difficult anything else in the encounter may seem. And remember, you probably should have taken the initiative yourself before it had to come to this (cf. Matthew 5:23,24). There is not one of us who, from time to time, would not be all the better off for having had just such an encounter.

Now, let us consider a second way that you can further the counseling movement in the days ahead. I can report that there is a significant amount of concern about becoming involved in biblical counseling

---

11 Ed. note. Many reading this will not even know what a cassette tape is. Today, the opportunities to learn how to counsel have exploded exponentially since the time Dr. Adams gave this lecture. Students can even still learn how to counsel from Dr. Adams online at www.nouthetic.org.

abroad in the land today. During the last two years, I have been receiving upwards of a hundred or so letters each year from young men who are majoring in psychology and who have decided to enter the field of Christian counseling. A fair number even come for personal interviews. Most of them want me to make some recommendation about the proper graduate training to get in order to prepare themselves for a ministry of Christian counseling. I make one reply: "If God has called you to the work of full-time counseling, then go to a good theological seminary. *That* is the proper place to obtain the training that you need. When you are through, get ordained and serve Christ in a pastorate because that is the proper place to do Christian counseling as a life calling.

"Incredible! What do you have in mind when you steer them into the seminary and then into the formal ministry of the Word? Are you interested in luring more students to Westminster?"

No, that is not my goal. As a matter of fact, I consider it just as much my job as a seminary professor to keep the wrong men out of the pastorate as it is to persuade the right ones to enter it. We already have too many men in pastoral ministry who do not belong there. We don't need any more of the sort. What I have in mind is just this: a *number* of those who write are precisely the sort of men who *ought* to consider the gospel ministry seriously. They have exactly the right qualities and the proper concerns, but they have never considered the ministry. Reasons vary, of course, but for many, I discovered, it is the model of the pastor, and the model of the pastorate they have known that has turned them off. A part of this grows out of the matter of balance, which I spoke about in the previous chapter, and the weaknesses of both the members of the congregation and many pastors in the areas of Christian living and personal confrontation. But when I sketch for them something of the biblical picture of a pastor and something of his work as it could be carried on, some begin to reexamine their goals. A number of these men are now preparing to serve Christ in the pastorate.

Now, in order to give you some indication—and of necessity what I say must be greatly abbreviated—of what the pastoral ministry of the future will be like when carried on by men well-trained in biblical counseling, who intend to do the proper work of the pastor (rather than all sorts of things to which God did not call them), I shall offer a slice of an imaginary, but typical sort of conversation with one of these men.

"The pastorate? Why do you suggest that? All of that visitation, organizational work, and preaching is not for me. I want to work with people and help them get out of their problems."

I am certain that you do, but that's exactly why I suggested that you consider the pastorate. You see, there is no better place to do what you want to do than in the pastorate. And it is just the very combination of factors that you think would keep you from truly helping people out of their difficulties (organization, preaching, and visitation) that God designed to accomplish that purpose. Any other sort of counseling endeavor that you undertook would be severely truncated, in comparison to the work of the pastoral ministry, by the omission of these factors.

"Frankly, I don't see it. You are going to have to spell it out a lot more clearly than that before I can buy it."

Gladly. Let's begin by taking up one of your previous comments. You want to help people get out of trouble, is that right?

"Exactly. I can think of few things more rewarding."

Fine, but let me help you consider one that might be. Here you are, five or six years from now, deeply involved in the work of counseling. You have just said goodbye to the third person this week who came in with the same problem. Who knows how many times before and after you will see others with that problem? Under your breath you say to yourself as she leaves, "If only I could get on the housetop and warn people before they got themselves into this mess; here is the third case this week!" But, alas, you can't. The counseling that you do is remedial, not preventive. It is repair work after the fact. But God designed a place where there is a rooftop from which to issue the warning—the Christian pulpit. There you can warn, rebuke, encourage, and guide men, women, and children around those potholes into which so many have stumbled. Preaching, among other things, is preventive counseling. Organizational work gives you an opportunity to plan for proper teaching in the church, school, youth group, etc. You can't do preventive work without access to people early enough to help them avoid the dangers. And nothing can reach them like an organized program. Moreover, before things grow so bad that it is hard to do anything about them, as a pastor you have the opportunity and the right to initiate counseling. Nipping problems in the bud, before they ever get so large that the person might think about consulting a counselor, is a significant part of true pastoral concern (which, incidentally, is what the word visitation means in the Bible). That word does not mean making all sorts of useless house calls, as some have misunderstood it to mean. It means shepherdly concern that leads to whatever help is needed. When the Bible speaks of "visiting widows and orphans," for instance, obviously it does not mean to make house calls on them; it means to look after them and to care for their needs. So, if you are really concerned about helping people get out of difficulty, you certainly should be equally as concerned, if not even more concerned, about keeping them out of those difficulties in the first place. And the person who can do this best is someone who has had to help pick up the pieces in remedial counseling. Only the pastorate provides a balanced opportunity to do both preventive *and* remedial counseling.

"O.K., I can buy that, but what about all of the other organizational activities that a pastor has to become involved in?"

Well, the problem is that some pastors have become involved in many things that they have no business doing, and have failed to do the things that they ought to do. I am interested in seeing you consider the ministry because I suspect that you would not be like many of the pastors who have failed in this way. You see, you are not rejecting the pastorate that is described in the New Testament; what you dislike or fear is a model that originated in modern times. For example, organization in the New Testament was structured in order to do two things: to allow the pastor to become a pastor and teacher (and nothing else) and to allow the entire congregation to exercise their gifts in mutual ministry to one another and to the world around, and to assist the pastor in his work. It is all found in concise form in Ephesians 4:11,12, but it is worked out in detail in many other places. Let me quote those two verses for you:

> *God gave some… to be pastors and teachers, for the equipping of the saints for their work of ministry.*

That is the New Testament picture. A pastor is a shepherd; the prime task of a shepherd is to know and care for his sheep. You get the picture when you read the twenty-third Psalm this way: "The Lord is my pastor; I shall not lack." It is the shepherd's task to provide the concerned care for the sheep that God requires. A large part of that will involve personal counseling (cf. Acts 20:31). Christ, the chief Shepherd, set the pattern for all of His undershepherds, by laying down His life for His sheep.

"I never thought of it that way."

You haven't heard the half of it. The pastor can counsel with authority—the authority of the living God Himself, as he counsels in His Name. He has the power of church discipline. Moreover, he can provide *total* care for the counselee, not merely care that extends to one hour one day a week. He can follow up his counseling as no other counselor is able to. And think of the resources that are available to Him. He has an entire congregation to draw upon. To assist him in counseling, he has their prayers, their strengthening re-assimilation of a forgiven offender, and their many specialized abilities, to name but a few. Take the latter. Why should the pastor spend his time as a counselor helping a counselee to get his finances in shape when he has a half-dozen men in the congregation who are experts in such matters? At that point in his counseling, he simply makes an appointment with one of them for the counselee and thus provides expert help while reserving his own counseling time for what could not be supplied by others. Moreover, by involving him, he has helped another member to use his gifts in ministry and thus has brought blessing to someone else. If a place is needed for a young person to stay while he is trying to kick a drug habit, he has six homes in his congregation ready and able to provide the needed care. He has trained the members of those homes himself. If ....

"Wait a minute, I don't know many churches like *that!*"

I agree, you probably don't. That is one reason why you have not considered the pastorate. But there are *some,* and increasingly we see more; there will be *many* more when young people like you catch the vision for the pastorate that is set forth in the Scriptures rather than shying away because they see in most of today's congregations and in many of their pastors something quite foreign to this. I do not say that it will be easy to make all of the changes that are necessary to bring this about. Pastors who are now working at it have discovered that it can be hard. But it is possible. And by God's grace it can happen all over. The idea must be taught, and Christians everywhere must be convicted of the need. The change will require nothing short of a revolution. Even if you are not called to counseling as a life ministry, you can help by supporting such efforts, as indeed a growing number of laymen are today. I did not say that it would be easy. But a man with the heart of concern for people that *you* show is just the sort of man that God loves to use to bring about such things.

And let me mention one final fact. The place to study for a counseling ministry is in a good theological seminary, because *that* is the only place where an adequate education for counseling as a life calling can be obtained. I am not referring primarily to the counseling courses offered in such institutions. Rather, I am thinking of the Greek, Hebrew, theology, exegesis courses, and so forth, those studies that enable one to become intimately and accurately acquainted with the Bible. That is what a counselor needs above all. If he is to withstand the pressures of the age, if he is to rely on the living God and not upon the wisdom of men, if he is to help counselees to love God and to love their neighbors as they should, he must have "the Word of Christ dwelling in him richly" (Colossians 3:16). That is the basic need for counselors today.

Well, you have heard me out. I don't know whether you have been influenced by what I have tried to say or not. But one thing I know—you are already involved in counseling more than you may recognize, and that involvement will increase. Remember, what you do to support biblical counseling may make a great deal of difference not only to you and someday to your children, but also to the future course of the church of Jesus Christ in the land. May God convict you all of the great need, and of the great opportunity that lies at hand, and move you to do whatever you should.

The Student Pastor/Counselor Today

Introduction[1]

IF I were a seminarian today and were shortly entering the pastorate, I would have in view the prospect of engaging in a significant counseling ministry. But if I entertained this purpose, I would also like to know what I would want from my theological training, what other resources were available, and what I should do about them.

It was those sorts of questions that I asked myself as I began to prepare for this lecture. I thought if I could deal with them clearly and concretely, then I might be of more help to you than if I simply chose some aspect of counseling that was of interest to me.

As I see it, there are three major facets of preparation for a counseling ministry that we should explore:

1. I must consider what evangelical students entering the pastorate today are like—what their dispositions, characteristics, and concerns are (i.e., their *stance* toward counseling);
2. I must take a look at the resources presently available to them and
3. I must say something about how such students may best use such resources to become effective pastoral counselors.

---

[1] This lecture was delivered at Concordia Theological Seminary, Ft. Wayne, Indiana on October 7, 1976.

Chapter 1

Let's begin with today's students. I am not intimately acquainted with the typical Lutheran student, so it's possible that I could be speaking past you rather than coming to grips with your particular problems, interests, and aspirations. I hope not. But I shall tell you what I do know from close association with one seminary and a rather good knowledge of a number of others. I'll have to leave it to you to judge whether I have scored or struck wide of the mark.

Now I want to make some observations about the seminary student as I see him First, the evangelical student of today has had it with traditionalism, i.e., with tradition for the sake of tradition. However, let me hasten to say that he is totally unlike the student who, as late as five or six years ago, wanted to overthrow the establishment simply because it was the establishment. There is a new balance in today's student. He has reasons for what he opposes — some of which he gladly admits grow out of tradition (not traditionalism). Yet, while he is freer to question and reject established practices and values than was his counterpart of the forties and fifties, he also can retain them more freely than the student of the '60s and early '70s, so long as he believes they are true to the Word of God. Within the biblical framework, he can think independently, slavishly following neither the traditionalist nor the iconoclast. This sort of freedom to hear the Scriptures afresh makes him open to new ideas, but it also makes him critical of newness for newness' sake.

Thankfully, his immediate predecessor — yesterday's student who thought that freedom from traditionalism meant reacting to everything traditional simply because it was — has gone. Because he found it difficult to accept anything associated with the past, he rejected much that was biblical, and, as a result, this determination to reject locked him into a destructive bondage to the very traditionalism from which he sought to free himself. This bondage — to say the least — was every bit as serious as that of the unthinking traditionalist that he abhorred.

One who only *reacts* — as did this predecessor of yours — is still tightly bound to what he wants to throw off. Because he reacted to traditionalism, he could not *act* on his own. The one who reacts acts only against what exists doesn't move into new, unexplored areas of creativity demanded by the recognition of unnecessary limitations and boundaries. For all his talk about the new, his stance is still backward, not forward. He does not look ahead or move forward because his sight and actions are yet controlled — negatively to be sure — but yet controlled by the past. Thank God, I say, that we are through with this sort of student mentality, a mentality that will tear down something simply because it is there.

But no significant trend — and for a while it was that — leaves those who live through its heyday and those who follow in its wake totally unaffected. In God's providence, there is always something worthwhile to gain from every movement if one has a biblical perspective from which to view it. Today we are all able to capitalize on the concern for freedom that the rebels of the sixties sought but never attained, if we care to do so. In spite of the inevitable failure of such a destruction-oriented movement, it shook many things loose, opened a number of sealed compartments, and provided a general sense of freedom that I, for one, appreciate. I refer not only to the more superficial matters like freedom to grow beards and eschew neckties, but to more substantive questions.

I guess what I am saying is that the door was opened for us to attack the *evils* of traditionalism today in a way that was not possible when I began my ministry twenty-five years ago. So long as that attack continues to take the responsible course of questioning what hasn't been questioned adequately *according to biblical presuppositions and principles,* while accepting and cherishing what proves to be truly scriptural, no matter who believed it or how old it may be, I am for it.

But there is another side, too. Today's student not only wants to reject error in thought and practice wherever it may be found, he is concerned to press beyond traditional thought and practices. He will correct what he must by offering new ways and means, but he also will explore new territories and push back the frontiers of ministry that for too long have been circumscribed by arbitrary and artificial barriers that no longer exist.

And he wants to get on with his work, yet he is unwilling to settle for the mediocre approaches that characterized so many in the past. He is a high-caliber exponent of the view that one stands on the shoulders of his fathers for one reason only — to reach higher than they could! Though he appreciates and appropriates the enormous amounts of truth inherited from the past, he is not content with eating fruit from the same branch as his teachers. He will reach above us; he is not satisfied with apples already well-picked over.

As you have gathered, I like this student. He is exciting to teach. He is challenging, but he is also devout. He is balanced. God has screwed his head on right, but at the same time, He has warmed his heart! I know his ambition is dangerous, but look at his potential! We simply can't hold him back because there is danger. He is needed in the church. We must warn him not to lose his balance. Then we must thrust him ahead. What God has provided, let not man reject.

There is one outstanding characteristic of this new student that especially thrills me as a professor of Practical Theology: he has a decidedly practical bent. That is one reason why he is so interested in pastoral counseling. While he is concerned about theory, he will not leave it there to stand on one leg. He demands that every presupposition and principle be carried to its conclusion — in *life*! In one sense, this means that he is even *more* theoretical. His theory concerns theory about theory. It holds that God gave man all truth to change life. He believes intensely — whether he can fully articulate it or not — in the study of the Scriptures, not merely to gather or communicate facts and data, but to discover the *telos* or purpose of each passage. He recognizes that he must provide more in his ministry than doctrine, accurately understood and faithfully taught. He wants to know and share the implications of every doctrine for family life, for business life, for social life, and so on. He staunchly believes in exegesis, but finds little satisfaction in discovering the grammatical-historical facts about a passage if that is what he is left with. As much as an evangelical biblical theology that finds the redeeming Christ as the heartbeat of every book of the Bible, including Proverbs, excites him, he does not want to join others who take biblical-theological excursions through the Bible merely to visit all of the Christocentric landmarks. He will not become a biblical sightseer. He wants to know (and to show) how the Christ of all the Scriptures can bless men in their daily activities. He is no tourist; his travel in the Bible is for business purposes.

Your fear that his practical inclinations may lead him to buy a bill of goods because, in his zeal to help others, he doesn't do the hard work of study to undergird his practical efforts may be well-grounded, but I doubt it. If I know him at all, I know that he is aware of and guards against this danger. He is not simplistic about all of this. His concern for a *telic* understanding of the Scriptures is insurance against it. Actually, it leads him to ask more of the text than some of his fathers did. He will wrestle with a passage in all of the old ways, but will not let go until it blesses him! He will make it disclose how the Holy Spirit intended to change him (and his congregation) through it. He will do the work of solid exegesis coupled with theological and historical reflection *so that* he can come to a correct *telos* of every passage.

Of course, a shallow pietism is the nearest pothole into which he may fall. And if he successfully avoids it, his how-to emphasis that insists upon cheering the discouraged, and therefore lethargic, Christians by showing them that there are (after all) practical ways of achieving what the biblical writers told us even without first becoming an apostle Paul, could lead him into the even deeper pits of legalism. Yet if he holds to a scholarly concern for exegesis and theology, tempered by the fires of church history, as the *means* for obtaining his *telic* and how-to emphases, he will avoid both.

I like this new student because of these and other unmentioned factors that make up his profile. If I were to describe him in a word or two, I think I'd call him a scholarly pastor — a man who begins to approximate Paul's pastor/ teacher of Ephesians 4:11. And it is because he is such a man that he recognizes the importance of discovering, developing and deploying the gifts of all the members of the body as verse 12 of that same chapter directs him to do. He is not going to throw away his ministry doing things that God gifted others to do; rather, he will concentrate and focus his efforts on those tasks that are peculiarly pastoral and didactic. But I cannot pursue this tempting area any further.

Let me conclude my discussion of today's evangelical theological student — incomplete as it is — with this one word. In short, he has the makings of one of the most biblically well-balanced—i.e., to say Christlike — students in the history of theological education. I hope he makes it!

Chapter 2

It is this sort of student who enters the ministry with a growing concern about pastoral counseling. I'm glad he is the sort of person he is. Any lesser man would fail. But what is there to help him? Our second task is to take a hard look at the resources available to him, which purport to enable him to become a counseling shepherd to needy and careworn sheep.

That the student I have described is interested in doing such work, pursuing the best training he can get, and utilizing all of the resources that he may, cannot be questioned. His orientation toward counseling necessarily accompanies the highly pastoral orientation that he brings to his scholarly endeavors. All over this land and abroad, there is an awakening to the need for offering better help to Christians who are confronted with the catastrophic upheavals stemming from the technological revolution, the ascendancy of the New Morality, and a galloping humanism —just to mention a few of the forces facing them today. People — Christian people everywhere — are crying out for help as never before. Today's student wants to be prepared to give it.

But as he looks about, the resources available seem woefully inadequate. Experience in the pastor's study frequently shows the sterility of past training (or lack of training) in counseling and provides few models for the student. Seminary curricula are heavily weighted toward other concerns, and counseling courses often are eclectically conditioned. Books are disappointing. The general situation is confusing. The resources seem slight, and what is on the market, for the most part, seems thin, outmoded (speaking to issues long since dead), or just outright wrong. It will no longer do — for that matter it *never* did — for a pastor to tell a couple whose marriage is on the rocks, "Read this Scripture verse, pray, and I'll pray for you too." There is nothing wrong with the verse or the prayer, but to leave people, who have already demonstrated their failure to relate God's Word to their marriage, merely with that — thrown out in such an abstract manner — is to court disaster. What makes you think that they will be able to use this passage in their present condition without explanation and concrete application? Why do you think they would be able to pray together at home when they can't seem to talk civilly to one another even in the counseling room? No, pastor-to-be, you must work and struggle with them, from the Scriptures and in prayer, not once but as often as necessary — perhaps over a six to eight-week period. They need counsel of a caring, orderly, directive, systematic sort that grows out of a *telically* understood and ministered study of the Scriptures.

But since such concerns are recent — indeed, not yet existent among some older pastors and professors, there is little systematic, scholarly biblical pastoral material on counseling available. True, there are popular books and booklets, pamphlets, and tracts in abundance, but many of these are superficial and offer little more than the prayer and Bible verse approach. But even the best do not provide what the pastor needs — to show him how to show others. On the other hand, there are plenty of theoretical studies about counseling, but while providing at times some aid for the more creative men, these too miss the mark for the average pastor who has not been trained to think in terms of the concrete how-to. These books almost universally circumvent such problems, leaving him to pursue them strictly on his own. They may tell him the ins and outs of the divorce question, for instance — and this can be valuable — but they don't tell him how to use this otherwise excellent material to prevent a couple from getting a divorce. Know-what is not know-how, and even know-how is not the same as show-how.

Of course, there are other avenues that he can take. One leads away from the church to the office of the psychiatrist or clinical psychologist. But the pastor who opts for this route recognizes sooner or later that he has made a wrong turn. Not only does he see few persons helped, but far too often he discovers that the advice given — if any *is* given — is quite contrary to what he teaches on Sunday from the Bible. Moreover, if he allows himself to think about it, the man in the office down the avenue with the couch doesn't have more to offer than he does. He doesn't have as much. What is needed to help people learn to love God and neighbor is the Bible. Psychology and medicine don't have the answers; he himself does in that Book about which he has learned everything else except how to use it to minister to men in need. It is not "psychology for living," but Scripture that we must have for living, after all. How can Freud, Rogers, or Skinner — men who loathed the Bible and Christianity and developed systems that not only omitted God, but were opposed to His teachings — help wayward, suffering, sinning parishioners to repent and to grow in grace? How can counselors who rely upon these systems help the members of your congregation to exhibit the fruit of the Spirit when they neither use the Spirit's Word nor rely upon Him — Who Christ said is the great Counselor — for help? Such musings disturb today's ministerial student and recent graduate. They are dissatisfied with the referral route — and for good reason.

But what of the books, tapes, lectures, courses, and short-term training sessions available for ministers today? These are — almost wholly provided by the same sorts of psychologists, psychiatrists, and secularly trained pastoral counselors. Why should the pastor think he can achieve what his friend down the street with a shingle couldn't by using the same approaches, gleaned in a half-baked manner? Moreover, the evangelical student who thoroughly immerses himself in the contents of this material is likely to come away disillusioned even more quickly than his friend who does referral. Sadly, he finds no consensus or agreement about anything, and that — unlike other disciplines in which there is a growing pool of accepted information — the disagreements among counselors continue to grow greater every day as new systems, challenging others at every point, are added to the scene! To read of the dissension and despair among the practitioners in this field is warning enough for him to stay aloof. On top of that, he senses that there is an almost total lack of concern about value, even though that is the stuff that every counselor (without exception) is working with. Counselors of every stripe try to change lives. Yet how can they take it upon themselves to do so when so many show not even the slightest concern about the fact that they have no standard for determining what man's basic problems are, what man *should* be like, what is the goal and meaning of life, etc? They simply adopt their own values, the values of the counseling system, or the counselee's values, usually without careful thought about what they are doing. What pastor can be unconcerned about the values inculcated in his sheep by others?

No, there is no help there. The student that I described is willing to do two things: (1) He will scrap these approaches, eclectically incorporated in the past into existent patterns of pastoral ministry because they do not square with the Bible and (2) He will gladly follow the lead of one who is biblically-oriented, even though this means plowing new ground in the field of pastoral counseling. But that's the problem on the horizon. There is hardly anyone for him to follow. Nearly everything offered is an eclectic potpourri that dishonors Jesus Christ by offering an unequal yoke of man's wisdom and the wisdom of God. In most instances, moreover, the Bible is bent to fit the psychological system into whose mold it is poured. Today's student rejects this; he will not play fast and loose with the Scriptures. So, where will he turn, and what will he do to become the effective counselor that he yearns to be and that his people will need?

Chapter 3

Since almost all of the resources available are either meager, superficial, or erroneous, what must he do? The answer is that he must do a lot of his own spade work. Since there is little for him to rely upon, he must break much new ground himself. That is the crux of what I have to say today. He will waste his time leaning on the bent reeds of the past. He finds that they snap under the weight of serious pastoral concern. Instead, he must saturate himself with the Scriptures to discover there what God says about life on this planet as well as life in the age to come. He must break up the clods and dig out the stones himself if he really wants to become a biblical counselor. He must tap the rich reservoirs of biblical truth lying offshore from mainland operations that are now petering out. This requires commitment and life investment. I call you to nothing less. I urge you to join me and the growing number of pastors, professors, and seminary students who are engaged in the task of opening up the tangled forest. This work is new, demanding, and exciting. And its early returns show that it is a worthwhile investment of one's labors.

"But can I do it?" you ask. It is like you, today's student, to be humble about the matter. But that, too, is a necessary quality for the work because it requires nothing less than absolute submission to the authority of God's Word.

Yes, you can! With God's help you can! That is why I have taken so much time to describe today's theological student. God is doing things with him. No student in the history of American Christianity was more ready to take on this work. His pastoral concerns, his freedom from unbiblical traditionalism, and his dedication to scholarly but practical, life-directed exegesis and theology form just the proper combination for it. What a tragedy if he fails! So, in the name of the Lord Jesus Christ, let me challenge you to join the ranks of those who are now beginning to undertake the task. There are few human guidelines, but what does that matter? That only serves all the more to drive us back to our Bibles. The risks are great, but the opportunities are greater. May God bless and use you in this task!

Nouthetic Counseling

Nouthetic Counseling[1]

Nouthetic counseling was born out of desperation. Because both the referral method ("refer and defer to more professional help") and the integration model (some Bible, some psychology, etc.) had proven unsatisfactory,[2] it became necessary to strike out on new paths. The new proved to be the old.

At length, the Scriptures of the Old and New Testaments were found to contain "all things necessary for life and godliness" (2 Peter 1:3), not only for normal everyday living but also for the change of attitudes, beliefs, values, and life patterns.[3] In other words, we discovered that counseling was not the business of a caste of self-styled and self-appointed professionals, but was the work of pastors (when practiced as a life calling) and the task of every Christian (in informal contexts). While physicians have a valid work to do (in medically treating those whose abnormal behavioral patterns stem from organic causes like brain damage, brain tumors, ingestion of toxic substances, etc.), and psychologists rightly may study human functions experimentally, descriptively reporting these (I am thinking of such work as the studies done by the Harvard Sleep laboratories on the effects of sleep loss), neither physicians nor psychologists have biblical warrant, training, or standards provided by their training for doing counseling.

Counseling has as its object the task of changing the way in which people live their lives. It involves the alteration of values, attitudes, beliefs, behavior, and the like. Where can the proper standard for such change be found? Nouthetic counselors see the Bible as the one source.

---

1 This essay first appeared in Gary Collins, *Helping People Grow, Practical Approaches to Christian Counseling*. The book is a compilation of contributions from representative authors of numerous counseling approaches.
2 Jay Adams, *Competent to Counsel,* Chapter 1.
3 Cf. 2 Timothy 3: 15-17. See expositions of this passage in Jay Adams, *Competent to Counsel* and *The Christian Counselor's Manual*.

From the Bible alone, generations of Christians living before Freud were able to advise one another rightly, and Jesus Christ (using only the Old Testament) was able to become the world's perfect Counselor. God did not leave His people without adequate instruction for living and changing all those years before modern psychotherapy appeared. The Bible, with its messages of salvation and sanctification, has all that anyone needs to live in patterns that are pleasing to God and beneficial to one's neighbor. Indeed, the advent of psychotherapeutic counseling meant that unbelievers had determined to develop new and different ways to teach man to live and to handle his problems—ways that did not include either salvation or sanctification—ways that ignored Jesus Christ. In thus wrongly entering the area of counseling in this way, psychotherapists of all sorts have (in effect) set themselves up competitively over against God and the Bible. That is why the integration of *counseling psychology* (or psychiatry) and *biblical counseling* is impossible.

Nouthetic counselors see the admitted chaos in the field of counseling (Zillborg says that the field is in "disarray," just as "at the beginning")[4] as the direct result of the failure to use the Bible, God's textbook, as the basis for counseling. There is no consensus in the field of counseling (unlike most others) because the one book that could have brought consensus has been set aside for human substitutes.

Over the years, since 1969, when Nouthetic Counseling was introduced, it has enjoyed a phenomenal acceptance among Bible-believing pastors and Christians. Literally thousands today are successfully engaged in doing Nouthetic Counseling. Training is offered at several centers in the U.S.A. as well as in Bible colleges and theological seminaries. Books on Nouthetic Counseling have been translated into twelve languages, worldwide interest has been expressed (training centers for other countries are being planned), and lecture tours have been conducted on four continents (with invitations from a fifth). Recently, I even had the opportunity to lecture about Nouthetic Counseling at the University of Vienna psychiatry clinic to a capacity audience.

---

4   Cf. Jay Adams, *Competent to Counsel,* p. l. Zillborg is both right and wrong. The field *is* in disarray, but the problem is *worse* than at the beginning.

Austrian Christians claim that this was the first time that the gospel had been publicly presented there. Master's theses and doctoral dissertations have been written on Nouthetic Counseling. Interest in biblical counseling has grown immensely since its inception. God has blessed beyond all expectations.

Negative evaluations by those who hold other viewpoints (some of whom are writing other chapters in this book) increasingly show concern over the spread and acceptance of Nouthetic Counseling. Yet the systems they offer instead are highly unsystematic and usually eclectic in nature. "How-to" material is significantly lacking. It is not the desire of Nouthetic counselors to argue and debate with them; rather, their concern is to continue to help those who want to become better counselors. Already, the influence of Nouthetic Counseling can be seen in the writings of some who have been opposed to it. Our hope is that, at length, many others will join forces to help us become even more biblical in our approach.

In 1977, the National Association of Nouthetic Counselors was formed. The purpose of this organization is to promote and upgrade biblical counseling by certifying counselors, counseling centers, and training centers.

Theory

The Greek word *nouthesia*, frequently appearing in the Greek New Testament in counseling contexts,[5] is the term from which "Nouthetic" has been derived. There are three distinct but interrelated elements in the word *nouthesia*:[6]

1. **Change** is needed because the counselee is living in a manner that is inconsistent with biblical standards;
2. **Confrontation** of the counselee by verbal means (counsel) designed to bring about the desired change must be given, and;
3. **Concern** for the counselee's welfare is uppermost. The confrontation and change flow from love. This love is familial.

---

5 *Parakaleo* also speaks about counseling, but less frequently in counseling contexts, and in John's writings has the idea of "counselor-at-law."
6 It was because no English word combines all three that the Greek term was brought over into English.

Love, then, is the motivating factor in Nouthetic Counseling—love by the counselor that seeks to promote love for God and neighbor in the counselee.

All non-organically caused problems[7] are considered to be hamartigenic (sin-caused). Sinful living (failure to express love toward God and one's neighbor, as such love is defined in the Scriptures) is at the heart of the counseling focus.

Even when a child has been tragically sinned against (and Nouthetic Counselors do not minimize the tremendous influence of parents and others, as some falsely claim), it is possible (and always necessary) for the counselor to discover the sinful patterns of response to such sin that the counselee developed (perhaps as a child). Others, though very influential, exert their influence only through such responses. A child, born a sinner (because of his sinful nature), will develop many such wrong habitual responses that may persist into adulthood and cause him much difficulty. But—and this is important—others cannot *cause* those patterns. Nor can they cause the ulcers, etc., that at length also may appear. Others are responsible for their sin against God and the counselee, but God also holds him responsible for his response to it. Jesus did not agonize over the wrong done to Him on the cross. Rather, He prayed for those who crucified Him. He assumed responsibility for His response to such sin and handled wrongdoing toward Himself righteously. He has required His disciples to do the same.[8]

Change occurs in Christians because Jesus Christ died for them, paying the penalty for their sin and freeing them from its power. He did not die to change their genes, to heal so-called "mental illnesses,"[9] or to change the counselee's past. He did not come to heal our memories (there is absolutely nothing in the Bible about this) but to pardon our sin and change our relationship with God and our neighbors. Through biblical direction by the Holy Spirit's power, He enables us to recognize and overcome sinful

---

7   Nouthetic counselors work closely with physicians to help determine what behavior is caused by organic factors.
8   Cf. *How to Overcome Evil*, a book that deals with this portion of Scripture.
9   For more on this euphemistic and misleading term, see "Is Society Sick?" in *The Big Umbrella*.

patterns so that more and more we may walk in God's new righteous ways instead. Biblical counselors, like all other counselors, are concerned with change. However, these alternative patterns of life are not merely tacked on or substituted for the old sinful ones; they issue from a changed heart (the inner life of the believer) that transforms outward behavior.

Because of this commitment to change at a level of depth (in the heart), Nouthetic Counselors consider evangelism an absolute necessity when attempting to help non-Christians. They are unwilling to offer unbelievers something less than the gospel[10] because

1. God has not authorized us to reform people outwardly;
2. To do so would misrepresent the true nature of His magnificent redemption in Christ; and
3. They see a danger in effecting outward change—counselees may rely upon it with false assurance that problems have been solved when what has happened is that one outward set of ungodly responses has been exchanged for another.

Problem-oriented evangelism (or what I call "precounseling"), however, must be adapted to each situation as (indeed) all evangelism must. Minimal initial help (never offered as counseling, but rather clearly distinguished from it) may be given

1. to clear the way of encumbrances for a presentation of the gospel to the unbelieving counselee;
2. to raise hope when there was none or when it has been lost.

But in all that he does in "precounseling," the counselor makes it plain that this is preliminary to the real counseling that can really solve the counselee's problems. At some point, he will explain that such solutions are the right and privilege of those who become members of God's family. Regeneration, then, is *the* prerequisite for change at a level of depth.[11]

Counseling proceeds on the basis of the four-step biblical process for change outlined in 2 Timothy 3:16.[12] The Christian counselor:

---

10   1 Corinthians 2 sets forth the two points of the gospel: 1) Christ's substitutionary and penal death for sinners; 2) His bodily resurrection from the dead.
11   That is why Nouthetic Counselors look on all other counseling as shallow and inadequate.
12   I have discussed this in a number of books in detail, especially *The Christian Counselor's Manual*, *Competent to Counsel*, and *Lectures on Counseling*. For

1. Confronts the believing counselee with God's requirements for faith and life found in the Bible ("teaching");
2. Uses pertinent Scripture portions (with exposition in context—not as if handing out a prescription) to bring about acknowledgment and confession of sin ("conviction");
3. Helps the counselee to get out of his predicament through forgiveness, leading to a change of relationship with God and others ("correction") and;
4. Shows him the alternative biblical lifestyles that please God and helps him to develop these in place of those patterns previously adopted ("training in righteousness").

The Scriptures are used as the basis for all counseling. This is what makes Nouthetic Counseling unique. "Why do you use the Scriptures as the textbook for counseling when you don't use them as the textbook for engineering, medicine, or a hundred other disciplines?" is a question frequently asked. The answer is simple: the Bible was not intended to be a textbook for engineering, medicine, etc., but it *was* intended to be the textbook for helping people come to love God and their neighbors. It is *the* textbook for living in this world and, preeminently, for learning all that is necessary to change from a sinful to a righteous way of life. All that is needed to form values, beliefs, attitudes, and behavioral styles is in the Scriptures. Indeed, no other book can do so, and all other books that attempt to do so thereby become competitive.

In the training of biblical counselors, the Bible again is the guide. The discipleship method is used. In John 8:26, 28, 31, 38; 5:19, 20, 30; 3:32, there is a theological base for the method. Jesus Christ entered into a Father/Son discipleship relationship that became the model for Christian training. He tells us that He learned by seeing and hearing. In contrast to the Greek "academic" model (derived from the academy), which emphasized hearing alone (and spawned the textbook/lecture method), the biblical method is fuller and stresses teaching by both verbal instruction and observation. The whole man is taught in an integrated manner by

---

more on this see comments on "example," "imitation," and "modeling" in *Competent to Counsel* and other books.

the whole man. Truth is integrated into life. In order to teach counseling this way, Nouthetic Counselors have established centers in which counseling is taught not only by lecture, reading, and discussion, but also by role-play, case study, seminars, and participant observation in actual counseling sessions. Content and skills are taught in an integrated way.

One of the principal concerns of Christian counselors is to introduce God into every counseling problem and every counseling session—not in some peripheral way, but at the center of all that is said and done. Pleasing Him—not relief from the problem—must be uppermost. Every counselee is called upon to "seek first God's kingdom and His righteousness." He is shown that what has happened has not happened apart from God (even a sparrow that falls does so only in His providence). Quite to the contrary, God is deeply involved in it all, working for His honor and the welfare of all His children (two things that always go together). Counselees do not always see this readily, but when presented in depth and accepted as the working basis for all else, everything changes.

This stance toward one's problems, along with the many details that grow out of it, leads to Christian hope[13]—an essential ingredient in all effective counseling. Recently, views aimed at countering the idea that Christians can change in their own strength (this idea is often called "depending upon the arm of flesh") have begun to stress that the Christian's only responsibility in solving his problems is to assume no responsibility for doing so. The more he "lets go and lets God" the better. The intention behind this is good, but the alternative offered is erroneous and dangerous. Galatians 2:20 is often misinterpreted to mean that the believer must let Christ (instead of the believer) live His life through him in such a way that he is quite passive. Actually, the verse says that the believer is responsible for living his life. It is the Christian—not the Holy Spirit (Christ in us)—who does the believing and the obeying. The true biblical teaching combines human responsibility with divine power. Changes (sanctification) must be made by the Holy Spirit's power (not ours) and at His direction, but by His power *enabling the counselee to accomplish*

---

13 This is never a "hope-so" hope, but a confident expectation based upon the unfailing promises of God in the Bible.

them. If Christians had no responsibility to do anything other than to get out of God's way (as it is often put), most of the New Testament wouldn't have been written. First Corinthians, for instance, could have been reduced to about a page's length. The details of the responsibilities for change that are set forth in such depth would have been unnecessary. No, the Holy Spirit does not do *instead of us* what He *requires of us* and instructs and empowers us to do.

Methodology

Nouthetic methodology is not borrowed from other systems. A distinction is made between "means" and "methods" (which are means committed to achieving the ends of a particular sort of talk designed to accomplish one or more of the goals of a system). All sorts of means may be used by Nouthetic Counselors in developing biblical methods, but methods must always grow out of and be designed to effect those ends that are set forth by God in His Word.

This means that Christians cannot be eclectic in their use of methodology, but are obligated to do the hard work of understanding problems biblically, addressing biblical answers to them, *and doing so by means that are consistent with biblical presuppositions and principles.*

Among the numerous counseling methods that have been developed from biblical sources are these:

1. Attempting to have all involved parties present in the counseling session (cf. *Competent to Counsel*);[14]
2. Allowing no slander or gossip in counseling sessions about persons not present (cf. *Competent to Counsel; The Big Umbrella);*
3. Sorting out each counselee's personal responsibility before God and his neighbor in the problem (cf. *Competent to Counsel);*
4. Analyzing and defining problems in scriptural (not medical, psychological, or euphemistic) language (language has sign value; labels are signposts: "sickness" points to a physician for help, "sin"

---

14   In this section the references in parentheses all refer to books listed earlier in these footnotes, unless indicated below.

points to Jesus Christ. Cf. *The Use of the Scriptures in Counseling);*
5. Laying out biblical plans of action founded on adequate data gathering (cf. *The Christian Counselor's Manual);*
6. Emphasizing the two-factored nature of sanctifying change ("from" and "unto"; the put off/ put on dynamic) that is in accord with the basic change that has already occurred "in Christ" (cf. *The Christian Counselor's Manual);*
7. Working within the framework of the church by its care and discipline, with its full authority and employing all its resources (cf. *Your Place in the Counseling Revolution; Shepherding God's Flock, Vol. 2);*
8. Expecting change following every session, and planning and prescribing for it (cf. *The Christian Counselor's Manual);*
9. Focusing upon the period (usually a week) between sessions as the time when change principally occurs in ordinary life situations (cf. *The Christian Counselor's Manual);*
10. Teaching counselees the biblical dynamic of the change that occurred, how to avoid future failure, and what to do (without running back to a counselor) to get out of it should they happen to fall into it (cf. *The Christian Counselor's Manual).*

Limitations

While much has been achieved, much more needs to be. Nouthetic Counseling is in its infancy. And even though all sorts of problems from depression to marriage difficulties have been solved biblically, more scriptural teaching, more sophisticated methodology, and much more are yet needed.

There are, of course, no limitations to what God can do. Other than those limitations that we impose upon the counseling sessions by our failure to understand fully or apply adequately what He has revealed in the Scriptures, there is no limitation in a biblical system of counseling that deals with sin. The unlimited power of the cross is at the disposal of every counselor who seeks to change the life of his counselee.

Conclusion

Biblical counseling is a growing movement. It is of no importance for a counselor to call himself a *Nouthetic* counselor (I have used the term merely for convenience). But it is of the utmost importance for him to use the Bible and the Bible alone as the basis for his counseling. Biblical counselors know that they simply cannot talk about man (or about changing man) without wading knee-deep into theology. It is important, then, for a Christian counselor to have a background in the Scriptures-in exegesis (the interpretation of Scripture), in theology (the systematization of scriptural teaching), and in practical theology (the application of Scripture to life in preaching and counseling). In short, Christian counseling is one important aspect of the ministry of the Word.

Reflections on the History of Biblical Counseling

Reflections on the History of Biblical Counseling[1]

Historical Roots of Pastoral Counseling

PRIOR to the Reformation, not only was counseling done in an unsystematic manner (except in certain specialized areas, largely having to do with the confession of sin and church discipline), but it was not often identified as a distinct ministerial task. That is not to say, of course, that pastors did not counsel. Faithful ministers of the Word met with members of their flocks, dealt with problems, wrote manuals concerning counseling issues such as melancholy (now called depression), and, in general, through letters and personal conference, carried on an embryonic, unsystematic form of counseling. The term *cure of souls (seelsorge,* which is still the identifying title in Germany) gradually emerged as the first and most enduring name for that branch of pastoral work that has to do with helping people deal with the problems of life from a pastoral perspective. Yet to this day in Europe, where it is often heard, that term is imprecise and refers to differing responsibilities according to the person using it.

Calvin was the first to distinguish sharply counseling (the term he used was *admonition,* a translation of the biblical Greek word *noutheteo*) as a regular, formal obligation of the pastor. As a result, he "is justly famous for devising and establishing in Reformation Geneva a system of pastoral visitation of daily life that aimed to reconcile every aspect of human affairs with the Sovereign God's revealed law.[2]

---

1 This essay was originally published in *Practical Theology and the Ministry of the Church, 1952-1984, Essays in Honor of Edmund P. Clowney.* Presbyterian and Reformed Publishing Company, 1990.

2 William A. Clebsch and Charles R. Jaekle, eds., *Pastoral Care* in *Historical*

Calvin wrote:

> What would happen if each is allowed to do what he pleases? Yet that would happen if to the preaching of doctrine there were not added private admonitions, corrections, and other aids of the sort that sustain doctrine and do not let it remain idle. *(Institutes,* 4.12. 1)

Where did Calvin get such notions and, more precisely, what was he talking about? His view of counseling (admonition or nouthetic confrontation) came from the Scriptures. He believed such work was an absolute obligation of the minister of the Word. This belief came from his exposition of Paul's sermon to the elders at Ephesus (Acts 20). Commenting on that passage, he noted that Paul refused to hold back anything that might be beneficial to the Ephesian church as he preached publicly; further, Paul also insisted on these truths becoming a part of life, individually adapting biblical principles "privately, as every man's necessity did require." In his commentary Calvin continues,

> Common doctrine will ofttimes wax cold, unless it is holpen [helped] with private admonitions [the word used in the Greek of Acts 20:31 is *noutheteo].*

Indeed, he goes so far as to chide those preachers who "having made one sermon, as if they had done their task, live all the rest of their time idly; as if their voice were shut up within the church walls," calling such behavior "inexcusable." Moreover, he calls this private ministry of the Word a "necessary duty" of the pastor. Here, as in so many things, if succeeding generations had only followed up the truly advanced insights of the Reformation, pastoral counseling might well have become long ago a vital factor in the life of the church, systematized and functioning in a biblical way.

Perspective (New York: Harper Torchbooks, 1967), 224. This book contains perhaps the most useful compilation of writings of various thinkers in the field over the ages. Luther also believed in and practiced pastoral counseling. In his *Babylonian Captivity of the Church* he wrote, "For a bishop who does nor preach the gospel or practice the cure of souls-what is he but an idol in the world (I Cor. 8:4). who has nothing but the name and appearance of a bishop?" And, in the same book he spoke of his own counseling: "Now suppose I counseled her to procure a divorce from his husband. . . . Then I would further counsel her ... "

The Puritan emphasis upon "cases of conscience" was an adaptation of the Reformation concern for counseling. But it was largely deflected from concern for the life of the believer when it frequently degenerated into a discussion of the problems of salvation with which many Puritans busied themselves. A schematic approach emerged in which they attempted to analyze and program conversion in a manner unknown to Scripture (breaking it down into definable steps or stages). Those Puritans who became involved in the preparationist teachings that grew out of this, like many psychologists at the present time, themselves probably unwittingly created most of the "cases of conscience" with which they subsequently dealt. Such Puritans (not all engaged in the activity) were the first Protestant psychologizers of religion, and the effects of their efforts were not unlike those confusing effects currently seen among evangelicals busy mixing psychological schemes of problem-solving with the pure teaching of the Word of God. An in-depth study of this matter in Puritanism might have a salutary effect on the contemporary problem.

In addition to the book cited in footnote 2, three other volumes are especially important to a study of the various periods of pastoral counseling.[3] But while they tell us much about the history of pastoral counseling through the years, when these studies reach the modern period, they fail to· take any note whatsoever of the emergence of the counseling movement in the evangelical churches. For that reason, I shall try to fill in the gap.

Pastoral Counseling in the Last Three Decades

The modern pastoral counseling movement in America is of recent origin and may be said to have begun with the publication of an article entitled "Challenge to Our Seminaries" by Anton Boisen, which appeared in *Christian Work* (1926). It stressed the need for instructing pastors in

---

3   John T. McNeill, A *History of the Cure of Souls* (New York: Harper and Bros., 1951); E. Brooks Holifield, A *History of Pastoral Care* in America {Nashville: Abingdon, 1983); H. Richard Niebuhr and Daniel D. Williams, *The Ministry in Historical Perspectives,* rev. ed. (New York: Harper and Row, 1983). Note that only the last two chapters of Holifield's book deal with the period we are treating in this essay; and, unfortunately, what he had to say pertains entirely to liberal Christianity, totally ignoring counseling in the evangelical church.

pastoral counseling. Boisen set forth the thesis that "in mental disorders we are dealing with a problem which is essentially spiritual." Ten years later, in *The Exploration of the Inner World*, Boisen argued (against Freud) that mental disorders arise from a bad conscience occasioned by real guilt rather than inner conflict over "false guilt."

Had the pastoral counseling movement developed along the lines suggested by Boisen, its subsequent history might have been considerably different. Although a liberal in theology (he held the moral influence theory of the atonement), Boisen saw clearly that this area, which increasingly was slipping away from the church into the hands of the psychiatrists, should be retrieved and made the object of theological discussion. He was right in claiming that counseling about life problems was the province of the church. His call, if heeded, might well have returned evangelicals to their Reformation moorings.

But instead of heeding this challenge, the pastoral counseling movement—even among Bible-believing churches—soon was redirected into Freudian channels and early succumbed to the idea that the pastor's major task is to defer and refer to the psychiatrist. Ministers of all theological descriptions bowed to the unending stream of propaganda published and disseminated under the aegis of the mental health movement, which insisted upon the medical model advocated by Freud and others. According to this model, counselees must be considered mentally ill, their problems the result of sickness rather than sin. This medical model removed responsibility from the counselee, who was now considered a victim rather than a violator of his conscience, and necessitated referral by the pastor, who was considered incompetent to counsel persons suffering from difficulties more severe than a psychic scratch.

With no biblical perspective on the matter and no imperative such as that which Calvin saw in Acts 20, ministers in liberal churches easily adapted to the propaganda and even began to spread it. Many of them, wishing to help others, saw psychiatry as the great answer to our needs that would replace the faith they themselves had abandoned. They studied psychology and psychiatry with a vengeance, incorporating its teachings into their preaching and doing counseling based upon its supposed findings. Early in the period we are discussing, Norman Vincent Peale, in conjunction with psychiatrist

Smiley Blanton, developed a counseling center. Perhaps the first of its kind, it incorporated the views of those psychologists and psychiatrists with whom they agreed as part and parcel of the ministry of the Marble Collegiate Reformed Church in America. This unnatural wedding was a statement of the supposed compatibility of psychology with Christianity while acknowledging the separate but equal territories of the pastor and the psychotherapist. A number of pastors and prospective ministers (including Carl Rogers) went over completely into psychotherapy, abandoning the church and becoming psychologists or psychiatrists instead.

Such capitulation by liberals is understandable, but how was it that conservative, Bible-believing ministers and institutions alike did much the same thing? Could they not see what Boisen, himself a liberal, saw? There were circumstances that do not excuse, but do explain, the nearly wholesale capitulation of the evangelical church to the mental illness viewpoint—a capitulation that was almost total by the 1950s. These circumstances clouded the picture so that Christian leaders failed to understand what was happening. With far lesser reason, many to this day are still engulfed by that cloud.

During the period when psychiatry and counseling psychology were gaining a strong foothold, the church was fighting a battle that took almost all of the time and resources it had. This was the battle for the Bible and the faith being waged against unbelieving science and liberalism in the church. Many evangelical churches and institutions had been taken over by liberals. Consequently, the airwaves, publishing houses, schools, and buildings built by evangelical money were all falling into their hands, and Bible-believing people were fighting for their very existence.

Great blows had been struck at the church. Evolution had all but destroyed belief in the doctrine of creation for many. Adam was considered but a mythical character, and the fall of man was denied. Christ's death had become an embarrassment and a problem. Few wanted to eliminate Him from the picture altogether, but His ministry and death had to be redefined. Higher criticism declared the words of Scripture untrustworthy so that each person, according to the latest "findings of the experts," was free to accept or reject what he or she wished. This made it possible to regard the Jesus of one's own preferences to be the "Jesus of history" behind the gospel records. Such attacks had to be answered. As a result, many important matters were wrongly relegated to a position of low priority. Much teaching about the Christian home, for instance, was totally abandoned for abstract doctrinal discussions. Moreover, with supplies, personnel, resources, and strategic positions all in the enemy's hands, evangelicals found themselves faced with the mammoth task of rebuilding a church that had crumbled. Critics jeered, Samaritans sniped, vast amounts of energy were consumed in battles for the faith, and even capitulating Christians (of which the woods were full) heaped discouragement upon the faithful few who undertook the task. The infighting had been exhausting; the opposition, bold and ruthless. But in spite of everything, today, a new church built out of the ruins of the old is perhaps better and stronger than the one that fell. Yet, much was lost during the fighting and rebuilding—particularly in the field of counseling. Rather than developing as a definite task of the minister of the Word in true Reformation fashion, counseling was handed over lock, stock, and barrel to the psychotherapists. As a result of its understandable but faulty prioritizing during the last three decades, the church easily succumbed to influences that destroy the home and make a mockery of the relationship between Christ and His church that Christian marriage is to reflect. Similarly, the church's place in the broader counseling enterprise, so clearly enjoined by Scripture, as Calvin pointed out, was simply overlooked. Overburdened pastors, often with relief, accepted the propaganda that assured them they were not competent to handle "mental illness." Under such circumstances, it was easy to ignore added burdens. It was easy to refer.

At the same time there grew up within the Bible-believing church a self-appointed caste of practitioners who encouraged "mental health" ideas of pastor incompetence and counseling as the province of psychology. All over the evangelical map, counselors trained in psychology rather than theology began to call themselves "Christian counselors" and hung out their shingles in competition with the church. Such people also found their way into seminaries, where they convinced a large proportion of the ministers now serving evangelical churches that the Reformation emphasis upon counseling as the task of the minister was wrong.

Chief among those evangelicals who have taught eclectic views are Donald Tweedie, Vernon Grounds, Clyde and Bruce Narramore, Gary Collins, Tim LaHaye, James Dobson, Frank Minirth, Paul Meier, and Larry Crabb.

An exception is Henry Brandt, whose counseling and writing go back to a period almost as early as Clyde Narramore's (their work began in the '40s and became well known in the '80s). Trained as a psychologist, Brandt soon realized that, in practice, his training was both ineffective and unbiblical. Discarding this training, he made an intensive study of the Bible to discover what God said about human problems and His solutions to them. When he began to apply Scripture in counseling, God blessed his efforts, and he became an effective counselor, helping many. Brandt has published a number of books and booklets for laymen, but he has never systematically set forth his counseling principles and practices in writing for the benefit of counselors.

Founder of a counseling institution located in Rosemead, California, speaker on an ongoing radio broadcast, and author of a steady stream of books and pamphlets, Clyde Narramore has done more to establish eclectic counseling among evangelicals over the years than anyone else. His radio program, for many years called "Psychology for Living," sets the theme: in serious difficulty, one turns to psychology—or more to the point, to psychologists—for answers. Following a trichotomistic view, Narramore parceled out the body to the physician, the spirit to the preacher, and the soul to the psychologist. In his books, one finds a strange mixture of fundamentalist belief side-by-side with Freudianism or some equally objectionable viewpoint. In his work there is little systematization of thought and an amazing tolerance of inconsistency.

Donald Tweedie early advocated an adaptation of Viktor Frankl's logotherapy approach, in which the pursuit of meaning (logos) is the foundation for all counseling. His views during the '50s and '60s were rather influential but have not been widely accepted, and his influence has waned.

Vernon Grounds, Christian statesman and former president of the Conservative Baptist Seminary of Denver, was another prime mover during the '50s and '60s. His eclectic, Freudian-based writing and lecturing early seduced a large portion of evangelicalism into such thinking.

His approach is best summarized in his article on "Christian counseling" in *Baker's Dictionary of Practical Theology*.

Clyde Narramore, Brandt, Tweedie, and Grounds were the principal spokesmen for counseling in the evangelical church during the '50s and '60s. Since Brandt's contributions were largely as a practitioner and not as a theoretician, his views failed to spread, while the efforts of the others yielded so large a return that they set the course of mainstream evangelical counseling down to the present time. Since the '60s, others, such as Collins, Bruce Narramore, LaHaye, Dobson, Minirth, Meier, and Crabb, have gained prominence.

From the '60s to the Present

Gary Collins of Trinity Evangelical Divinity School, Deerfield, Illinois, unlike most of those mentioned above, mainly writes and teaches about, rather than practices, counseling. His writings, as much as those of any other individual, represent the continuation of the movement begun by Clyde Narramore in the '40s.

Bruce Narramore began the Rosemead Graduate School of Counseling under the auspices of his uncle Clyde Narramore in conjunction with the Rosemead Foundation. This school later joined forces with Biola University of La Mirada, California. The school's orientation is avowedly eclectic, emphasizing a more scholarly, academic approach. Together with John Carter, Bruce Narramore founded *The Journal of Psychology and Theology*, which reflects their position.

Tim LaHaye, while pastor of the Scott Memorial Baptist Church and president of Christian Heritage College in El Cajon, California, through several books, popularized a modern adaptation of the old Greek temperament theory of the four humors set forth by Hippocrates and, more recently, by O. Hallesby. LaHaye originally acknowledged the pagan origin of the system, which he expanded to include combinations of the original four temperaments, but later "found" the big four temperaments set forth in an obscure passage in Proverbs.

Much stronger in their impact at this time are James Dobson, Frank Minirth, and Paul Meier, who, through their books and radio shows, regularly promote psychological views throughout the church.

Larry Crabb, writer, lecturer, and teacher, has expressed a desire to divorce himself from the mainstream evangelical-eclectic movement in favor of establishing a cognitively based "biblical counseling" system. So far, he has failed in the attempt because he continues to tie tightly the foundational principles and practices of this approach to Adler, Freud, Ellis, and Maslow. As in the case of others mentioned above, there is little exegesis. The Bible is used to support positions arrived at apart from Scripture, and biblical material is molded to fit views and practices the Bible itself does not teach.

All in all, one can say that in the evangelical church, theology and exegesis have had little to do with the positions and viewpoints adopted and taught. This is largely because most of the principal promoters of the eclectic view have little or no training in theology and exegesis, but much training in psychology. The (faulty) assumption seems to be that a Christian who is a counselor thereby automatically becomes a Christian counselor, regardless of the beliefs and practices inherent in his or her counseling.

The problem is that while these practitioners themselves, for the most part, are Christians, their counseling is anything but. It was, and largely still is, true of such counseling that the counselor's Christian orientation only served to confuse and delude the Christian counselee, who uncritically imbibed pagan thought and advice, thinking it was Christian. For instance, Vernon Grounds quotes Quentin Hyder as saying:

> The actual psychotherapy I had given him was not significantly different from that which he would have gotten from a non-Christian psychiatrist. However, there were three factors which were different. First, he felt more easily able to express his problems in biblical terms and knew that I understood what he was trying to say. Second, being reassured that I was myself a committed believer, he was much more readily able to accept my explanations and respond to my suggestions. Third, I was able to read a few relevant passages of Scripture to him and we often concluded our sessions with prayer together.[4]

---

[4] Vernon C. Grounds, "Christian Counseling: Who Has the Answer?" *Eternity* 26, no. 1 (January 1975): 19.

Significantly, Grounds comments, "It is this stance and spirit that most Christian counselors appear to identify with today."[5] Notice that Hyder considers neither the Scriptures nor prayer to be part of the psychotherapy as such; such matters seem to constitute little more than trimmings, which create more acceptable conditions for psychotherapy. Through these Christian accouterments, the counselee was led to let down his or her guard, being assured of the counselor's Christian commitment and, accordingly, as Hyder notes, finding it easier to accept the non-Christian explanations and suggestions given. Such "Christian counseling," in which Christianity is only in the packaging, Grounds describes as typical.

The Rise of Nouthetic Counseling

Only during the 1960s was a belated challenge to such counseling issued. At Westminster Theological Seminary, under the impetus of Cornelius Van Til's insistence that every movement be examined presuppositionally according to the Scriptures, basic questions were asked concerning the foundations of the pastoral counseling movement and the teaching and practices forming an integral part of it. Plainly, it was shown that the Reformers and Boisen were right: counseling deals with changes in people having to do with their values, behavior, beliefs, and attitudes. The task involves changing and improving relationships—with God and our fellow human beings, as Christ explained when He declared that the Bible could be summed up in the two commands to love God and our neighbor. Therefore, the school began to treat counseling as a theological matter. Man could not be viewed as he was by Freud, Rogers, Skinner, or other unbelieving theorists and still be helped. Their teachings and practices are not neutral; they were shown to be nothing more or less than bad theology. The counselor's anthropology must be biblical. Moreover, sin, guilt, and the fruit of the Spirit are all theological matters that bear directly on counseling and, therefore, could no longer be ignored. The place of the Scriptures, not as trapping but as integral to the process of change itself, and in this

---

5   Ibid.

regard, the work of the Holy Spirit in and through the ministry of the Word was emphasized.

Thus, a new movement, sometimes known as nouthetic counseling, grew up, calling for a return to counseling by pastors (as a life calling) and Christians in general (in more informal ways) within the church according to biblical principles. The necessity for a systematic approach to biblical counseling, built upon biblical principles and presuppositions, was acknowledged, and such a system has been under development since 1965.

Books in a steady stream have been published during the last fifteen years, setting forth various aspects of the system; courses and audio and video tapes have been produced. The movement has spread across America and Europe, where three national associations of biblical counselors have been set up for the purposes of certifying and networking, and nouthetic counseling works have been translated into thirteen different languages. Centers for counseling and training counselors have been started in churches, and conferences are held regularly in various parts of the world to teach the biblical viewpoint. Seminaries and Bible colleges, in increasing numbers, now provide training in biblical counseling. Doctoral work in biblical counseling can be taken at several Seminaries.

Briefly stated, nouthetic counseling sees the work of pastoral counseling as part of the work of sanctification, a ministry of Christ's church in which one Christian helps another to put off old, sinful life patterns and to put on the new biblical responses required by God in their place (cf. Eph. 4:22-24). This work of ministry must be done in the power of the Holy Spirit, who, in His way, honors His Word as it is ministered faithfully. Unbelievers are not counseled but pre-counseled (i.e., evangelized). Such verses as Galatians 6:1, Colossians 3:16, and Romans 15:14 depict counseling as the obligation of believers in general, whereas Colossians 1:28, Acts 20:20, 31, and similar passages describe nouthetic confrontation as the work of the pastor in particular. Thus, there are such activities as informal and formal counseling. The latter, the work of the eldership of the church, involves the official and authoritative ministry of the Word.

The word *noutheteo*, singled out by the Reformers as relating to the counseling of individuals from the Word about their lifestyles, has no adequate English equivalent. It embraces three ideas:

1. -the *confrontation* of a Christian whose attitudes, beliefs, or behavior must be
2. -*changed* by appropriate verbal means
3. -out of *concern* for him.

Rather than a harsh sort of confrontation (as some wrongly suppose), this third element is especially prominent in the Word, and such concern never loses the familial connotations firmly adhering to it.

All nouthetic counselors worthy of the name strive to help people solve life's problems God's way from His Word. Moreover, they see Paul's words in 2 Timothy 3:16-17 as a description of the process of change that God effects by means of His Word ministered in the power of the Spirit by a "man of God" (minister). They will find that the Scriptures "fully equip him" for every task of changing people to which God has called. They see no need, therefore, to "integrate" biblical counseling with those counseling systems which present alternative patterns of living that compete with God's. When God has said that peace, joy, and other blessings are the fruit of the Spirit, biblical counselors cannot conceive of these qualities of life as equally the fruit of Rogerianism, Freudianism, or other schools of thought. They plainly recognize that integration is impossible since the Bible teaches God does not bless His competition. Moreover, they point out that for over nineteen hundred years prior to the birth of Freud, the church was not without the resources to help its members make those changes which please God!

Of course, the findings of legitimate (non-counseling) psychology may indeed prove useful, though never necessary, to biblical counseling. But competitive *counseling systems* and *methods* designed to attain the goals of those systems can never be integrated with biblical teaching. Moreover, since the outset, nouthetic counselors have worked hand in hand with physicians, provided they stay in their own province (treating the body and not trying to tell their patients how to relate to grandmother). Nouthetic counselors have advocated the establishment of a significant relationship with Christian physicians so that they may work in tandem.

According to 2 Timothy 3:16, biblical counseling proceeds from scriptural *teaching* as the standard of faith and practice, to a *conviction* of failure to conform to that standard, moving next to *correction* of sinful ways by confession and forgiveness, and finally to the putting on of God's new ways through *disciplined training* in *righteousness*. That is not to deny that in the simpler forms of counseling, the mere impartation of information or the encouragement of the counselee is all that is needed. However, in 2 Timothy 2, Paul looks at the process of *nouthesia* (nouthetic counseling, or admonition and correction) and not at these simpler tasks, which are performed under such biblical labels as *encouragement* and *teaching*.

Biblical counseling demands counselor involvement, taking counselees seriously about their sin, prayerful use of the Bible, discipline, teaching, the fellowship of the flock, and the worship of the church—all in the context of the activity of the Holy Spirit, who is the *Paraclete*. In its broadest sense, *paraclete* means "assistant, one who comes alongside to help." The help may be of any form, but when specified as of a particular type in the New Testament, it is "comfort," "counsel," or "advocacy." As the *Paraclete* in counseling, the Holy Spirit is the counselor. But He is also the one who convicts and comforts.

The biblical counseling movement has made an impact on evangelical churches and drawn the line between the two sorts of counseling approaches now in use. According to Collins, who is no advocate of nouthetic counseling, "few others have been courageous or creative enough to attempt ... to build a counseling system which begins with and is built on Scripture." He admits that "there is no alternative system which is as clearly biblical."[6] There is a great difference between

1. building a system from biblical presuppositions and principles and then developing practices out of these, that are consistent with them at every point, and
2. stuffing biblical material into the pigeonholes of a system built from nonbiblical materials.

There is a great deal of the latter. Collins has the insight to see that apart from the nouthetic system, the former does not exist.

---

6   Gary Collins, *How to Be a People Helper* (Santa Ana, Calif.: Vision House, 1976), 169.

The nouthetic approach is yet incomplete. Unlike many other systems narrowed to the thinking and experience of men, nouthetic counseling is based upon the limitless Word of God. It is an open system—but unlike other open systems, it is open only to God's Word. Thus, as new biblical insights are developed, they may be added without upsetting those discovered previously. Such is not the case with other open systems, where opinions of men are replaced by more opinions, none of which is complete. In saying this, nouthetic counselors do not deny that they may have wrongly or incompletely understood the Scriptures at various points or claim that everything in the system as now construed is complete or perfectly reliable. It would be sheer arrogance and stupidity to say any such thing. But they do affirm that insofar as they have accurately understood and construed the Scriptures in relationship to human problems, their system can be amplified by true biblical insights without significant alteration. Because nouthetic counselors work with the inerrant Word of God, whenever they are correct, they build unshakably for the future.

This leads to one more factor—the effect of the counseling system upon the counselor. Whatever a counselor spends his or her efforts, time, and energy thinking about and using day by day will affect that person as well as those counseled. Indeed, such principles and insights probably affect the counselor far more than any individual counselee, since the counselor is exposed to them for a much longer period of time and in a more intensive and thorough way. Thinking regularly about people and their problems as Adler, Ellis, and Maslow do, and building a worldview and lifestyle around their pagan presuppositions is dangerous, not to say discouraging. But the biblical counselor, confined to the limits of the Scriptures alone, spending time in the exegesis and application of the Bible to the problems of people, is continually blessed by the work itself.

The extent to which the infiltration of pagan ideas into evangelical circles has now progressed can be seen in two recent publications: William Kirk Kilpatrick's *Psychological Seduction* (Nashville: Nelson, 1983) and Dave Hunt and T. A . McMahon's *The Seduction of Christianity* (Eugene, Ore.: Harvest House, 1985). Furthermore, in a recently published book, *The Biblical View of Self-Esteem, Self-Love and Self-Image* (Eugene, Ore.: Harvest House, 1986), I have demonstrated how the evangelical church has become filled with Adler-Maslow teachings that threaten to revolutionize the church of tomorrow if not successfully met and overthrown.

The period under study has been an exciting one, but full of confusion, experimentation, and (as two of the aforementioned volumes note) seduction. Yet, out of it all, God has raised up, for the first time since the Reformation, a viable biblical counseling movement in which biblical principles of counseling have not only been put into practice but also codified in the form of a working system. As Collins indicates, this is unique. Practical theology has been the stepchild of the seminaries and the church. But it is a Johnny-come-lately that has come!

While most other aspects of Christian ministry, doctrinal and ecclesiastical, have for many years been determined by creedal affirmations and denials, those pertaining to preaching and the work of counseling have not. Today, the church is becoming aware of the great dangers of the infiltration of its ranks by those who advocate psychological doctrines—many of which are every bit as bizarre as those held by the most extreme cults. My hope is that the church in the near future will not only cleanse itself of such teachings but will, for all time, set down its abhorrence of, and warning against, them in doctrinal statements about the work of the minister and that such statements will eventually issue in generally agreed-upon creedal forms. This is the lesson about pastoral counseling that the church should learn from the last three decades. If it fails to do so, who knows how many decades of disaster may lie ahead?

The Physician, The Pastor, Psychotherapy, and Counseling

The Physician, The Pastor, Psychotherapy, and Counseling[1]

For years when I was a pastor, I attended mental health meetings for pastors sponsored by various organizations, at which psychiatrists and psychologists addressed us. The pastors always listened, the psychiatrists always talked. It was never the other way around. It troubled me that the data flow was so one-sided. Therefore, I appreciate the opportunity, as a minister of the Word, to come to a gathering of medical personnel to speak to you, rather than merely to be on the other side of the fence. Thank you for the opportunity.

At these conferences for pastors, we were told that the pastor is a "gatekeeper." That word kept coming out all the time. Because the pastor is one of the first to see people with problems (the statistics bear this out), he was taught by the "experts" at these meetings to defer and refer. That is the particular task of the "gatekeeper." His job is to send to the psychiatrist or psychologist people who have anything worse than a psychic scratch. The problem was that, as a pastor, when I followed this advice, I found it didn't work! Sending people off to the psychiatrist and psychologist more often than not meant that they came back later on as bad (or worse). So we weren't getting results. It became quite a problem.

I know you physicians have a similar problem. I don't know whether we have any psychiatrists or psychologists here, but most of you are "body" people. You're not working on problems about how to relate to grandmother. You're dealing with *body* problems. So you have much the same problem that I had as a pastor. You also frequently must send

---

[1] This article was originally published in the *Journal of Biblical Ethics in Medicine*, Volume 3, Number 2. The article is based on a 1988 presentation in Birmingham, Alabama. It is edited for publication, yet retaining an informal style.

people off to someone else for help. Many of my physician friends have spoken to me about this problem. I've read the literature that says, in some places, up to fifty percent (other literature sixty to seventy percent) of the persons that a physician sees have no organically-based problem and probably shouldn't be there. Their problems are "psychosomatic" (or whatever you want to call it). The difficulty is that you've got to do something for those people.

Many physicians, of course, give them some kind of a pill or prescription to make them happier and send them on their way. People aren't happy if you don't do something for them. This is one of the reasons for the enormous amount of over medication going on. When you send people off to psychiatrists or psychologists, you still have the problem. You might take the Weed or Cross approach to Problem-oriented Medicine, but I've been through much of that, and it looks so complex that I guess most people wouldn't want to get very heavily tied into it. Also, it is not biblically oriented, though it attempts to look at the whole person in trying to do the job.

Well, then, you say, "I'll try counseling myself." Some of you have tried counseling people. You are Christians. You know that their real problem is that they need to get certain things squared away with the Lord, with their family members, their boss, or others. So, you try doing counseling. That, however, creates a new problem. You have too little time to do an adequate job. It destroys your own family if you stay late night after night, extending your time with such people. Taking extra time, you create new and worse problems than you faced to begin with. You can't do much counseling plus all the body work you must do in the ten or fifteen minutes (perhaps a little more for Christian physicians) typically allotted for a patient. Counseling takes time—much more time. If you give them that kind of time, you're going to have to charge exorbitant fees in order to keep your salary level up to where it belongs, because you'll see far fewer people.

So, you are in a dilemma again. You're wrong if you don't and you're wrong if you do. What are you going to do? Well, you refer, reluctantly. If you've read *Medical World News,* you know that the difficulties with psychiatry and psychology are serious. About ten years ago, that periodical first reported an experiment in which a psychiatrist thought he would check out his fellows on their ability to diagnose problems. Into twelve of this nation's leading mental institutions he sent seven persons (I hope the next statement is accurate) as sane as you or I. When they entered, they lied only about one thing. They said, "I hallucinated." They didn't act strangely in any way, and they didn't tell any other lies. Any questions they were asked they tried to answer factually. In these seven instances, how many times do you suspect that they were declared to have serious mental illnesses? Would you believe half? You'd be wrong. Three-fourths? You'd still be wrong. In seven of seven instances these persons were labeled mentally ill. They were called schizophrenic in six cases, and manic depressive was the label gummed on the file in the seventh case.

Such serious labels put on people's files follow them throughout the rest of their lives. Yet, in all cases, seven of seven in this instance, the diagnosis was absolutely false. A person can hallucinate for all sorts of reasons, as you are well aware: hallucinogenic drugs, sleep loss, etc. Just because a person is hallucinating doesn't say anything about etiology. If a person here in the audience had a red nose I would have no right to accuse him of boozing just because of that. It may be that his wife punched him in it, because he is growing a pimple on it, or because he fell asleep under the sun lamp. There are various causes for red noses. The same effect may have various causes. The same is true of hallucinations. Yet in all cases where these persons said, "I hallucinated," they were labeled as having a serious mental illness.

When that experiment hit the fan, it splattered all over the medical and psychiatric world and made quite a stir. When it settled down, the fellow who did this went to one of these institutions and said, "I'm going to do it to you again." But he didn't. Then he waited a while and checked the intake records of that institution. He saw that before he said he was going to do it again, virtually nobody was turned away as a malingerer (or fake). However, after he had said this, all sorts of people were being turned away as malingerers. He got them going and coming.

There is a mess out there in psychiatry. Zilboorg, in his two-volume history of psychiatry, concluded: "The field is in disarray, just as it was at the beginning." I agree with him that the field is in disarray, but I disagree that it is just as bad as it was at the beginning. If you take as the beginning somewhere around Freud and Charcot, at the beginning of modern psychiatry and psychology, you had only five to twelve different viewpoints, depending on how thinly you slice the psychiatric sausage. Today, in America, we are told that there are over 230 different viewpoints on counseling psychology and psychotherapy of various sorts. You can't even adequately study them all in a lifetime to evaluate who is right (if any). Nor can you determine what pieces are right if you are going to eclectically make an amalgam of these viewpoints. Day by day new ones come on the market, and, like breakfast cereals, at each trip to the store, you discover new offerings making stupendous claims.

These new systems invariably say, "At last we've found it! **All** the rest were wrong up until now. You've finally got it!" Thus, all your study of Freud and Jung and the others is worthless, because now, at long last, truth has appeared. Who knows who's right? You don't even have time to study Jung in a lifetime. Jung is a mystic. Jung is tough. Jung's teaching about the animus and the anima is esoteric. He speaks of a "collective unconscious", mystical "archetypes" that go back to the early days of man's history. Just to begin to understand Jung's viewpoint, let alone evaluate it, is a tremendous task. Then there is Freudianism and all its types: early Freudianism, later Freud, and neo-Freudianism, which emphasizes the Ego rather than the Id. You find it in all its strange manifestations, such as in Harris' "I'm O.K., You're O.K."

There are the "third force" fellows, who have become more dominant than the behaviorists and Freudians. These people have filled our country with humanistic ideas of self-love, self-esteem, and self-worth.

Practically every book coming off the press today by Christians purports to see in the Bible teachings of self-worth, self-love, and self-esteem. We are told to bolster every human being in order to raise his self-worth. This is something we have never seen before, but rather condemned for many years. But now the church has been brainwashed into believing that this is true. Even our hymns are being changed so that we no longer sing anything about being "worms". And so it goes - just continued change after change. We go from one thing to the next. But there is nothing solid, there is no consensus.

Leading psychologists and psychiatrists first met together about three years ago in Phoenix. Time magazine reported that there was only one conclusion coming out of that meeting: that nobody agreed about anything! I was on a jury last year, and we had a psychiatrist testify in the case. It was interesting when the district attorney asked the forensic psychiatrist, who testifies regularly for $500 per appearance, whether psychiatrists agree on anything. Under oath, he said, "No". That was the honest answer. Only ignorance or arrogance leads anyone in this field to say, "This is right. This is correct." He'd either be ignorant of the varieties of viewpoints and the lack of consensus, or he'd be arrogant to say, "I know which one is right.

The only way in this confusion that anyone could testify that he has the answer and knows he is right is either to be ignorant of the situation or to be arrogant.

Where, then, is the answer to your problem? You physicians see these people; you have to do something about them. You must work with people whose lives are full of difficulties and problems. Should you send them off to the shrinks? Should you try to treat them yourself? Is there hope anywhere?

I want to tell you that there is an answer to your problem. It is coming slowly but surely. Though not as widespread as we'd like, it is in place in a number of areas. There is a new kind of person to whom you may refer people. It is someone who doesn't try to play shrink, who wants to work with physicians, and who can be of great help to these people who need counseling rather than medicine. I refer to the new breed of ecclesiastical cat that is prowling around much of this country today.

But first, on behalf of all concerned ministers who see matters this way, I want to take advantage of this opportunity to ask your forgiveness on behalf of preachers of the gospel who ought to have been working with you and serving you over the years, but who have not done so. The dilemma in which you physicians find yourself is not of your making. It is not your fault. You're in a dilemma that the church created. Specifically, preachers have brought it about. They are at fault, not you. What has happened is understandable, though not excusable. Pastors used to do counseling. At one time they wrote the books on melancholy (now called depression).

But, in the history of the Church something happened. There came the great liberal onslaught into American Christianity. That movement was so powerful and had such an impact upon the church, that many things were lost in the battle that ensued. Institutions were taken over by liberals, as were church buildings, denominations, publishing houses, and radio broadcasts. The conservatives who were holding on to the truth became so zealously engaged in the battle with liberalism, while barely hanging on by their fingernails, that they allowed many things to slip by the wayside. And much of what went by the wayside affects our homes and has brought on the chaos that we experience in our communities. The teaching of family responsibility, of husband-wife relationships, as well as parent-child relationships, dropped through the cracks. Everything became a doctrinal issue. The battle had to do with whether the Bible was the Word of God or not. That issue was central and basic, and we could never evade it. However, many important things disappeared because of the desperation of the circumstances.

One of those things that disappeared was counseling. Pastors stopped doing biblical counseling. At this very time, the psychiatrist and the psychologist were coming to the fore. They claimed there was a third category in life beyond the organic category and the spiritual (or moral) category: a non-organic, non-moral category. They introduced this to provide an area in which to work.

This unnatural third category the Bible knows nothing about. The Bible knows about the organic problems people have (sickness, injury, bad health), and the Bible knows about spiritual problems, which have to do with one's relation to God and his neighbor. But it knows nothing about a "mental illness" category, in which a non-organic bug of some sort creates a non-organic problem which has to be treated non-organically under a medical aegis, though there is nothing medical about it. What is peculiarly medical about someone telling how to live with grandmother? This new category forced its way between the two biblical categories that we have always known and believed in. Many pastors were glad to have it so! They were exhausted from the battle with liberalism. They were preaching in storefronts with few resources, trying to make a comeback. They were in bad shape materially and physically, and had little time. They were all too glad to have somebody else take over their counseling work. They let it go. Thus, the problem grew, and you are faced with it today.

All the while there was a better answer to people's non-organically based problems. But that answer was buried. The reason there is no consensus today in the field of counseling is because the one Book that could have brought consensus was rejected early on and laughed at by people in the new category. They said, "We can enable people to love, experience joy, peace, and self-control apart from the Bible. But the Bible calls these desirable qualities the "fruit of the Spirit." God has said through His Word, "I am the one who brings those qualities of life into a person's experience through faith in Jesus Christ as that individual appropriates the Word and as the Spirit of God enables him to fulfill that Word in daily living. I am the one who does that."

They said, in effect, "No, we can do all that without the Word, without the Spirit, without God, without the Church, without any of these things, by means of Freudianism, Rogerianism, Behaviorism, Skinnerianism - or something else. Competitively, these organizations and viewpoints set themselves up over against the Church. Many Christians, now realizing that there was a need to help people in these areas, began to take training. The trouble was that they went for training with these same people who were opposed to God's way and who were in competition with God.

Many of you may not realize that psychotherapy has set itself up in competition with God. Whatever you call it, that is all I can call it. If I set up a store on one corner and I sell auto tires, and three other people set up tire shops on the other three corners, I call that *competition*. We're claiming our product can do the same thing. We're trying to get the same people for the same purpose. Here is God saying, "I can give you love, joy, peace, self-control, etc., through my Spirit by my Word." Here are other people saying, "No, *we* can enable you to experience love, joy, peace, self-control, *without* the Word." That is competition. They have set up shop over against God saying, "We can do a better job, in a different way." I don't know how you can integrate those two things. Surely, there is no way they can be integrated. If the Old Testament teaches us anything at all, it is that God doesn't bless His competition! I don't believe you can have it both ways. You must choose between them.

So there it laid buried in the Word of God—the idea that there were answers, qualities of life, that God promises to people who love and serve Him obediently through Christ. Christians went off to study with all kinds of pagans. Then they tried to integrate these competitive viewpoints with Christian beliefs. They then proclaimed themselves as "Christian psychologists, Christian psychiatrists, Christian counselors". What they did was hold their Christianity, which in most cases they genuinely believed, in one hand, and their therapeutic methods in the other hand. The right hand didn't know what the left hand was doing. The two were never really brought together. They didn't think presuppositionally, they didn't see contradictions, they didn't recognize the competitive nature of the situation. They said on the one hand, "I go to church, I am a Christian and I try to live that way in my community." On the other hand they said (in effect), "This is my job and I will give them Freud and Rogers, with a little prayer and Bible sprinkled on top."

They thought integration could take place very simply because these people had PhDs in psychology and a Sunday School degree in Bible. When you put a Sunday School degree together with a PhD, which one do you think is going to take over? Obviously, the Bible is likely to be bent to fit the degree. Many of our seminaries, lax as they are in other ways, always seem to be interested in accreditation. So they brought in psychiatrists and psychologists to boost accreditation rather than theologically and exegetically trained people who knew the Word in depth to teach pastoral counseling. What did they teach? "Ministers, you're gatekeepers. You must learn to refer and defer to the Christian psychiatrists." That is, self-styled "professionals" who have hung up their shingles outside of and in competition with the Church. Thus, even in Bible-believing circles, the Bible was laid aside in favor of psychotherapy, which is now firmly entrenched inside the Church. The competitive camel has come under the tent - its nose, its body, its hooves, its tail.

But, long overdue, something else has been happening in the last 20 years. The new breed of ecclesiastical cat I mentioned has begun to flex his muscles. He says, "No, we must not turn to pagans out there to find the answers to people's problems. And we must stop bringing pagan ideas into the church. We must turn to God and determine what He has said must be done. We must develop a methodology that is not borrowed from the pagans but which grows out of biblical presuppositions about what is wrong with human beings and what the Bible says must be done about these problems. The methodology must be appropriate to basic biblical presuppositions at every point." These ecclesiastical cats are multiplying and becoming available in more and more areas today. They are persons who want to cooperate with the Christian physician.

Last Monday I was talking to a group of pastors, men who are concerned about these matters. In the question and answer period one of them said, "How do you find a Christian physician who will work with you? How do you find a physician who, when you send him someone for a medical workup, won't shoot him off to a shrink but will send them back to you so that you can counsel him?" I get this question all the time from the other side of the fence. Here are people who are longing to work with you.

They care about people and are more and more equipped to deal with people who have non-organically generated problems.

There are all sorts of training institutions in this country, now well over 30, that regularly turn out pastors trained to do truly biblical counseling in a sophisticated way. There is a national organization. There are programs of continuing education for pastors who were originally trained in wrong ways. There are video and audio courses and books galore. This has all mushroomed in the last 15 years. More and more of these pastors are ready to work with Christian physicians in a significant alliance.

These counselors recognize what James 5 is all about. James wrote, "Call for the elders of the Church if you are sick." The passage goes on to talk about what they do when they get there. These elders don't just pray. James continues,

> Let them pray for him, rubbing him with oil in the name of the Lord, and the believing prayer will deliver the one who is sick. The Lord will raise him up and if he has committed sins he will be forgiven.

The verb that I translated "rubbing him with oil" is rather significant. The King James and some other translations render it "anointing him with oil" as though it were a ceremonial event.

There are two New Testament words for anointing. One of them refers to ceremonial anointing *chrio*, the term from which the word *Christos* (or Christ, the "Anointed One") comes. That word speaks of the Spirit coming upon people as a *chrisma* (Cf. I John). But that is not the word used in James 5. It is *aleipho*, and is distinct from it. It is a word that, for example, Hippocrates used to speak of how people were helped physically by doctors in his day. Greek physicians mixed herbs and various medical potions with oils and wine. The person was rubbed with these, medically. That is what this verse is talking about. It is talking about rubbing or smearing. It is not talking about ceremonial anointing at all.

James, therefore, is saying that the elders are to do two things. First, they were to administer medicine: rub him with it. Of course, doctors weren't available on every street corner in those days. He called the elders. Anyone could administer medicine. The elders were to pray, but also to use the best medicine of their day. Secondly, they were to pray for his healing. Exercises by people who carry a little bottle of oil around and make ceremonial noises are out of the spirit of this passage. If the person is ill because of some sin, he is to confess it, and it will be forgiven. So the elders were to recognize the dual responsibility of dealing with people who have both organic and non-organically caused problems. They ministered medically and spiritually.

There are, finally today, men who want to work with physicians as a team, fulfilling both aspects of James 5. But in what circumstances might you want to work with such men and refer patients to them? One instance is when medicine won't work or shouldn't be given. A brief check by you of some of the attitudes of some of those people, and the nature of their life problems, might indicate that the source of the difficulty is something you ought not to be handling. To prescribe tranquilizers as so often is done to deal with marriage problems, etc., is the wrong solution and bad practice. That is not the way to deal with marriage or many other problems. Tranquilizers don't resolve such problems. They only make people incapable of dealing adequately with problems as they remove the initiative to deal with them.

Complaintive, self-pitying persons may be those you should think about referring. They need someone who will face them with their responsibilities before God and their neighbors. Depressed and suicidal persons need to be dealt with by someone who is going to take the time.

Anti-depressants are not the answer to depression, but help in getting one's life squared away so that he or she (more frequently she) meets responsibilities. Such people must be taught now to discipline their lives so as not to follow their feelings but their responsibilities before God and their neighbor.

At our counseling training center (we have 5 of them now, some operating for over 17 years), we have had hundreds of depressed people helped quickly and lastingly by the application of biblical principles. In four to six weeks, we have these people not only out of the depression (that usually takes a week or two) but functioning as they ought to, so as to stay in that condition. Concerned homosexuals and lesbians can benefit from biblical counseling. You have no pills for those problems, but there are people who can deal with them. In I Cor. 6:9, Paul states, "Such were some of you." There are ways of dealing with such people, but they take some time. Often, a counselee has to be convinced that there is hope for him to change because he has bought a lot of propaganda that says he is genetically flawed. Pastors, trained biblically, know how to counter such ideas. Also consider referring to these pastors, persons acting in a bizarre manner, who are not on drugs and who show no other indications of an organic difficulty. Bitter, resentful people or fearful, anxious, and worried persons can benefit from biblical, pastoral counseling.

Moreover, consider referring husbands and wives who are troubled about their families, their marriage, or divorce. Also, people undergoing tragedies and grief. You can't adequately support them during such times, though you may give them a word of encouragement and pray with them. You have so much else to do, so if you try to do counseling in addition to medical work, you and your own family will soon need counseling. I find this to be a problem with many Christian physicians. They neglect their own families because they care so much about their patients, and they spend more time with them than they really should. But then nothing gets done properly. They spread themselves too thin. I even find physicians wanting to get into the ministry to do counseling more effectively.

In general, I'd say anyone who needs to deal with values, attitudes, or behavior change is one who should be referred to a biblical counselor. Today, more and more, you can find such counselors in or near your community. It is worth a trip. We have known people to come 150 miles or more for biblical counsel. Finding the person who knows how to deal with a problem in the right way will solve many difficulties.

I'm suggesting that these pastors are out there, available and ready; more and more they are on the scene. There are gaps, but there is a network you can utilize through our national organization, called the National Association of Nouthetic Counselors. The word "nouthetic" is simply a New Testament Greek word that means to counsel people. It means "to counsel." There are three elements in the word which was brought over directly from Greek since no English word approximates it. The three elements in it are *change*, effected by *confrontation*, out of *concern*. The word also has a warm familial matrix, in which deep family-like concern is exhibited.

The Bible doesn't deal so directly with medicine as it does with lifestyle. Medicine is mentioned, and it is commended. The physician is not looked down upon in the Bible so long as he does not get in the way of God.

The Bible, of course, forbids trusting physicians instead of God. Also, physicians involved in some kind of incantation or pagan cultic practices are looked down upon. But the Bible deals less directly with medicine than with lifestyle. There is some direct data on medicine. Those data ought to be known by every physician. Many physicians aren't aware of what the Bible has to say about medicine. An example is the James 5 passage discussed earlier, which may not have been well-focused in some of your minds. There are other passages in Proverbs and elsewhere that have a direct bearing on medicine. Probably, if you were closer to some theologians concerned about this matter, they could help you to get some of those data on the table where you could work with them.

The Bible also gives us definite principles and presuppositions related to ethics in medicine, which is the topic of this conference. If you want to find presuppositions for ethics in medicine or anything, you must go to the Scriptures. In extant ethical textbooks, there is total confusion, as each person is left to decide what he is going to do. You see norms derived from some sort of natural theology which is, supposedly, universally agreed upon. The confusion in the field of ethics is simply horrendous. Until you realize that God is the one Who, in His Word, sets the norms, Who gives us the principles and practices, Who tells us what the human being ought to look like, you're stuck. However, few physicians have a good biblical training in their background. That is understandable. So you need to get together with some people who have that training if you want to make ethical decisions that are biblical and pleasing to God. You must know biblical principles. This means sitting down with theologians. You need to talk with them about passages. You need to consult reliable exegetes who will answer your questions about given passages and what they really mean, rather than the way well-meaning but uninformed Sunday School teachers may have interpreted them.

For example, take the Proverbs passage which says, "As a man thinks in his heart, so is he." How often have I heard in a Sunday School class or elsewhere, "Here is an important philosophical principle for us to follow in life." Well, it isn't anything of the sort. This is one of the few Proverbs that has a little bit of context. It is talking about going to eat with a man who serves you a meal. He asks you, "Would you like a second pork chop?" But the whole time he is thinking in his mind, "I hope he doesn't take it, that pig. I want it for supper tomorrow night." What the passage says is that what he may be thinking in his heart is what you really need to take into consideration, not what he says. It has nothing to do with a philosophy of life. It is more nearly a philosophy of eating.

It is necessary, also, for the theologian and Christian physician to work together to determine what the biblical data are and how they apply to medical practice. On the one side, you have people who can produce something in the way of organic data, and on the other hand you have those who can produce exegetical data. We need to bring those together. Too often we have people with organic data who don't know the biblical side well enough and vice versa. What we need is a fruitful union if we really want to get some ethics moving here. Such an alliance would help both the pastor and physician. I'd like to see, over a period of years, opportunities for solid Christian physicians, theologians, and exegetes to meet together to iron out some of these things. We get too many books in which either one or the other tries to do the job without recognizing the data in the other field.

Casuistry will be the outcome. Casuistry is a good thing that has a bad name. It only has a bad name because of the way it was carried on in medieval days. It simply means the application of biblical principles to life situations. That is what we have to get down to - understanding what the Scriptures say and what the circumstances are- to bring these together in a way that grows out of our biblical presuppositions according to our biblical principles and practices. I am calling today for a fruitful relationship between theologians and physicians. May God grant us a day to come when we will see that. It is my hope and prayer.

Response to the Congress on Christian Counseling

Response to the Congress on Christian Counseling[1]

ADDRESSING this body strikes me as an anomaly, nearly as extraordinary as the time many years ago when, in Korea (which was yet a backward nation), the famous dog story writer, Jack London, was told that an entire city had gathered to see him. As he viewed the vast crowd from the top of a platform erected especially for him, he couldn't help but congratulate himself that his fame had reached so many in this far-off region. But when he opened his mouth to speak, the official in charge stopped him, saying, "Please, Sir, remove your teeth." Somewhat taken aback by the request, he nevertheless did so. The crowd applauded. Then, amidst continuous applause, for the next half hour, he stood there removing and replacing his artificial teeth.

I want you to know that tonight I'm not so foolish as to congratulate myself over this appearance. As the coordinator rightly indicated when he invited me, I have been a source of irritation to many of you. I also know that I can't consider myself one of you, except as we are brothers and sisters in Christ. Indeed, I came not knowing why you asked me. I do know, however, that, as London's experience so vividly shows, there can be a number of curious reasons for inviting someone to participate in such a gathering. Why, it even occurred to me that you might have brought me here to induce me to remove my teeth! Of course, that's not so easy to do; you see, only false teeth can be removed. On the other hand, my presence here may only prove what I've been saying all along: most Christian counselors are eclectic—so eclectic, indeed, that I could

---

[1] Dr. Adams' response to being awarded a plaque for pioneering in Christian counseling on November 10, 1988, in Atlanta, Georgia.

be included tonight. So, since I can't occupy the remainder of the five minutes allotted to me as London did, I want to take advantage of this occasion to do two things: give you an explanation and extend you an invitation.

First, the explanation. Contrary to what you may think, I have not spent the last fifteen to twenty years trying to refute (or even irritate) so-called Christian professionals (psychiatrists, psychologists, sociologists) like yourselves. Had I intended to do so, I assure you I would have done a better job of it! No, I have not had you in mind. My efforts have solely been to help pastors who, according to II Timothy 3:17, are God's professionals. That's why the approaches and arguments in my writings are not tailored to you. Rather, I designed them to expose pastors to the futility and dangers of attempting to integrate pagan thought and biblical truth.

Moreover, while these negative measures are necessary to alert and inform pastors, my work is fundamentally positive. I am more at home with the construction gang than with the wrecking crew. Even a superficial survey of my books reveals that my greatest efforts are positive. In them, I endeavor not only to provide concrete help in specific areas but also to set forth a biblically based system of theory and practice in a usable form that may be communicated easily to any pastor out there on the front line.

Finally, whenever I mention names of those who publicly propagate views I believe detrimental to pastoral counseling and the welfare of Christ's church, I want you to know that it's their opinions I am assailing, not their persons. Anyone who puts forth ideas in order to influence the church (including me) should be ready to stand the criticism of the church. The important thing for you to recognize is that there is nothing personal in my critique.

So much for the explanation; now, the invitation. With all that is within me, I urge you to give up the fruitless task to which I alluded: the attempt to integrate pagan thought and biblical truth. In his latest book, Gary Collins admits, "It's too early to answer decisively if psychology and Christianity can be integrated." Too early? Think of the millions of hours, the more than one generation of lives, already spent on this hopeless task! Why are there no results? I'll tell you why: because it just can't be done.

Remember God's words: "My thoughts are not your thoughts, neither are your ways my ways" (Isaiah 55:8). What does God tell us to do to resolve this radical antithesis? Integrate? No! In that passage He commands us to forsake our thoughts and our ways and turn to His Word, which He promises will not return void.

Counseling has to do with changing people. But, you see, that's God's business. There are only two ways to change people: God's way and all others. You simply can't build a Christian counseling system on a pagan base, nor can you incorporate pagan teachings and methods into Christian counseling. Pagan thoughts and ways are at odds with God's. God proposes to produce fruit (love, joy, peace, self-control, etc.) by means of His Spirit through His Word. Then others come along and claim they can produce love, joy, and peace apart from the Spirit and the Word. The two proposals and the methods that go with them are essentially competitive. That's why they can't be integrated. If the Old Testament teaches anything, it's this: God doesn't bless His competition. That's why integration won't work.

I invite you to abandon this useless endeavor. Instead, come, join the growing number of those who are discovering that the way to construct a truly Christian counseling system is to begin with biblical blueprints, use biblical brick and mortar, and find Christian workmen to construct it from the ground up. Steer clear of the 'me too' approaches of those Christians who emulate the world. Rather, get out in front of the pack, showing that world what God by biblical counseling can do!

At the conclusion of one of Sam Jones' evangelistic messages, an irate woman said to him, "I'll never listen to you again. You've insulted me. You stroked the fur the wrong way!" "No," Jones replied, "I stroked the fur the right way; the cat was facing the wrong direction." Tonight I, too, have been stroking fur.

Change Them?... into What?

Change Them?... Into What?[1]

It's truly a great pleasure to bring you greetings from friends in the United States. The subject before us tonight has the German word *seelsorge* in the title.[2] I must do something to limit that term so that you understand what I'm talking about. That word is much larger than the subject before us. Perhaps your word *beratung* comes closer to it, but that misses it a bit, too. Because the latter word can have more of the idea of consultation (as I understand it), in which two people speak to one another on much the same level, there is still some problem.

I'm really talking about the subject of *counseling* (as we call it in English), a word that envisions one person bringing something to the consultation in order to help another who needs it. It also has the connotation that the counselor is in charge and moving ahead in a purposeful direction. With that brief introduction to the word and the title, perhaps you will understand where I am coming from more clearly. I'm certainly not going to cover the whole area of *seelsorge*, which involves all sorts of pastoral care.

I would like to begin by briefly informing you about the counseling situation in the United States.

Divergence and Disillusionment

In the United States today, there are no institutionalized schools of counseling.[3] The idea that any psychotherapeutic, psychiatric, or other kind of counseling viewpoint is supreme in the United States is quite false. An article in the *Saturday Review of Literature* stated that there

---

1 In the Fall of 1977, Jay Adams, was invited to address the faculty and student body of the University Psychiatric Clinic in Vienna, Austria.
2 The German title was "Psychotherapy and Pastoral Care" (*Seelsorge*).
3 By that, I mean widely accepted by most theorists and/or practitioners.

are at least 230 distinct schools of psychotherapy and counseling in the United States at the present time. When I speak of some 230 different viewpoints (or schools) of counseling, I am not talking about minor differences. The differences between these schools are vast, with each one claiming to have a corner on the truth. If you were to survey the many differences among the members of each school, I'm not sure how much higher the numbers would go. One thing seems apparent as you survey the differences between the schools: this diversity has arisen from a number of causes, and it has brought about some very interesting results. Tonight, I shall focus on the principal one.

There has been a growing lack of consensus in America for the last forty years, during which time this rapid growth of diversity has taken place. This lack of consensus has troubled people greatly because it has resulted in a great deal of confusion, mistrust, and popular disillusionment over counseling. Books that pour from the printing presses, claiming to have the answers, are so common that anyone trying to keep up with the field today is constantly bombarded with new assaults upon his thinking. Immersed in a pile of new ideas and new challenges, he cannot even begin to think of reading and thoroughly understanding it all, let alone deciding who—if anyone—is right!

The general American population is becoming more and more disturbed over these differences, as popular articles and reviews indicate. People don't know if they should turn to someone with a medical orientation who believes that their problems are organic, whether their difficulties stem from sociological factors, as others claim, or whether their problems have to do with environmental difficulties (as Skinner and others in the behavioristic movement say). The number of jokes and cartoons about psychologists and psychiatrists shows something of the popular concern. There is even a television program about a psychologist, Bob Newhart, who is one of the most confused people on the program. *One Flew Over the Cuckoo's Nest*, a dramatic and important film that appeared a year or two ago, was an extremely strong attack upon mental health institutions in America. The tremendously positive reviews, not only of the participants in the film but of the film's message, perhaps as clearly as anything, have brought out this concern that has shattered the faith of the American public in counseling.

A few years ago, Zilboorg, in his two-volume history of psychotherapeutic work, made this statement: The field is "in disarray, just as it was in the beginning." His statement was, in part, correct and, in part, incorrect. When he was talking about the disarray, he was exactly right, but when he said that it was in disarray *just as it was in the beginning*, he understated the present situation. Initially, there were about three or five views to choose from, depending on how you divided the offerings. But now—230? That's impossible to deal with!

Therapeutic Failures

An added factor has led to more disappointment and disillusionment. There is a general failure of the psychotherapeutic community to succeed in doing anything significant for people and their problems. This was highlighted two and a half years ago when one psychiatrist decided to test the ability of his fellows to diagnose problems. Into twelve of the nation's leading mental institutions in five states, he sent eight persons (and I hope that the statement I am about to make is accurate) as sane as you or I, telling this one falsehood as they entered: "I heard voices." They lied about nothing else, and they did nothing to deceive in any other way.

As I'm sure most of you are aware, such hallucinations can be caused by any number of factors. Two and a half days of significant sleep loss in some people can lead to every effect that the ingestion of LSD does. So by saying "I heard voices," they were not saying anything about *causes*; they were simply talking about effects. No conclusions about causes should have been made without a thorough diagnosis. But in how many instances out of the twelve attempts do you think they were diagnosed as having a serious mental illness? Would you believe in half? Wrong. Would you believe in three-quarters of those instances? Still wrong. In all twelve instances, those individuals were diagnosed as having serious mental illnesses. That was a one-hundred-percent failure.

This news was broadcast throughout the psychiatric community in the important journal, *Medical World News*, and it caused quite a stir. But our friend the psychiatrist was not yet through. He then announced to one of the twelve institutions that he was going to do it again, but he didn't. After a period of time, he studied the intake record of this institution and discovered that after his second announcement, in the history of the institution, there had never been as many people turned away as malingerers (or fakes) until that time.

Of course, this is humorous, but it is also tragic. The general public has become painfully aware of these things through the many media that continually expose them. But the psychiatric community is becoming concerned, too. Karl Menninger, perhaps our oldest and most loved psychiatrist in America, commented on this event. After eleven of the twelve were declared to be schizophrenic,[4] Menninger said, "Schizophrenia? That to me is just a nice Greek word."

I recently wrote a chapter in a book on schizophrenia, and in that book, entitled *The Construction of Madness*,[5] a number of different viewpoints on schizophrenia were expressed. No two were anywhere near one another. The diversity was great. There was the behavioristic view, of course, and the Hoffer-Osmond organic chemical problem view, among a number of others. But because I was presenting the Christian view and another man presented a "religious" view too, they lumped our two views together in one section. I was very interested in discovering what the other religious views were. It turned out that the other writer believed that schizophrenics were people who had broken through from this earthly plane to some kind of religious plane where they were having greater religious experiences than the rest of us. While his twist was a little different from that of R. D. Laing, who sees schizophrenics as more stable than the rest of us, it was in that direction, though with religious overtones.

Why should there be so much diversity? We don't have such a lack of consensus in other fields. In fact, there is some kind of growing consensus in almost every other field. Why is it that when we start dealing with human beings, we seem to become fuzzy and vague? If there were as many different points of view in aeronautics, for instance, with as many basic differences among pilots concerning the principles of flying, I can guarantee that I would not be here lecturing tonight: I wouldn't get near an airplane. That is something of the spirit of the American public today:

---

4   The twelfth was said to be manic-depressive.
5   That chapter is included in another section of this book.

it has backed off from counselors, with their grandiose claims and poor results. People have crashed often enough; they want no more forced landings and desperate escapes from "planes." However, the question still remains: Why is there so much diversity in this field? I shall address that question, but I'd like to tell you about another development.

The Crisis in Pastoral Counseling

About twenty years ago, Christian pastors in America were involved in doing two things in reference to counseling. Some were under the impression that they could not help people who came to them for help, largely because of the mental health propaganda that said, "Don't touch those people if they have more than a single psychic scratch—you dare deal with nothing deeper than a scratch." Out of fear, pastors simply referred everyone to a psychiatrist or psychologist.

There were others who bought the psychiatric viewpoints and tried to adapt them to their own counseling practices. They tried to incorporate various psychotherapeutic principles and methods that they found around them into Christian counseling. But this assimilation of psychiatric views was usually done in an extremely uncritical way. You might say that these methods and viewpoints were brought in totally unbaptized. So, a disillusionment grew within the church that was parallel to the disillusionment popularly found among other people.

As the leadership in the church became increasingly concerned about what it was offering to its own people, and as they began to see the failure and the confusion all around outside, it led to a reevaluation of the whole situation. Over the last fourteen years, this has developed into a new approach to counseling that we call Christian counseling. Christian counseling is entirely fresh; it is totally different from anything that has been offered in our generation in America.

The Need for a Standard

When asking why there has been no consensus, particularly in this field in which people are trying to change the lives of other persons, many of us came to the conclusion that it was because there was no standard by which this was attempted. You may say that society is the standard, or you may say pragmatically that what works is the standard, or that the counselee is the standard; but when you finally boil it all down and strip off the externals, what you have left is this: the individual psychotherapist determines the standard. The problem of subjectivity is enormous. Something from outside of the counselor and counselee is needed; something far more solidly grounded than any limited and biased individual is required. Otherwise, the kind of splits and divisions that occurred at the very beginning right here with Freud are inevitable.

You see, if Freud was the final standard (which he must have been), he could not allow heresy within the ranks. This same spirit has continued so that various new schools develop whenever there is a difference in the standard. Why do we need a standard, a yardstick, a rule? Because we are dealing with the problem of changing human lives. What man has the right or the ability to say to another, "I know how you shall live"? What man will take it upon himself to say, "This is wrong in your life, this is right in your life, and this is how I want to change you"? Some think they can divorce themselves from the ethical issues. They think that value can be cast aside. But you can't; you continually get involved in the realm of values when you deal with people and their lives. When you endeavor to change another human being—i.e., to change his values, his beliefs, his behavior, his attitudes, his relationships—are you willing to say, "What I think his values, his relations, his attitudes, and his behavior should be like is best"? Are you willing to say that? Unless you are ignorant or arrogant, you must hesitate.

And yet from the very outset, that has been the problem, hasn't it? There has been no one standard by which to bring about consensus.

If there is one school that seems to be most dominant in our country today, it is the behavioristic school under the leadership of B. F. Skinner. They maintain that it is possible to produce any sort of human being that you may want to produce. It's their view that if given the proper contingencies—the proper schedule of rewards or adversive controls (or you might prefer to say punishment)—they can control the behavior of an individual to produce any sort of person consistent with his physical limitations. In other words, they say, "We have a sausage grinder, and we can grind whatever kind of sausage you wish."

But you get four Skinnerians together in a room and ask them what kind of sausage they want, and you are going to get four different answers. Each will want the person who comes out of the sausage grinder to look like the human being that he thinks is ideal. There is no common standard for what a human being ought to look like. We sometimes read in popular writings that "psychologists say …" or "psychiatrists say …," but anyone who knows the confusion behind those statements can only take them humorously rather than seriously. The fact is that there is no agreement on the most basic issue of all—what sort of man is normal? We won't get that norm from sociological studies either because they will only tell us about the average attitudes and behaviors that human beings have in a given period or place.

I'm not sure that you or I want to produce more of the kinds of persons that we now are: the kind that have brought about the number of wars that our world history records, the kinds of people who do the things we read about on the front pages of our newspapers all the time. There has to be a standard and a model that conforms to it, so that we can both know and see what a human being should be like. We have to have a picture of what a human should look like if we're going to try to change people. Where are we going to get such a picture? This is the question that Christian pastors in America have been dealing with for the past fourteen years, and they say that they have an answer.

Jesus Christ, the Standard

They say that human beings should look like Jesus Christ! They say that the Bible not only gives a description of what a person should be like in abstract terms but that Jesus Christ is the model of such a person in terms of action and speech. Indeed, in contrast to the psychotherapeutic confusion, it has been most powerfully demonstrated in America that a true consensus can be developed when there is such a standard.

In America, we have no national churches (*landeskirke*). We have only free churches, and there are many different churches in America. Most of them are in agreement on the major issues, but they differ on many minor questions. Now, it is interesting that in the last fourteen years this movement has swept over many different denominations with a force and power that has led to a movement involving literally thousands of pastors and lay people (*mitarbeiters*) who are now doing counseling according to this new, Bible-based approach. They have been drawn together in a counseling consensus by the Bible.

This movement has had quite an impact in American churches, and it has also spilled over onto a number of continents. In my case, as a representative of this viewpoint, this has led to visits just this year in Ireland, Brazil, New Zealand, Australia, Mexico, Germany, and Switzerland.

I am here in Vienna too, but you didn't invite me because of widespread interest. There were just a couple of people who showed interest. But the fact that we have such a large turnout here tonight shows me one thing—that you, at least, are curious, and I'm glad for curiosity, if nothing more. A lot of things can begin when people get curious.

I want to do one thing here tonight. As an advocate (a very strong advocate) of this viewpoint, I have something to give to each one of you, and I hope you'll take it. I'm here to hand out some candy to each of you. This candy is not soft enough to swallow all at once, nor is it so brittle that you can bite down on it and crack it readily. I hope that it will be like good hard candy that you take into your mouth and that you'll suck on it for awhile when you leave.

A Look at Nouthetic Counseling

Perhaps you'd like to know something about this Christian view, what it looks like, what it does, and how it operates. Let me give you just a few suggestive thoughts that may constitute that piece of hard candy. We call this counseling *nouthetic counseling*. We have incorporated the Greek term from the New Testament into the title because the English language has no word that is exactly equivalent to it. It is my understanding that the German language is also deficient. This Greek verb, *noutheteo*, and its equivalent noun form, *nouthesia*, have three elements that correspond to the three basic factors in Christian counseling. The first element describes the person who is being counseled as responsible for his sinful actions and in need of change. So a need for change in the thoughts, attitudes, and behavior of a responsible person is the first element.

Nouthetic counseling, for instance, would be at odds with any Freudian or neo-Freudian viewpoint that makes man totally irresponsible, saying that all of his activities and motivations are carried on below the threshold of consciousness.

The second element in this word is confrontation in a verbal form. In the Scriptures, it means verbal confrontation according to a scriptural norm. Previous counseling programs for pastors in America have been dominated by the thinking of Carl Rogers and his non-directive counseling, in which he teaches that a person at the core of his being has all of the essentials necessary to solve his problems. His difficulty is that he has not realized the potential within, so the counselor's task is to evoke these answers from within him. The one heresy with Rogers is to bring in any kind of confronting force or offer any outside information or advice. And so, just as the first element of *nouthesia* contrasts sharply with any view of man as a non-responsible creature, so the second element contrasts sharply with Carl Rogers's view that a person needs no outside intervention.

The third element in *nouthesia* is concern. But it is more than concern; it is concern for the welfare of the individual confronted. In B. F. Skinner's view, for example, as you might find it expressed in his philosophical works *About Behaviorism* and *Beyond Freedom and Dignity*, there is only one value, the preservation of the human herd. He thinks about people as animals to be bred as any other group of animals might be. So, by controlling human life (at both ends), you must breed a new human herd. Of course, we heard talk like this before by other people back in the thirties. Now it is hooked to a more sophisticated scientific method that makes it a lot more powerful. This herd mentality contrasts quite sharply with this third element in *nouthesia*: concern for *individuals*. There is no place for an individual in behaviorism—that is silly sentimentality. So this new Christian approach is not eclectic; it has a standard of its own that enables it to look around and compare and contrast itself with other counseling approaches.

Change at the Heart Level

This view is also concerned with change at a level of depth. It is not concerned about changing people on the surface alone; man and his actions and his attitudes must be changed at the inner core of his being so that his set of values and the springs of his motivation are affected.

The Bible calls this inner power man's heart. It is from the heart that people's problems stem. This means that a new power from the outside is necessary for him to realize the goal of Christian counseling—to become more like Jesus Christ. In other words, Christian conversion is an essential element in this kind of counseling. If he is not a Christian, the counselee's relationship to God must be changed. He must come to the place where he recognizes that the Christian message about the cross is real. This old message from the Bible is that Christ died on the cross in the place of guilty sinners in order to transform their lives, beginning at the very heart of their being and then leading to needed outward transformation. Christian counseling has depth because it goes to the heart of human difficulty.

This old message has been found to be a very new and vital force in the lives of many people. It is possible that you've even heard in the newspapers here, as others around the world have said, words like "born again" that have become popular in America these days. That's precisely what we're talking about. In this counseling system, God Himself is asked to give the counselee a new life with new purposes, new goals, and new power. This counseling draws upon the wisdom of God in the Scriptures and the power of God in the Holy Spirit. Two things happen: the counselee's eyes are opened to God's standard for human living, and God enables him to begin to measure up to that standard for the first time. This is the basic Christian approach.

Under these fundamental rubrics, every kind of problem that has ever crawled, walked, or flown through the psychiatrist's door has similarly entered the doors of our counseling center for this counseling approach. Here, hundreds of pastors have been trained and, through actual observation of counseling sessions, have seen how the use of the Scriptures has transformed lives dramatically and lastingly.

That is a glimpse of *nouthetic* counseling. Doubtless, some of you have spit the candy out already. Some of the rest of you are having a little difficulty with it sticking to your teeth. Nevertheless, I hope that you will continue to suck on it because when you deal with that question of the standard, you're dealing with *the fundamental issue in counseling*. Problems that have to do with people ultimately can be resolved only by their Creator and Savior.

If you think seriously at all, after you've talked about everything else, you will come back again and again to the issue of the standard. I ask you not to close the door on this matter too quickly. Until it is resolved, you can do nothing. You are planning to help people; fine. But that means changing them. The question is not only how, but, most basically, into what? The Christian replies, "Into the likeness of Jesus Christ." Is there *any other* answer?

The Christian Approach to Schizophrenia

The Christian Approach to Schizophrenia[1]

The word "schizophrenia" has become a non-specific wastebasket term covering a multitude of problems (and often covering up a vast amount of ignorance) that have but one common denominator: the inability of the counselee to function meaningfully in society because of bizarre behavior.

It seems to me that we must abandon the word as misleading and confusing, particularly when its use provides such a convenient temptation for diagnostic abuse. Add to all of the other possible factors that might be mentioned the hopelessness generated by labels, the tendency of many counselees to play the role they think the label implies, the irreparable damage that cavalier use of this label by careless, irresponsible, overworked, or even malicious parties can have upon a client's future, and you have an almost airtight case for rejection of the term. Whenever the word "schizophrenia" appears, I shall be referring not to any definable, diagnostic category representing a specific illness or behavior. Rather, I shall view it solely as a broad, collective term having no one clear-cut referent, but rather pointing to bizarre behavior that is the result of any cause—contrived or otherwise—or any complex of causes that may lead to severe inability to function in society.

Descriptive versus Explanatory

I consider the words "red nose" to be on precisely the same communicational level as the word "schizophrenia." To observe that one has a red

---

[1] This article is adapted from an essay that Jay Adams contributed to *The Construction of Madness: Emerging Conceptions and Interventions into the Psychotic Process*, edited by Peter A. Magarow (New York: Pergamon Press, 1976).

nose is to say nothing more than that; the statement carries no necessary causal implications. That is to say, the observation refers to an effect that may have any number of different and widely diverse causes. Thus, the statement, "You have a red nose," does not necessarily carry with it the insinuation that the person addressed has been boozing. He may have fallen asleep under a sun lamp, his wife may have punched him, he may be growing a pimple on it, etc. Similarly, to say that one is schizophrenic is merely to observe that his behavior has become so bizarre that he is unable to function (or is not allowed by others to function) in society.

As an additional complication, it must be remembered that the line between the abnormal and the normal is not always clearly definable in a society whose values are in flux. What is tolerated (or even prized) in certain communities or cultures may be rejected by others.[2]

Two Sources of Schizophrenia

To summarize, then, it may be noted that all of the problem behaviors generally identified as schizophrenia stem from two sources: (1) forces distorting one's ability to perceive or evaluate the world as it is in reality, or (2) self-induced forces that cause one to misread or mislead one's self or others. Within each of these two very broad categories, the varieties of situations and types are manifold. For instance, poor perceptual intake may lead to proper brain functioning that turns out badly because it is based on faulty data; on the other hand, the behavior may stem from the malfunctioning of the brain because of a tumor, while the perceptions are intact. Therefore, to speak of schizophrenia as if the term denoted any clearly definable condition, distinguishable from all others, is to misunderstand entirely.

For convenience sake, we may classify (roughly) the causes of schizophrenia as organic/inorganic (or from a telic perspective as misreading/misleading activities), always keeping in mind the fact that even the boundaries between these categories are not fixed and impassable. What may have begun largely as misleading activity (i.e., deception) may at length turn into a misreading activity (self-deception), or a bit of both.

---

[2] This is the same sort of basis upon which R. D. Laing and Timothy Leary argued for the schizophrenic state as preferable.

"Narcotics agents are after me," John insisted. The charge—as his "evidence" proved—was ludicrous. Yet the reality construct by which he justified the claim was perfectly reasonable to him. It was so because the construct of reality into which he pigeonholed data had gradually emerged over a period of time as the result of a long history of flight. John's problem originated within a reality construct that was true to life. There was a time when he was a drug pusher. At that time, it was realistic for him to be suspicious and wary. But the life patterns developed then continued long after he had abandoned drugs. The pattern of looking over his shoulder persisted. The guilt of the past, the patterns of life, etc., all continued until he came to forgiveness and put on a new and Christian reality construct. As Proverbs put it, "The wicked flee when no man pursues" (Proverbs 28:1).

Conversely, what began as a misreading activity (dysperception) in time may develop into a life of misleading (deception of others or self). Visual perceptual distortion may lead one (for instance) to dysperceive the shapes of the faces of loved ones who appear (to the person whose chemical processes are malfunctioning) to be scowling at him when in fact they are not. Visual cues that do not fit auditory communication may lead him to suspect the motives of others and to respond with caution, etc., which is appropriate to the faulty data but not to the reality situation. Such action will be interpreted as bizarre. He may develop a suspicious attitude toward others that, at length, may become a reality construct for falsely interpreting all of life.

The Christian Perspective

How does a counselor in the Christian tradition begin to handle the many problems of schizophrenic behavior? That a person experiencing such problems may be subject to (or may subject himself to) internal and external forces that may impair his ability to function, that he is capable of intentionally and unintentionally stimulating and simulating such impairment in order to mislead, and that over a period of time (or suddenly) he can develop such faulty responses to stress situations that he loses a grip on reality (i.e., he may misread it) is to picture him at once as a frail, conniving, self-deceptive, and foolish being. That is to say, as Christians look at it, the person is a sinner, who, according to the Bible, has been subjected by God to vanity because of his rebellion against his Creator.[3]

Sin, the violation of God's laws, has both direct and indirect consequences that account for all of the bizarre behavior of schizophrenics. That is why Christians must refuse to ignore the biblical data. From the perspective of these Scriptural data, *all* faulty behavior (which for the Christian is behavior that does not conform to the law of God) stems ultimately from the fundamental impairment of each human being at birth in consequence of the corruption of mankind resulting from the fall. No perfect human beings are born by ordinary generation. They all inherit Adam's fallen nature together with its organic and moral defects, which lead to all faulty (including all bizarre) behavior. No aspect of a human being, no function, has escaped the distorting effects of sin. To some extent, therefore, the same problems seen in schizophrenics are common to all. The differences lie in (1) what bodily functions are impaired, (2) how severely, and (3) what sinful life responses have been developed by the counselee. It is also vital to ask whether the individual is redeemed by the grace of God, since redemption involves a gradual renewal of human nature (cf. Ephesians 4:22-24; Colossians 3:10).

The identification of the problem of schizophrenia as a theological difficulty points toward a theological solution. In the same way, a non-theological diagnosis ("mental illness," etc.) leads to a non-theological solution.

Wrong labels point in wrong directions which, in turn, end only in more frustration. *Schizophrenia* is a psychological or psychiatric label that leads toward psychological or psychiatric solutions. If, on the other hand, investigation shows that a particular kind of bizarre behavior should be labelled as a chemical malfunction (stemming not from personal sin, such as sleep loss, but is rather solely the result of the fall), that conclusion leads toward a medical solution. If it indicates that the problem comes from sinful living, the term "sin" points in the direction

---

3   Romans 8:20. "Vanity" (*mataioteti*) in this passage refers (among other things) to the consequences of the corruption of the world and of human nature due to sin. The New International Version interestingly translates *mataioteti* "frustration."

of a theological solution. It is a serious fault thus to suggest that anything less than God Himself can solve a problem that fundamentally has to do with one's relationship to Him.

The Christian counselor's approach, therefore, will begin with an attempt to discover whether the behavior of any given counselee stems fundamentally from organic defects or from sinful behavior on his part. In the case of bizarre behavior, whenever indicated, he will insist upon careful medical examinations to detect any glandular or other chemical malfunction, brain damage, toxic problems, etc. But when he is reasonably assured that (at base) the problem is not organic (or that it is not only organic), he will counsel on the supposition that such behavior must stem from sinful life patterns. He will be aware, of course, of the vital fact that the counselee is a whole person whose problems cannot always be divided neatly into the categories *organic* and *inorganic* (or into categories of misreading or misleading). There are often elements of both. And most assuredly, the organic affects the nonorganic and vice versa.

When Philip smashed a chair on the floor, attacked his counselor, wept uncontrollably, whined in self-pity, and spoke of hearing voices and taking trips on a flying saucer, more than one problem lay behind these difficulties. Sleep loss, possible chemical malfunction, twelve years of frustration with an inexplicable problem, resentments (and suspicion) toward physicians, psychiatrists, and ministers, bitterness over scores of shock treatments, a severely distorted reality construct, sinful patterns of living and institutionalization, all influenced and motivated by a sinful nature, combined to produce the bizarre behavior.

The Heart-Body Connection

The Christian has always been aware of the psychosomatic (or, as he might prefer to call it, *hamartiagenic*)[4] nature of much illness because the fact is taught throughout the Bible.

Studies in biofeedback have extended our awareness of the great extent to which man controls his physical condition. They appear to show: (1) that we have much more control over our bodily functions

---

4   *Hamartiagenic* means "sin-engendered."

(blood pressure, heartbeat, muscle tone, galvanic responses, etc.) than heretofore was realized; (2) that we are, therefore, more responsible for our organic condition than we had suspected; (3) that we can control and are responsible for many (if not all) of the glandular and neurological responses that occur in some forms of bizarre behavior. It is altogether possible that the chemical/electrical processes that govern perception may be controlled by attitude, etc., in a manner that makes man more responsible for these functions than most have thought. That is to say, beliefs and attitudes (in addition to other factors) may also be at the root of perceptual dysfunction (misreading of reality).

The Christian, in harmony with biblical promises (e.g., Psalm 32:1, 2; Proverbs 3:1, 2, 8, 16; 4:10, 20-22; Berkeley Translation), has affirmed that the fundamental biofeedback that he has needed for *hamartiagenic* problems is the Scriptural criteria themselves. Conformity to biblical patterns of life, with the emotional states and attitudes that grow from them, enables one to regulate his bodily functions (albeit unconsciously) in ways that promote good health. Conversely, failure to do so produces malfunctioning. The biblical principle to care for the body as "the temple of the Holy Spirit" means that he must not ingest hallucinogenic drugs that will distort perception; it also means that he will not push his body beyond its capacity through subjecting it to significant sleep loss that could cause similar dysperception. The principle "Do not let the sun go down on your anger" (Ephesians 4:26) is filled with implications concerning the healthy functioning of the glandular processes and their effects. Moreover, the principle "He who conceals his transgressions will not prosper; but he who confesses and forsakes them will obtain mercy" (Proverbs 28:13) implies the fundamental benefits of a clear conscience plainly enough so that there is no need to expand upon it. These, and a large number of similar exhortations and promises, when followed, promoted healthy living because the body was properly regulated by the attitudes that were created growing from self-evaluation of one's behavior. The Christian may have known little or nothing of the functioning of the human body. But he (nevertheless) benefited from living in ways that promoted proper functioning. It is fair to say that Christian living will, itself, preserve (reclaim) one from those harmful bodily functions which are autogenically controlled and that may lead to bizarre behavior. Christian living, of course, will not prevent or counter such behavior when it is produced indirectly as the result of bodily defects or breakdown due to purely somatic factors.

Roughly, then, we may break down *schizophrenia* into several categories as this figure visualizes:

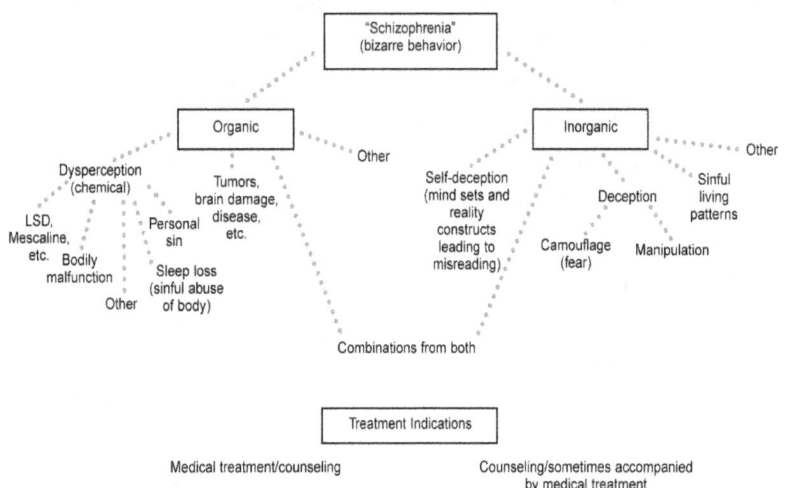

All of which leads to the Christian conviction that man is largely (or in many instances totally) responsible for his behavior, even when it is of a bizarre nature. Passages such as 1 Peter 3:14 ("Be neither terrified nor troubled by their threat") more fully come alive under such considerations. It is not impossible to *command* the control of one's emotions. By proper attitudes and actions, the Christian *without biofeedback* controls his bodily functions and states as God intended him to. Except in those relatively infrequent cases (such as brain damage) that are validly organic at base, the Christian counselor seeks to deal with schizophrenia in the same manner as he would in confronting those who have other problems occasioned by sinful living patterns. In this large measure of responsibility lies hope. What is due to sin can be changed; there is no such certainty if, as some think, schizophrenia is largely due to other factors.

A Case Study

When Barbara received the unpleasant news that her son, George, had gotten his girlfriend pregnant, she was unprepared for it. This news came in the wake of other unsolved problems that had been piling up in the family, some of which were due to Barbara's own sin. John, Barbara's husband, phoned a nouthetic counselor and described the scene: upon hearing the bad news, Barbara had gone to their bedroom, sat down on the bed, and had frozen—stiff as a stone. This would classically be called a catatonic state. She had been in the position, staring ahead at the wall, totally uncommunicative, acting as if she were "out of touch with reality," for seven hours. The counselor arrived and did three things:

1. From the data gathering he did with others in the home, he surmised that there was no organic cause for this behavior.
2. He assumed that Barbara was *not* out of touch with reality and could hear, understand, and act upon what he was about to say.
3. He then spoke to Barbara in a firm, loving manner, stressing hope and issuing a warning. Greatly summarized, here is what he said:

> Barbara, I know that you can understand everything that I am saying, and I want you to listen carefully. First, you are running away from your problems this way. That is wrong; it is not God's way of handling life's disappointments and dilemmas and will create only larger difficulties for you and your loved ones if you persist in it. Not to respond is sin. I recognize that your problems are serious and that you don't know what to do about them. I do not want you to think that I minimize them one bit. They are probably worse than I could now realize. Yet, your Lord Jesus Christ is greater, and if you will let me, I shall help you to work out the answers to them from His Word. The sooner that you begin to talk, the sooner we can begin to lay out a biblical plan to solve these problems. But apart from your willingness to face the situation God's way, there is no hope.

Barbara stirred a bit, but did not respond. The counselor went on to describe the alternatives:

If you will not face your problems, you will force John to take the only other and far more unpleasant course of action that lies before him. First, it will be necessary for him to let you sit here for a day as you are. You will find that lack of food and toilet needs will make the situation exceedingly uncomfortable. If, even under those circumstances, you still do not budge, John can do only one more thing—he must send you to a mental institution. Do you have any idea what it is like to live in a mental institution? Let me describe …

It was not too far into that description that Barbara broke down. She wept in relief, then poured out the story of her disappointments, anger, and fears. The counselor, as a result, was able to help her meet these God's way.

As one can see in this abbreviated account, much of the seemingly bizarre behavior (if not most) is not bizarre to the person himself. The behavior makes sense to him *from his viewpoint*. Even original schizophrenic concepts of a split between affect and behavior (and/or speech) are explainable on this basis. There is no split for the counselee; the affect and behavior seem out of sync *only for the counselor*. Thus, to speak of the schizophrenic's evasions, suspicions, silly grins and giggles is to speak as one who is evaluating another's behavior from the point of view of what, at times, can be entirely different data. Here, Barbara did not know what to do, so she did nothing. She was afraid that any action that she might take would worsen rather than help the situation, so she took no action. She was angry, her pride was hurt, but rather than reveal this in the outbursts that she was afraid these emotions would occasion, she restrained her feelings to the point of immobility. It was wrong behavior, but not irrational; the rationale behind it is clear.

The Counselee's Perspective

To a person with perceptual difficulty resulting from chemical malfunction, the world may seem all askew. Chairs may appear to fly off the ground toward one's head, lights may pulsate strangely, faces may seem grotesquely distorted, etc. Given such dysperception, one's actions, although strange or bizarre from the point of view of an onlooker, to the counselee are not strange but explainable. To protect oneself from a flying chair by leaping from its path is rational behavior, but it seems outlandish and irrational to one who does not perceive the chair as moving at all. Indeed, in time, his rationality may be questioned by the counselee himself. After all, the chair never arrived!

Of course, all such bizarre behavior may be simulated *in order to appear* insane.[5] There is a mounting conviction that much bizarre behavior must be interpreted as camouflage intended to divert attention from one's otherwise deviant behavior.[6] The explanation of much behavior as coverup or camouflage runs something like this: bizarre behavior some time in the past (perhaps far back in the past), was rewarded positively when it succeeded in deflecting attention from one's deviant behavior. Bizarre behavior of this sort must be viewed (like all other sinful behavior) as the product of a "deceitful heart" (cf. Jeremiah 17:9). Therefore, on succeeding occasions, the client again attempted to hide behind bizarre actions and discovered that frequently this ruse worked. If this occurred frequently enough, a pattern of such action was established. Bizarre behavior then became the natural (habitual) means to which he resorted whenever he sinned.

However, such behavior, though often successful at the outset (frequently enough to become a deeply etched pattern and thus the first resort when one does wrong), does not continue to work as successfully as it did in the past. As one grown out of childhood and into adolescence, for instance, he finds it more difficult to hide. Now he is expected to give rational explanations for his behavior. Rather than change, the habit-dominated person will endeavor to continue to resort to bizarre behavior as his solution. But repeated failures of recent attempts at length force him to make some change. Yet, even then, he changes not the nature of his response but its intensity. So, in order to continue to cover up

---

5   Cf. the case of David cited in 1 Samuel 21:13.
6   Cf. O. Hobart Mowrer, *Crisis*, pages 81–102 (especially pages 83–91) where Mowrer sets forth Tim Wilkins' "Dick Tracy Theory of Schizophrenia." In this view, the counselor is thought of as Dick Tracy rather than Ben Casey. An illustration of this viewpoint is found in Walter C. Stolov's work at the University of Washington's hospital in the rehabilitation of patients with severe ambulatory problems. Cf. *Medical News*, Volume 209, No. 10, 8 September 1969, page 1442.

his behavior, his actions become more and more bizarre. If the pattern is not broken, his behavior eventually will become so deviant that, in the end, society will institutionalize him. In this way, behavior can become totally unacceptable in a very short time.

In the long run, the counselee finds that such behavior, even when it hides him from detection, is not really successful. Increasingly, as his actions become more bizarre, he finds that his behavior tends to isolate him. His social contacts are broken off, and the society which he needs so desperately drifts away from him as he hides from it. He knows he is living a lie, and his conscience triggers painful psychosomatic responses. So at last he becomes a very miserable person, externally isolated and alienated from others, and internally torn apart.

The Counselee's Choice

Steve was a young man of college age whom the writer met in a mental institution in Illinois. Steve had been diagnosed by psychiatrists as a catatonic schizophrenic. He did not talk, except minimally, and he shuffled about as though he were in a stupor. Upon sitting down, he became frozen in one or two positions. At first, communication with Steve seemed impossible. He simply refused to respond to questions or to any kind of verbal overtures. However, the counselors told Steve that they knew he understood fully what was going on, that though he might have fooled others—the psychiatrist, his parents, the school authorities—he was not going to fool them. They assured Steve that the sooner he began to communicate, the sooner he'd be able to get out of the institution. Steve remained silent, but was allowed to continue as a part of the group, observing the counseling of others. The next week, the counselors turned to Steve, and for more than an hour, they worked with him. Steve began to break down. His hesitant replies gave evidence that he clearly understood everything. There was no reason to believe that he had withdrawn from reality.

As Steve began to respond, the rough outlines of his problem emerged. By the third week, he broke down entirely. Steve had no mental disorders or emotional problems. Steve's problem was difficult but simple. He told us that because he had been spending all his time as prop man for a play rather than working on his college studies, he was about to receive a raft of pink slips at the mid-semester marking period. This meant that Steve was going to fail. Rather than face his parents and his friends as a failure, Steve camouflaged the real problem. He had begun acting bizarrely, and discovered that this threw everyone off track. He was thought to be in a mental stupor, out of touch with reality—mentally ill.

Steve had done this sort of thing many times before, but never quite so radically. Over the years Steve had gradually developed an avoidance pattern to which he resorted in unpleasant and stressful situations. When the college crisis arose, he naturally (habitually) resorted to his pattern. Steve's problem was not mental illness, but guilt, shame, and fear.

As he spoke with the counselors, Steve recognized that they were asking him now to make the basic decision he had previously sought to avoid. Steve knew that now he must decide whether he was going to tell the truth to his parents and his friends and leave the mental institution, or whether he was going to continue the bluff. When we left, on the fifth week, Steve was still working on that decision. He was actually posing the question himself in these words: "Would it be better to continue the rest of my life this way or to go home and face the music?"

In working with Steve, it became clear that the more others treated Steve as if he were ill, the more guilty he felt. This was so because Steve knew that he was lying. It is important for counselors to remember that whenever clients camouflage, whenever they hide to avoid detection, whenever they purport to be ill when they are not, sick treatment only makes them worse. To act as if they may be excused for their condition is the most unkind thing one can do. Such an approach only compounds the problem.

When Steve was approached by those who held him responsible, he responded. For the first time since his commitment, he gained some self-respect. He began to talk about his condition. Contrary to much contemporary thought, it is not merciful to be nonjudgmental. To consider such counselees victims rather than violators or their behavior as neutral or not blameworthy only enlarges their lie and increases the load of guilt. Such treatment, Steve explained, had been for him sheer cruelty because of the mental anguish and distress it engendered. Nothing hurt more, he said, than when his parents visited him and treated him kindly, like an innocent victim of circumstances.

Hope Amid Despair

Many persons with problems serious enough to be labelled schizophrenic are persons who (if their behavior is autogenic) are desperate and who already have reached a point where they are willing to take radical measures to solve their problems. Their behavior itself is evidence of this fact. Herein lies hope for the counselor. A person in despair may be ideally suited for dramatic change. The seemingly most difficult cases often afford the most unique opportunities. Sweeping life changes are frequently recorded. This should not be thought strange: a person with a scratch will settle for a band-aid; someone with cancer will submit to radical surgery. In the providence of God, often persons who have reached the end of *their* rope are ready at last to take hold of *His*.

In recognizing the rationality of such behavior, the Christian seeks to penetrate to the factors involved in each case taken individually. To these, he brings Scriptural solutions. He refuses to lump all cases in one simplistic category. In doing so, he tries at every point to begin with the good news of salvation and then moves to the specific implications and applications of this basic solution that are appropriate to the circumstances of each case. The presupposition that salvation provides the basic solution for human problems will also lead him to combine evangelism and counseling whenever indicated, and it will always require second-level solutions that grow out of and are in every way consistent with biblical principles.

Schizophrenia, for the distinctly Christian counselor, provides no more or no less of a challenge than any other problem involving original sin, personal sin, and the consequences of both. He believes that the resources provided in the Scriptures, coupled with the power of God through His Spirit, are more than adequate. As the Scriptures themselves put it: "Where sin increased, grace abounded all the more" (Romans 5:20b, NASV).

Biblical Interpretation and Counseling

Biblical Interpretation and Counseling[1]

Part 1

A person who can't interpret the Word of God properly can't counsel biblically. It is wrong to talk about being biblical and then all but ignore serious biblical study. To use the Bible in a shallow, simplistic fashion that, in many cases, misrepresents what God is saying in the passages to which one refers is inexcusable. Is there really a problem like that? Let me tell you there is. If you've read even a small portion of the counseling literature out there (and I'm talking about Bible-believing, "Christian counseling" literature), you know that there's a problem with the way the Bible is being used.

Misuses of Scripture

If you're still not sure about what I'm saying, judge for yourself. Here are a few examples. One counselor who is a Christian quoted Oscar Pfister, Freud's confidante, as saying this: "Tell me what you find in the Bible, and I will tell you what you are." He then went on to say, "The Bible is a mirror into which a person projects his own concept of himself and which in turn reflects it back." He said that was his understanding of James 1:22-24. What he did was turn the Bible into a Rorschach test.

Here's another: "God wants us to love in ourselves the person created by Him in His image." Do you think God wants you to love the person He created in you? Why did God create you in His image? So that you

---

[1] This essay is adapted from an address to the National Association of Nouthetic Counselors (NANC).

would love *Him*, not yourself! If I hand a picture of my wife to you and say, "This is my wife," what will my reaction be if you tear it to shreds, throw it on the ground, spit and jump on it? Do that and you're in trouble! Why? Because the paper and ink are so valuable? No. You're in trouble because that ink and paper *represent* what you've insulted, attacked, and tried to destroy—namely, my wife. The image of God in man is important because of the One whose image it is, not because of you or me, who are only the paper and the ink.

One counselor misuses Jeremiah's statement that God will not remember our sins (31:34) to support his view of the "healing of memories"—as if God ever forgot anything. This counselor wrongly equates *not remembering* with *forgetting*. He goes so far with this unbiblical interpolation as to write, "Perhaps God Himself has had some kind of healing of His memories." If that isn't misusing Scripture and insulting our God while doing so, I don't know what is. Where is his theology? Does he even have a doctrine of God?

The lawyer for a prominent counselor called the biblical process of putting a person out of the church, which is described in 1 Corinthians 5:5 as delivering him to Satan, a "Satanic ritual." Can you believe it?

Then, in writing a book on forgiveness, another one said this: "Christ's way was the way of giving forgiveness even before it was asked. He prayed, 'Father, forgive them.' That's forgiveness—unasked, undeserved, yet freely given." But even casual exegesis reveals that there was no forgiveness granted from the cross. This was a prayer that God *would* forgive, not a *granting* of forgiveness to those who were crucifying Him. Did God ever answer that prayer? Yes. He answered it on the day of Pentecost and on subsequent occasions, when Peter preached. Those who, by God's mercy, repented and believed were the first of many answers to Jesus' prayer. Forgiveness was not given apart from repentance and faith. This writer quite wrongly understands the passage.

How often have you heard an explanation of Romans 8:15, 16 in which we read, "the Spirit witnesses with our spirit," as meaning that He witnesses *to* our spirits? Just a little study in any good commentary would make it clear that the Greek preposition, *sun*, used there doesn't mean *to*. It means *together with*. The Spirit witnesses *together with* our spirit or *along with* our spirit. The idea there is clearly of two witnesses, as required by God's law. It's not the Spirit witnessing *to* us, but *along with* us.

When will be the last time that you hear someone misusing 1 Thessalonians 5:22? Paul urges us to avoid every appearance of evil. Almost any commentary of any merit explains that Paul isn't saying, "Avoid things that *look like* evil but are not." Rather, he's saying, "Avoid genuine evil in whatever form it appears and wherever it appears."

Recently, on a Christian TV broadcast, someone was trying to sell a hyssop tonic. She said, "The Bible teaches 'cleanse me with hyssop,'" and, of course, it does. She then went on to say, "You have to drink this tonic of hyssop to cleanse your inner organs." Anyone with a semblance of biblical training would know that cleansing or purifying with hyssop in Scripture refers to the sprinkling of blood on persons and objects by means of this springy plant. In Exodus 12:22 we are told, "Take a bunch of hyssop and dip it in the basin of blood and apply it to the posts and the lintel of the door." In Hebrews 9:19 we are told that Moses took the blood of calves and goats with water and scarlet wool and hyssop and sprinkled both the book itself and all the people. There isn't a word about hyssop *tonic* cleansing your *inner organs*!

The Key to the House of Knowledge

In the light of such statements I ask, Is it necessary to learn to interpret the Bible so that you can counsel from God's Word? Isn't there much work to be done? I'm not talking about expending superficial effort in that endeavor, but studying so deeply that you reach the real meaning of each passage you use. Does God just bless the use of His Word, no matter what we do with it? God has the right to do as He pleases with His Word. Of course, sometimes He is better to us than we are to each other. But that doesn't excuse us for misusing, misunderstanding, or misinterpreting the Word of God.

Jesus seemed to think that this was an important matter, as we can see in His words to counselors who were leading others astray by their erroneous interpretations of Old Testament law. Jesus said, "You have taken away the key to the house of knowledge. You didn't go in yourselves, and you have hindered those who were entering." That's serious. Not only did they jeopardize themselves before God, but they put others in jeopardy as well because they pointed them in wrong directions.

The Need for Study

Peter spelled out the severity of this problem in 2 Peter 3:16-18. Referring to Paul's writings, Peter says his letters contain "some things hard to understand, which the untaught and unstable distort as they do also the rest of the Scriptures, to their own destruction. You, therefore, beloved, knowing this beforehand, be on your guard so that you are not carried away by the error of unprincipled men and fall from your own steadfastness" (*Christian Counselor's New Testament*). It is dangerous, says Peter, to follow those who twist and warp the Scriptures. It is important to recognize, he says, that there are portions of Scripture that are tougher to understand than others. It will take extra time and effort and prayer and study, hard sweaty toil, to rightly interpret them. Paul, as well as others, did not always write things that are *easy* to understand.

The Bible is not a book to be read casually like a newspaper. It is a book into which you must pour your heart, and soul, and skills in study until you can mine from it the great treasures God has put in it. God didn't try to make it hard, but some parts are harder to interpret than others. Because we are so foolish, sinful, lazy, and blind, it is often hard for us to pry those truths loose. A surface reading of the Bible isn't enough. We have to do it the right way.

I am troubled by the word *devotions*. When people say they study the Bible *devotionally*, I don't know what that means. I'm afraid that too often it means, "I'm going to close my mind to what the passage might mean or what all the commentaries might help me to understand it to mean. Instead, I'm just going to let the words sort of trickle down through my being and filter out something that will be useful to me. Whether or not it's what God intended in the passage, it's going to do me good somehow."

I want to encourage you to **study** your Bible *devotionally*, not merely use Scripture superficially. When you come to the Word of God, you must never close your mind to study. Instead, you want to bring all your acumen and skills to it so as to understand the real heart of the passage. Take time to think through what a passage means. Stay with it until you do. Then thank God for the understanding and apply it to your life in whatever ways increase your devotion to God! Study your Bible devotionally by devoting yourself to a thorough *study* of it.

Twisting Scripture

In the book of Proverbs, the writer says that the proverbs are there for understanding and for interpretation. There are tough things in Proverbs, but the book is there to enlighten you. It takes effort, prayer, and work to get that enlightening truth out.

Unfortunately, because this is true, what we often see in so-called biblical counseling is "open season" on the Bible. Many twist the Scriptures. They bend and warp the Word of God to fit ideas previously found in some pagan book. And predictably, when somebody with a Ph.D. degree in psychology and a Sunday School degree in the Bible interprets the Bible, the Bible gets bent every time to fit the psychology. You can't properly study the Bible that way. When Scripture is twisted and tortured on the rack, Peter teaches that it ends up destroying people, both those who do it and those who listen to them. Scripture-twisting ruins the lives of counselors and of their counselees.

According to Peter, why do people twist the Scriptures this way? Why is there so much misinterpretation of God's Word? Why do people treat God's Word so superficially? Verse 16 puts the finger on it. They are untaught, and they are unstable.

God puts no premium on ignorance. God wants people who are enlightened with knowledge and wisdom. The first chapter of Proverbs teaches that understanding, discernment, and knowledge are part of God's will for our lives. The Bible is given that we might have knowledge. "The fear of the Lord is the beginning of *wisdom*." Counselors who are untaught in the Bible are untaught because they spend their time studying psychology rather than the Scriptures.

The Latest Wave

Recently, a secular book entitled Fad Surfing was published. Its focus was on organizations going through wave after wave of new ideas to re-engineer or reinvent their businesses and operate better. But with wave after wave after wave, managers in these organizations are now tiring themselves out, unsettling their people and their organizations. A lot of them are getting caught in the undertow. I think that also applies very much to developments in popular, so-called biblical counseling today.

When I began counseling, Freud was in vogue. He was the fad. Then Rogers became more important than Freud. After Rogers came Skinner; then Skinner disappeared from the scene. Next, an avalanche of stuff descended. "I'm okay, you're okay" came on the scene. Now it's no longer okay! After that, there was an emphasis on self-esteem. When I lived in California, self-esteem was permeating every aspect of the governmental and educational systems. I once drove 45 miles an hour in a 35-mile zone and was stopped by a policeman who came up to my window and said, "We don't think you're a bad person because you were speeding, but you're going to get a ticket!" What do I care whether or not he thought I was a bad person?! What I cared about was paying for that ticket! But his comment was offered to keep my self-esteem from draining away. Such efforts were disbanded when people finally were forced to acknowledge that they didn't do any good.

People who promote wave after wave of new psychological solutions have never learned how to interpret the Scriptures. They are untaught in how to get from the Scriptures what God put in them. They spend their time reading books on counseling while their understanding of the Scriptures is superficial.

Learning to Interpret Scripture

What should you do if you want to be different? If possible, take a course in Bible interpretation, hermeneutics, or exegesis, which are terms we will soon explain. Get some serious instruction in Bible study. If you can't take a course, my little book, *What To Do On Thursday,* will get you launched in that direction. The important thing is to learn how to interpret the Scriptures.

Not only is there an abuse of Scripture because people are *untaught*, but Peter also says that they are *unstable*. Their roots are not deep. They are blown about by every wind of teaching. This "fad surfing" goes on constantly in these circles largely because of people's own instability. Instead of people who deepen and refine their biblical knowledge of how to live for God with joy, these people adopt and then jettison one counseling system after another. They can't make up their minds about truth (cf. 2 Tim. 3:7).

I don't think I could go on for very long like that. If I had invested myself deeply in "I'm okay, you're okay," for instance, and then found that it was out of favor and I now had to retool for *another* system, learning its jargon and strategies, I wouldn't like that. But then, to find that this kind of overhaul was required with wave after wave of new counseling theories, I'd soon become very tired of it. I might even begin to suspect that maybe these guys haven't got the answers. I might conclude in time that the counseling crowd, for the most part, is unstable. James says that such people are like the waves of the sea. You can look at a wave, but when you go to touch it, it's gone! It's unstable. It constantly changes form, location, and color. A wave is in motion. All is flux. I couldn't counsel people while continually in flux. Could you?

The Word of God is *stable*. Counselors who plant their faith firmly upon it will themselves become stable, rooted in and founded on something that isn't going to change. As their knowledge deepens, in that sense, of course, they will change. But because Scripture remains the source and reference point for everything they believe and do in counseling, they will never have to retool for an entirely new model. They will learn more about what they have. Change will be a deepening of understanding, a building on the same foundation. What a difference that makes! You don't have to get discouraged. You can know that if you stay with the Word of God and spend your time learning more and more about it, you are doing something solid and worthwhile.

There's another blessing that should be mentioned. You are studying the Word of the living God. You can't do that without it having good effects on you, challenging you, bringing you to repentance, bringing you to a greater understanding of how to live with other people, how to deal with counselees, how to solve problems. What a wonderful thing to spend your time digging into the Word of God and learning what it says in the fullest way possible! It will benefit you, too. It is a great privilege to study the Word to preach and counsel. Why anybody would spend time seeking wisdom elsewhere is something I don't understand.

But, according to Peter, error is infectious. "You, therefore, knowing this beforehand, be on your guard so that you are not carried away by the error of unprincipled men." Some of these people are poor, sad, misguided people who mean well and have never learned any better. Others, as Peter says, are unprincipled. Some recognize the emptiness of what they're doing, but they have such a vested interest in it that, despite the hollowness of it all, and even though they're not really helping people, they go on pretending, practicing, and propagating it.

Three Elements of Interpretation

Instead, God calls us to focus on Bible knowledge, to grow in grace and in the knowledge of our Lord and Savior, Jesus Christ. There are three terms that are important to Bible interpretation.

Hermeneutics is the first word. The word comes from the name of an individual, Hermes. He was the messenger, supposedly, of the Greek gods and the interpreter of those messages. So hermeneutics came from the name of a fictional god in Greek mythology. Today, the word has lost its religious connotations, but it continues to carry the idea of a messenger who interprets someone's message to others. Thus, today, the word means simply to explain, to interpret. In Luke 24:27 Luke says, "Beginning with Moses Jesus went through all the prophets and *explained* to them in all the Scriptures the things that concerned Himself." Jesus was doing hermeneutics. He was explaining.

We use the word hermeneutics today to mean the science of biblical interpretation or explanation. It includes, as that word is commonly used among us, the theories, principles, and practices of Bible interpretation.

The actual practice of putting those principles into effect as you study is labeled by a different word. That word is **exegesis**, the second term with which you need to become acquainted. It is an intensive form of a Greek word that means *to lead out*. It refers to the act of leading or drawing a writer's thoughts out of his writing. In exegesis, you are pulling those thoughts out by using hermeneutical tools according to hermeneutical principles. You are leading those thoughts out of the book into your heart and mind, so as to be able to expose other people to the truths of the Word of God.

In other words, what we do when we do exegesis well is to apply the principles of interpretation (the hermeneutics) in such a way that we get what God put *into* that book *out of* that book. We don't pour some of our own ideas into it first and then dip those out later on. We come to the well with an empty jar; we want to know what God has to say. As we dip into God's truth, up come the life-giving waters of God's Word. That's exegesis.

Calvin wrote, "It is the first business of an interpreter to let the author say what he does instead of attributing to him what we think he ought to say." That's exegesis. In other words, exegesis involves the use of every piece of relevant knowledge and experience and every available help to bring out the Holy Spirit's meanings and intentions in the writing of the original book or books.

One other nontechnical term that helps us understand is the word ***opening***. This completes our list of three words. This word appears in Luke 24:32, 45 along with those other words. It means to explain by opening. Do you remember how Jesus said that the Pharisees had taken the key to the house of knowledge, locked the door, and thrown the key away? It kept people from going in and gaining knowledge. By contrast, opening is putting the key in the lock and opening the door of knowledge from God's Word to people. It's saying, "Here's what God says in His book," and explaining that to someone else.

This is what ministering the word in a counseling session is all about, explaining a passage to people so they are able to say in their hearts or out loud, "Ah! I see what that's talking about!" By the time they are through, they don't say, "That's a counselor's idea." They say, "I understand that's what God was saying to me in His Word. The counselor *opened* that passage to me in such a way that I knew what God was saying to me." This stands in contrast to a superficial use of a passage of Scripture, when a counselor (literally or figuratively) hands a passage to people and says, "Take this three times a day with prayer." That isn't *ministering* the Word. When we counsel well, we first study the Word of God for ourselves to understand it. Then, with counselees sitting in front of us, we *open* the passage to *them* so they may recognize that the authority for what we say does not come from us but from God—they can see that from the *opened* Word. Whenever Scripture is fully opened, counselees cannot rightly excuse themselves with a shrug, saying, "Oh well, that's just what the counselor thinks." If he backs away from a biblical injunction, he does so knowingly.

An Interpreter's Goals

Since the idea is to understand the thoughts and intents of the Holy Spirit expressed through the inspired writings of chosen men, the interpreter's goals ought to be three: (1) To neither add nor subtract from the thoughts and intents of the Holy Spirit but (2) to reproduce them exactly in words that are fully understood (3) by the interpreter and by those whom he counsels. This is a prerequisite of truly biblical counseling.

Why is this important? Because of what God says a true counselor does. In Isaiah 40:13, 14, we are reminded that God doesn't need man to counsel God's Spirit. God doesn't need to be counseled! However, in the course of his argument, Isaiah lists the things a counselor normally does; things a counselor, therefore, need not do for God. Isaiah says that a counselor normally *directs people*. Second, he *informs people*. Third, he *gives understanding or discernment to people*. Fourth, he *teaches people*. Then, in Isaiah 41:28, he adds that a counselor *gives answers to people*. So a counselor directs, informs, gives understanding, teaches, and gives answers to people's questions. If you're going to do those things biblically, you need to know how to interpret the book.

Part 2

Bible interpretation involves three important elements. Each of them plays a particular part.

The Human Element

The first element in Bible interpretation is the human element. It's your part. First Corinthians 2 makes it clear that unless the Spirit of God dwells within a person, he cannot interpret the Word of God. First Corinthians 2 says that Scripture is spiritually discerned.

A New Heart

Thus, the first requirement for faithful Bible interpretation is salvation. We cannot expect unbelievers to understand our Bibles. Sure, they can read the words and understand certain aspects of the Bible at one level, but to really grasp Scripture in a life-changing way, well, to put it mildly, they haven't a clue! Paul writes, "Eye has not seen and ear has not heard and neither has it entered into the heart of man what God has prepared for those who love Him" (1 Cor. 2:9). The unbeliever has eyes that read but do not see. He has ears that listen yet do not hear when the Word is preached. He has a heart that is stone-cold to the things of God. The way Ezekiel put it was, God has to rip out that heart of stone and replace it with a "heart of flesh" (Eze. 36:26). The "heart of stone" in an unbeliever resists the truth of God. It's dead to everything spiritual. Until the Spirit of God is poured into a man's heart and transforms it into a living, vital, warm, receptive organ, that person cannot understand Scripture. So salvation is the first prerequisite for Bible interpretation.

A Discerning Heart

Next, you have to come to the Bible in the right attitude and at the right stage of spiritual growth in order to understand it. There's nothing magical about the Bible or about how to read and understand it. Some people think that if they just read a certain number of words or passages every day at a certain hour, that's going to make a difference in their lives. And, by the grace of God, it might! The Word of God might snag them at some point. But just reading words in the Bible is not the same as studying and understanding those words. God places no premium on ignorance or sloth.

There have been times when I have sat reading the newspaper, and my eye has gone down a column of print from top to bottom. But I suddenly realized that though my eyes looked at every one of those words, I didn't have the faintest idea of what I had read. Why? Because I was listening to a conversation behind me. Has that ever happened to you? Unfortunately, that's the way a lot of people read the Bible—their eyes are just going over the print. Their minds are elsewhere. They don't understand what they're reading because they haven't studied it adequately.

Perhaps, also, those who fail to interpret properly fail because their own spiritual lives are in such a condition that even though they're Christians, they cannot really understand very well. Hebrews 5 talks about this. We read in verse 12:

> *"For though by this time you ought to be teachers, you have need again for someone to teach you the elementary principles [or rudiments] of the oracles of God; and you have come to need milk and not solid food."*

The writer was not speaking of people who had never attained any understanding of the Bible. These were people who once had some understanding but, because of a deteriorating spiritual condition, had lost it. The writer says, "Solid food is for the mature, who because of practice have their senses trained to discern between good and evil" (5:14).[2] In

---

2 Editor's note: For an in-depth study of discernment, see Jay Adams, *A Call for Discernment*.

verse 11 he gives the reason for their deterioration: "Because you have become dull of hearing." That word *dull* is used by Greek writers outside the Bible to describe people who are in a coma.

It's sad that Christians who have learned and known truth can come to the point of near unconsciousness. But it's also sad that others have never grown to the kind of maturity where they learn enough to teach others. They're still like babies, sucking on a bottle of milk.

Babies are cute. I have nine grandchildren and four children, so I have nothing against babies. But an adult sitting around sucking on a bottle is kind of disgusting. That's what the writer is talking about here. Solid food is for the mature. He said, "Everyone who partakes of milk is not accustomed to the word of righteousness. He is an infant" (5:13). That's sad. So if you want to interpret the Bible, you have to grow. You have to get beyond milk.

If you want to counsel people and use the Word in a way that can help them, you must first have that Word in your own heart and mind. You can't be dull of hearing. You have to be sharp and alert and have your senses biblically trained to discern between good and evil. You have to be able to come to the Bible and know how to understand and use it.

One thing that hinders a Christian's understanding of Scripture is his sin, often his sin of laziness in studying the Bible. A Christian counselor can't be like that. He has to be continually in the Word, continually growing and building up his understanding of it. So the human element is very, very critical. Sin clouds perception, causes distortion, and may even cause you to avoid certain portions of Scripture. Sin in your life may have a lot to do with how much you understand God's Word.

Some counselors will always steer around certain issues when they encounter them in their counselees because they've never applied them to their own lives. This is just one example of the human element in counseling, which has many other dimensions.

The Literary Element

The second element is the literary element. The Bible, of course, is literature. Everywhere that Christianity has gone, education and literacy have followed because people need to be able to read, study, and understand God's Word. People have no right to say, "I'm just going to sit and listen. I'm not going to study." When God was so gracious as to give us His Word in a convenient and accessible form so that we could keep it, study it, and spend hours learning from it, we are simply ungrateful people if we do not do so. You need to spend time in the Word.

But there are language issues to consider when studying the Bible because, though unique, it *is* literature. It is inspired, which makes it very different from every other kind of literature. The Bible is the one place in which you can know that everything you read is right. There is no error. It is the pure Word of God. We have been given something valuable, and we ought to treat it with great care and love.

But this literary element also means that you have to understand grammar. You have to understand history. You have to understand something about the genres of literature that exist in the Bible itself. In the Bible you find poetry. You find narrative. You find prophecy. You find apocalypses. You find gospels. You find parables. You find different kinds of literature, and each one has its own canons of interpretation. As a student of the Word, you have to become familiar with the kind of literature you're reading. God saw fit to give the Bible to us in a variety of literary forms. You must familiarize yourself with what a proverb is like, how to get the truth from it and use it, just as you must learn what a narrative is like and how to get the truth from it. You don't approach them in the same way. You must also dig for the *purpose* of the particular piece of literary material you're studying.

The Divine Element

Finally, there's a divine element in the Bible. Here inspiration and illumination come to the fore. The Holy Spirit alone can apply inerrant Scripture to people's lives so as to change them to think and operate the way God desires. Sanctification comes through the truth of God. "Sanctify them by your truth," Jesus said in John 17:17, "Your word is truth." What does the word "sanctified" mean? It means to set people apart from sin to righteousness, from their ways to God's ways (cf. Isa. 55:8). It means putting off what they've learned as sinners—the habits, the various thought patterns that are not God's—while putting on new habits and new thoughts to enable them to think God's thoughts after Him and walk in His ways. That's the divine element. The Holy Spirit didn't take thousands of years to produce the Bible only to do an end run around it by setting up some kind of special pipeline outside of the Bible. There is no new revelation today. God teaches you and your counselees *through His Word*. That's why He gave it to you.

The Spirit of God told the apostles that whenever they would speak, He would provide everything they needed. They didn't even have to prepare beforehand what they would say or how they would say it. There are two passages (Luke 10 and Luke 21) where Jesus says these things to His apostles. In them, you'll find four key things that the Holy Spirit promised the apostles. These four elements make counseling as well as preaching effective.

First, God promised to give them *the right thing* (the "what"). He would give it to them *in the right words* (the "how"). He would give it to them *in the right way* (with "wisdom.") And He would give it to them *at the right time* ("in that hour") when it was appropriate and needed. You ought to be concerned about those four things so that the people you counsel also receive the right thing in the right words given in the right way at the right time, so that the Scripture you use fits their situation precisely.

These are the elements of interpretation: the human element, the literary element, and the divine element. All three must come together in the counseling room.

God and the Counselee

In counseling, fundamentally, it's not you and the counselee who are involved; it's the Spirit and the counselee. Every counseling session ought to be a time when the Spirit and the counselee (or counselees) are brought into close proximity to one another. You want the counselee to know by the Word you minister that it is actually God who is addressing him. To bring this off, you must interpret Scripture accurately. Whatever transaction takes place is not between you and the counselee but between God and the counselee. Every counseling session should be an experience in which the counselee comes into the presence of God. It's the Spirit who changes people. You don't change anybody. You don't do it through your persuasion. It's the Word that changes them as the Spirit uses it when you minister it.

When all three elements of interpretation are in sync, God's meaning and purpose in a passage are understood. To the extent that one or more of these is out of sync, there is weakness in the counseling session.

Let's put it another way. Here is the hermeneutical triangle (Figure 1). This hermeneutical triangle gives you the elements that you're going to be dealing with as you interpret God's Word.

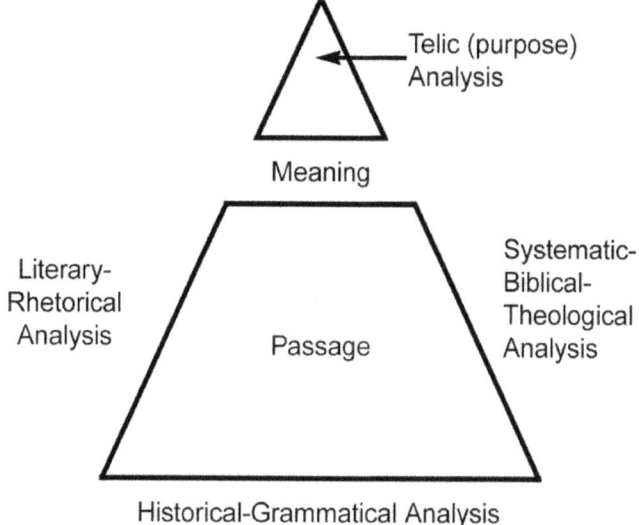

Figure 1. The Hermeneutical Triangle

Grammatical and Historical Analysis

If you were a student at a good seminary, you were told to do grammatical, historical exegesis, weren't you? Your professors warned you not to be an allegorist like Origen. They told you to get back to the grammatical and historical meaning of the Scriptures. That's what we want to look at here: the grammatical and historical aspects of the Scriptures.

The *first* presupposition we have is that God determined to use language to convey His will.

The *second* presupposition is that the book in which He did so was not designed to be a puzzle but a revelation of truth. It was designed to give us data, information, and exhortation. In history, that word was communicated through grammar and syntax. Take, for example, how this grammatical-historical approach unfolds. To begin with, understanding the grammar makes all the difference. If you understand the passage grammatically, you're way ahead of people who just read "devotionally."[3]

In Ephesians 4:22, 24, for example, Paul talks about putting off the old person and putting on the new person. But sandwiched in between those two verses is an important statement about the way in which Christians must be motivated to do so. Paul says you will make changes when you are "renewed"—or being renewed—"in the spirit of your mind." This phrase, "the spirit of your mind," probably means in the *attitude* of your mind. It's an unusual phrase, used only here. But the word "*renewal*" is the word I want to look at. Here's a grammatical issue, a vocabulary issue. In two other places in the New Testament, we're told that we need to be renewed. We read about renewal in the parallel passage in Colossians and also in Romans 12:2. These two passages use the same word, which simply means "renew, to make new again." But that word does not tell us how that renewal occurs. What is this "making new again"? Here in Ephesians, there is a different word that tells us *how* the renewal takes place. The word we read in Romans or Colossians, which is very bland, simply means "to make new again." But the term in Ephesians is a rich one, meaning "to rejuvenate, to make youthful again." That's how renewal takes place. *Anakaineo* (in Colossians and Romans) means "to renew," but *ananeo* (in Ephesians) means "to make youthful." What new light that throws on the whole business of renewal!

People become cynical early in life. All the sin they read about in the papers and see on television, and all the heartaches and sorrows that flood their own marriages and homes affects them. "What's the use?" they ask.

But as Christians, we don't have to be cynical. We're told in 1 Corinthians 15:58 that our "labor in the Lord is not in vain." What you do—the changes you make—are *not* all useless and worthless. It's worthwhile to serve Jesus Christ. There is an eternal dimension to temporal action.

---

3 Which so often means without understanding.

Adam was created with marvelous prospects that God laid before him. It must have been wonderful to look over God's perfect creation and be able to say, "God has given it to me to rule, have dominion over and subdue so as to use it for His honor and glory." But then sin entered the picture and scrawled a big "X" mark over the whole. Men became cynical because of what sin does in their lives and in the world. But Paul says that a youthful attitude like Adam's can be renewed. You can begin to have the youthful thinking of the young man who looks out on the world and says, "It's my oyster." You can *really* say that as a Christian because you have reason to say so in Jesus Christ. It is worthwhile to serve Him! The "spirit of your mind" can be "rejuvenated." You should have a youthful spirit in which you say, "Let me go out there and do things for the Lord!" It's that attitude you need to convey to your counselee so he'll want to put off the old ways and put on the new ones. You want him to serve with enthusiasm, knowing his efforts are worthwhile. But if you don't understand the vocabulary of the passage and pass a correct interpretation on to your counselee, you'll both just read words. There'll be no enthusiasm to go out to do a homework assignment for Jesus Christ. How important the interpretation becomes in the actual counseling hour itself!

Another example of a passage that's commonly misused among Christians is Proverbs 23:7. The King James Version reads, "As a man thinketh in his heart, so is he." I don't know how many times I've read or heard people speak as though this were a philosophical statement that gives deep insight into personality theory. It isn't anything of the kind! The sentence occurs in one of the few passages in Proverbs after chapter 10 where you have a little context around it. In the context the writer says, "Eat not the bread of him whose eye is selfish, neither desire his delicacies, for as one who inwardly figures the cost, so is he." The writer is giving a simple warning for times when you sit down at the table with somebody who says, "Go on, take another. Have another lamb chop." You'd like to have another, but this proverb says, "No, go slow. Don't take that extra serving. Your host might really want it for himself." That's all the passage is talking about! "Be careful when you sit down and people offer you more food." It's a practical warning, but by missing the context, we make a philosophical principle out of it. It is simply saying that one's words and one's intentions (to seem generous when one isn't) are not always the same.

The grammatical and historical analysis of a passage is important. "Take up your cross daily and follow me," Jesus commands in Luke 9:23. Some people say to their counselees, "I know that your wife is your cross," understanding this passage to mean that crosses are burdens we must bear. That's not what Jesus was talking about at all! "Take up your cross" meant "Carry it up to Golgotha and be crucified on it." There wasn't anybody in Palestine who misunderstood that. A cross, in the historical context, wasn't just a burden to bear; it was an instrument of death on which you were going to be nailed. When Jesus says, "Take up your cross, follow me and deny yourself," He's talking about crucifying and saying "no" to yourself, killing your own sinful desires, putting your ways to death, so that you can follow Him instead. The "put off" and "put on" are right there in that call to discipleship. Never weaken the passage to mean that a cross is a burden. Never talk as though when Jesus says "deny yourself," He meant to deny yourself *something* (like giving up chewing gum for Lent). You don't deny yourself some *thing* in some minimally ascetic sense. You deny *self*. You "say no" to *self*. That word "deny" means, literally, "to say 'no' to." You say no to that sinful self that says, "I want that woman. I want his house." "Say 'no' to" that desire, and "say 'yes' to" Jesus Christ! That is what you should be teaching counselees from Luke 9:23.

Another passage that is frequently misused is 1 Corinthians 7:10, 11 which speaks about divorce under the Greek term *choridzo*. The English translates that faithfully as "*separate*." "Ah!" says the counselor, "I can recommend marital separation." No, sir! You cannot. There's no such thing as a legitimate separation in the Bible—legal or otherwise. The word "*separate*" there is simply one of the three or four Greek words that were used to refer to *divorce*. Notice, if you will, that the passage is talking about separation that leads to an *agamos*, ("unmarried") state. It says if the wife separates, then let her remain *agamos* (unmarried). It's not talking about what we mean by separation today. The Bible doesn't know anything about that. You need to get this straight by understanding the grammar and history, as well as the context.

Another common example is the use of "*heart.*" The word *heart* is used all over the Bible. I have heard preacher after preacher (and I used to do so myself!) say that what we need is more *heart* knowledge, less *head* knowledge. But that's not a biblical dichotomy at all! Consider verses like, "As a man *thinks* in his heart," "the fool has *said* in his heart." The Bible penetrates, according to Hebrews 4, "to the *thoughts and intents* of the heart." These examples show that the biblical heart is full of thinking. *Heart* in the Bible does not mean emotions. In Scripture, emotions are talked about in terms of the bowels and kidneys.[4] Heart in the Bible means everything that goes on *inside* of you: "Man looks on the outward appearance, but God looks upon the heart" (1 Sam. 16:7). In the Bible the contrast is between the *lips* and the *heart*, the *mouth* and the *heart*, the *outward appearance* and the *heart*, the *outer person* and the *inner person*. It includes emotion, thinking, conscience, and everything that goes on inside of you that only God and you know about.[5] The Bible's view means the inner you.

Systematic, Theological Analysis

A good pastor and counselor not only knows how to study a passage of Scripture grammatically and historically, but also knows how to analyze a passage in a systematic, theological way. You need to do that when you counsel. For example, if you are teaching somebody that he should pray, you might turn to John 14:13, 14 in which Jesus says, "Ask anything in my name, and I will do it." But if you lead him to believe that that's all there is to prayer, you have given him a truncated view of the Scriptural doctrine of prayer. Because you are not giving your counselee a complete view of what the Scriptures say about prayer, you may lead him astray. Systematic theology is simply taking all that the Bible says about a given subject and putting it together in a way that enables you to relate each aspect of the subject to the other aspects so that you see the whole picture.

When you read John 14:13, 14, you have to remember James as well. James doesn't say you can simply ask for anything in Jesus' name and get

---
4   The seat of feelings.
5   And, of course, only God knows perfectly. The Bible calls Him "the Heart-Knower" (Acts 1:24).

it. It qualifies that statement by other statements. It says, "If you ask in faith believing ..."; if you don't doubt, because "whoever doubts can't expect to get anything from the Lord." And it says, "If you ask" (1:5-8; 4:2). A lot of people don't have because they *don't* ask. James goes on to say, "The effectual fervent prayer of a righteous man availeth much" (5:16). He also says, If you pray to satisfy your own desires, you won't get an answer, and so on. There are a lot of qualifications elsewhere (we've looked only at those in James) that you must keep in mind when you consider John 14:13, 14. You might not mention all of them when you are making a point from John 14, but you need to keep them in mind so that you don't contradict what you said about John later on when you expound James. You need to *think* systematically when you say something about John. Talk about it in light of the whole of Scripture. What John says is not absolute, in that it is conditioned by other biblical statements as well.

The hope referred to in Romans 15:13 gives us another example of ways in which we need to think systematically about Scripture. You need to give people lots of hope in counseling. You may gather all kinds of data about a person, but if you haven't given him hope, you may not have a counselee the next week. How do you give hope? Look at Romans 15:13: "Now may the God of hope" (i.e., the source of hope is God, from whom all hope comes) "fill you with all joy and peace in believing so that you will abound in hope by the power of the Holy Spirit."

But how do you get that hope? You get it from God. Yes, but how does God give it to you? Through the power of the Holy Spirit. "So what do *I* do to get it?" the counselee asks. "Do I sit here and ask the Spirit to give me hope?" No. That isn't how it happens; there's *more to be said* about *how* the Spirit gives hope. Look back at the fourth verse in the same chapter. Paul says, "Whatever was *written* in earlier times was written for our instruction so that through perseverance and the encouragement of the *Scriptures* we might have hope." The Holy Spirit gives us hope by His power as that power is released through the *Scriptures*, which alone provide hope from God. You don't get hope by sitting and asking the Holy Spirit to zap it into you. As a counselor, you have to bring both of these verses together to show that the Spirit brings hope through the Word of God.

Counselors are often concerned about *convicting* people. Who convicts your counselee? In John 16:8 we're told that the Holy Spirit convicts. But in 2 Timothy 3:16, we're told that the Scriptures convict. And in 2 Timothy 4:2, the preacher is commanded to convict people. So who convicts them? Is it the preacher? Is it the Spirit? Or is it the Scriptures? A systematic view will bring all three together. You must conclude that it's not the Scriptures alone that convict. It's not the preacher alone who convicts. It's not the Spirit alone, working apart from these other two elements, who convicts. It is the preacher ministering the Spirit's Word in His power that brings conviction.

We also need a *biblical theological analysis* of a passage to keep ourselves from moralism: "David was a great man. You be a great man. Love God and love your neighbor because the Bible says this is good." As a counselor, you must make it clear that no individual can obey the commands of God apart from the Spirit of God, first to convert him and then to enable him to do as God says. The law was given to show us that we can't do it on our own. It was intended to *drive* us to Jesus Christ. It was to bring us to the foot of the cross first and then, once we have trusted in Him, to look up into His face as our Lord and Savior to receive from Him the grace He so freely gives. We shouldn't attempt to do things in our own wisdom or strength. We should do them through *Him* as He supplies mercy, grace, and power.

Romans 5:5 is very powerful in this regard. There we read: "Hope does not disappoint because the love of God [the love He gives to us so that we can love Him and our neighbor as we should] has been poured into our hearts through the Holy Spirit who was given to us." You see, you can't even love as God requires on your own. An unbeliever can't love God or his neighbor in a way that's acceptable to God. Until the Holy Spirit is poured into the heart at regeneration, the love a person shows others is defective. The love which God requires of him, God *gives* to him in grace through the Spirit. So it's not David, Moses, or Elijah that we want to recommend to people; it's Christ working in David, Moses, and Elijah.

Literary and Rhetorical Analysis

A third element, literary and rhetorical analysis, is another important aspect of Bible interpretation. There are narratives, epistles, poems, proverbs, parables, apocalypses, and all sorts of literature in the Bible. Each is somewhat different.

In a parable, for example, there is usually one major point being made. The parable of the unjust judge is not calling God an unjust judge. At best, as A. B. Bruce puts it, it's saying, "When you think God is unjust, here's what's really going on." Not every element in a parable, then, is meant to be emphasized; the speaker is developing one main idea, and the rest of the elements are there to create the story. There will be confusion if you don't understand how to use a parable. The point of the parable of the unjust judge is, "Don't give up. Keep on praying when you think God isn't hearing, when you think He's like an unjust judge."

There are also different ways to interpret a narrative and a proverb over against one another. A narrative, like the story of Elijah and the prophets of Baal, may run for two chapters. A proverb may consist of two lines. You must approach these two literary forms differently since they must be studied according to the canons (rules of interpretation) for those particular genres of literature.

Take, for example, a narrative that is extended over several chapters like the one I just mentioned. It's like chocolate candy laced with cherry juice and a cherry in the very middle. You pop one in your mouth, you bite on it, and there's a burst of flavor that goes all over your mouth as the juice squashes out between your teeth and trickles down over your tongue. It's a lovely experience that's quickly over. It's soft stuff. That's the way a narrative is; there isn't a lot in every sentence. The message is spread out over a couple of chapters.

But a proverb is like a piece of hard candy that you put in your mouth. You don't dare bite down on it lest you break a filling. You suck on it and turn it over with your tongue and bite just a little off one edge and get some flavor out of that and then turn it over some more and suck some more. It lasts longer. The way you handle those two kinds of candy is the way you handle a narrative over against a proverb.

When you get to the proverb, you have to find all that has been packed into it. Lots of truth, experience, and applicatory material are packed into a principle that is stated briefly and memorably (often in picture form). This principle has a larger life, you might say, than the proverb that contains it.

Take, for example, the proverb that Paul referred to: "Don't muzzle the ox when it treads out the corn" (1 Corinthians 9:9). Paul asks, "Was God talking about oxen?" He answers, "No!" But God *was* talking about oxen, wasn't He? Certainly. Paul is pointing out that this was not *all* God was talking about; it was not even the principal thing God intended. There was a principle *embedded* in that proverb that was bigger than the proverb as stated and applicable to all sorts of situations. The proverb applied that principle in a visual way, to a circumstance everybody could understand. People could carry it in their minds as portable truth to be applied to a whole variety of situations, just as Paul did when he talked about paying a preacher. "Don't muzzle the preacher; he ought to get money from the work that he does." That's the way Paul used the proverb. Certainly, the proverb applied to the ox, but the principle that was embedded in it could be applied to other situations as well.

A student of the Word also must know how to analyze rhetorical statements in Scripture, things that are said in such a way that they make something memorable by shocking people into thinking. For example, Jesus says in Luke 14:26, "You have to hate father, mother," etc. Does He really mean you're to hate them, that you have to work up a deep animosity toward them? No. That isn't what he's talking about. What does he mean?

In the parallel passage, Matthew 10:35-37, he says, "You have to love God more than you love father, mother, brother, sister," etc. You can make the point either way. But if you simply say, "You have to love me more than others," a person *might* remember that. But when you say, "You have to hate them and love me," it makes him sit up and take notice! That way of saying it has shock value. It's memorable as well. Rhetorical devices are not to be taken literally, but to drive you to think and remember.

Take, for example, the words of Jesus in Matthew 5:29-30, where He talks about cutting off your right hand, cutting off your right foot, plucking out your right eye, lest they cause you to sin. Jesus is not speaking literally. He is using a rhetorical device, a memorable one that shocks you into thinking when you hear it—and, once you've heard it, you will never forget it.

Jesus talks elsewhere about passing a camel through the eye of a needle. If you say He is really talking about a little doorway, you take away the whole point. Jesus is using a rhetorical device called hyperbole. The picture is that of a teeny needle and a huge camel, the biggest animal in Palestine. You can picture, can't you, someone trying to thread a camel through that needle's eye?

When He talks about straining out a gnat, the idea is that you are concerned about removing a tiny gnat from your drink, but then swallowing a camel. It's a ridiculous picture: concerned about minuscule matters, unconcerned about mammoth matters! This, too, is the use of a rhetorical device.

You have to understand what the Bible is talking about. But you also need to learn how to use those devices to impress truth upon counselees to help them think and remember. Learn to invent and use crisp, startling aphorisms the way Jesus did. "Don't cast your pearls before swine," "Wherever your treasure is, there will your heart be also," are aphorisms applied to a given situation, but the principle beneath each can be applied to a variety of situations.

Telic Analysis

Finally, the most important of all is telic analysis, which many people ignore. Telic analysis asks, "What did the Holy Spirit intend to do to people through this passage?" In my book, *Teaching to Observe*, I try to get that point across. The counselor teaches his counselee not merely to know but also to *observe*, as Jesus said we should in His last commission to His church. The Great Commission is couched in educational terms, but not education of the Greek sort, which has influenced modern academia. Academia has it all wrong! Academia says "teach to learn meaning." But in the Bible, it's "teach to learn purpose in order to live"—"to *observe* all things whatsoever I have commanded you." Teaching must influence life, or it will lie on soil where it will never bear fruit. One *learns* to *live* to *minister*.

Telic analysis leads you to ask this question as you do all your other analyses of Scripture: "What's the Holy Spirit up to?" "What does He have in mind in giving us this portion of Scripture?" "How does He want people to change or be different as the result of it?" What's the *telos* or purpose of the passage? The Greek word *telos* means "purpose" or "end." What's the goal that God has in mind? When you can answer that, you've got it.

As an example, let's consider the *telos* of John's entire Gospel. Why do you think so many people have been converted through John 1:12, John 3:16, John 3:36, John 14, and so on?

Because that was the *telos* (or purpose) of that Gospel: "These are written that you may believe and that through believing you might have life in His name" (John 20:31). Use the Bible, whether you are discussing a book or just a section of it, for the purpose that it was given. Search out what the Holy Spirit had in mind. Don't use it for *your* purposes or anybody else's. Find the Holy Spirit's purpose, use it for *that* purpose, and you'll find it powerful. It will change people. It will do things to them.

I have sought to do four things as we have considered biblical interpretation and counseling:

1. To highlight the importance of careful, biblical interpretation in counseling.
2. To call on you to become a sound interpreter.
3. To urge you to do solid interpretation before and during counseling sessions. Don't just give people verses. Explain them, interpret them, open them.
4. To attempt to help you develop an exegetical conscience of your own so that you will never use a passage for a purpose for which it was not intended.

A biblical counselor deals with Scripture. When he does so, the Scriptures must be carefully selected, accurately interpreted, rigorously applied, and effectively employed.

Discipling, Counseling, and Church Discipline

Discipling, Counseling, and Church Discipline[1]

Basic Considerations about Discipline and Discipling

CHURCH discipline among modern American congregations almost does not exist. Where it does exist or where it is beginning to be revived today, you can almost—not always, but almost always—point to a man who is doing biblical counseling as the one who brought discipline to that congregation. It is an honest and accurate statement to say that nouthetic counseling has been a strong force in resurrecting and reestablishing biblical discipline in America. It may even be true to say that nouthetic counseling is the strongest force in the United States today.

Yet there's such a long way to go, and the churches are in such a pitiful state that it looks like nothing has been done; comparatively speaking, virtually nothing has been done. But what little has been accomplished has been done by some of you men right here in this room, as well as others like you who, for various reasons, could not be here. You are doing biblical counseling, and you have realized very early in the game, as every man who begins to do biblical counseling must, that one of the absolutely essential tools for doing biblical counseling is church discipline.

If we do not have church discipline, we can't really do an adequate job of helping people out of their problems. We can go just so far and then we're stymied. But we don't need to be stymied. Church discipline provides the means for enabling us to go all the way to the final stages of help.

---

[1] This essay was adapted from an address given to the National Association of Nouthetic Counselors.

In order to become an effective counselor, then, one must understand biblical discipline and its relationship to discipling. So the first thing we need to discuss is what church discipline is.

Interestingly, in English, both the words 'disciple' and 'discipline' come from a common Latin source; they are related. The word-family source in Latin has to do with education. 'Discipline' and 'discipling' are a matter of education. But when one talks about education today, because of the many wrong ideas stemming from Dewey and company, his view of education is quite different from the biblical view behind these words.

In the Old Testament, the word *musar* and in the New Testament the word παιδεω speak about a particular kind of education that incorporates a specific method. Biblical education is education that gets the job done. Today, we don't know much about education like that; all you need to do is read the literature on education to discover that. Book titles scream the fact: *Why Johnny Can't Read, Why Johnny Can't Write, Why Johnny Can't Do Arithmetic*. Education, in general, is a failure in our culture. Just about everybody in the field admits it. So today in America, we don't know much about the kind of education that gets the job done.

The kind of education described in the words *musar* and παιδεω is an education in which elements have been built to assure us that the job will be done. These elements enforce education. Biblical education is education with teeth. That idea is found in both of these words. In fact, these words are also used for chastisement and punishment. They have in them something of the idea of, "If he won't get it any other way, we'll beat it into him." Now we don't know much about that kind of education in our day. You may not like that, but that's in the Word, and I can't fight it. All you have to do is read Hebrews; there, the Old Testament word is quoted from the Greek Septuagint using the New Testament word. There you can see that words speak about the education that God uses, education in which He chastises us and scourges or whips every rebellious son of His. In fact, the writer says that's how we know that we're His sons—because we get a beating, because God gives us a whipping when we need it, because He spanks us. That's the kind of education to which these words refer. It's education that may not be pleasant for the time being; indeed, it may be very painful. It's certainly not something we like, says the writer of Hebrews. But, in the long run, it produces the "peaceful fruit of righteousness." Those ideas lie behind the word 'discipline' in English.

Now also incorporated in the word 'disciple' in the New Testament is the idea of one who is a student or pupil. There are different words in Greek for education and for student, but both ideas are merged in our expression 'church discipline,' due to the fact that it was a student or pupil who was educated by this particular form of education. Coming into the Latin and then to our English, these two words, 'disciple' and 'discipline,' merge with one another. So you can see how they are and are not related linguistically.

A student is one who is instructed or trained by a kind of education that involves discipline. He is trained in knowledge, skills, and wisdom. Knowledge is knowing what to do, skills are acquired by practice in doing it, and wisdom is knowing when, where, and how to do it. And all this comes together in various passages in Scripture. You will see that as you read carefully the wisdom literature. Then, when you read Christ's words about a discipline, you understand what He meant when He said, "When he is fully trained, a student (disciple) will be like his master." He did not say, "will think like him"—that's the modern Greek-based academic educational concept. (When Christian schools today talk about their high academic standards, I shiver down to my toes because I know they're chewing up and spitting out a bunch of kids who haven't got the gray matter to be as 'academic' as they'd like.) The biblical concept involves more: he will "be like him."

What I'm talking about when I speak of biblical education is this: truth is translated into life and life into ministry. The implications of truth are used not only for the benefit of one's own life (selfishly) but also for the honor of God and the blessing of others. That's education, biblically speaking. It is not the practice of stuffing heads full of facts to be repeated in a test, but rather, the process of transforming people by truth so that they may live for God and minister to others. Biblical education leads to love for God and one's neighbor.

All we see involved in the background of these words and the purpose of discipline leads to discipling. Discipline results in discipleship. Discipline creates learning conditions. If we do not have conditions conducive to teaching facts and knowledge, conducive to the practice and development of skills, conducive to transforming knowledge and skills into ministries that honor God, then these ends of education will never be accomplished. Discipline, the ways and means for getting the job done, provides the educational structure for discipling. That's the relationship between the two.

A discipline structure that accomplishes the task provides the atmosphere in which one's education in the knowledge and use of God's truth can take place. One of our modern problems is that we have so little structure. That's why so little education takes place. There's so little structure in our schools. Under modern conditions, it's pretty hard to get an education. And, unfortunately, the same is true of education in the church. Because the church is also an educational institution, discipline belongs in the church.

Maybe you've never thought about the church as an educational institution, but that's what it is. Worship has its place, fellowship has its place, and ministry has its place, but these activities are not primarily what the church does. Education is the fundamental task of the church. Education involves all the rest and is more basic than any one of them. In the Great Commission, we are told about the church's basic task in educational language: "teaching them to observe all things whatsoever I have commanded you." That's the commission the church is given. The purpose of the church is to educate people in the full sense described above. Education is the great thing. But notice, this education is not modern academic education. It is teaching (facts and data must be communicated) but also teaching that is to be 'observed' (i.e., lived and used in ministry). In true, biblical education, all facts must be related to life, but this cannot happen apart from discipline.

Therefore, the ultimate purpose of discipline is always positive, never negative. Most people, however, think of discipline as a negative activity because they associate it with troublemakers and what is sometimes called 'backdoor revivals.' In the public's mind, church discipline exists to get rid of troublemakers. On the contrary, although discipline occasionally involves excommunication, that isn't the purpose of church discipline. It's a sad thing when church discipline is reduced to that. The purpose of church discipline is to create good order in the church of Jesus Christ. Its goal is to produce order in the educational institution, order among the students, order that is conducive to all the educational activities in which they engage. Discipline provides, through structure and design, the climate in which it is possible for learning to take place. That's what discipline is all about. It has a very positive goal—enabling us to learn what God wants us to be and do.

If all of you were walking around here, praying or talking or doing whatever you wanted while I'm trying to talk to you, very little learning would take place. But you're in order, sitting there quietly listening with your mouths shut. Our host set you all up for learning. He got you to stand up; he got you to stretch and breathe deeply so you wouldn't go to sleep, and then he seated you again. He didn't say, "Everybody stand—now do whatever you want to do!" No, his last word to you was, "Be seated!" That was an item of order. Discipline is important in everything that has to do with learning. The entire learning process requires it—whether one is involved in understanding truth, in translating truth into daily living, or in using truth to minister to others in Christ's name. Discipline must begin at the very first stage, proceed into the second, and continue all the way through the third. Discipline is necessary not just in initial teaching but also in the correction of failures or refusals to obey Christ. Discipline is the structure that allows the whole three-step process of teaching-to-observe to occur. It is needed at every point.

When a person's thinking is out of order, he must be disciplined into thinking biblically. When he fails to transform truth into life, he needs discipline and structure to do so. When a person doesn't minister or doesn't know how to, discipline is required. Discipline is the essential factor in the whole process of making Christians like Jesus Christ, whether they are willing or unwilling.

Discipling is not what a lot of people call it today. It's not following some contemporary teacher and becoming like him. Discipling is becoming like Jesus Christ. He is the one we follow. Now, Paul did say, "Be imitators of me," but read the rest of the sentence: "… as I am of Christ." What he states in that command is, "If you see me do anything that isn't in direct imitation of Christ, don't follow it. But if it helps you to see it in another Christian like myself, who is a redeemed sinner like yourself, then learn from my example. But everything you learn has to be ultimately the imitation of Christ." So, we follow Him.

There is a discipling movement that has gone overboard in some areas. Some people dominate other individuals so much that they structure their entire lives for them. For instance, they may tell them whom to marry or not. I don't mean telling believers not to marry unbelievers—we ought always to exhort one another to marry "only in the Lord." What I mean is that they say, "Marry Jane and not Sally Sue." Dominating another person, doing his thinking for him, is not the sort of discipling about which the Bible is talking.

So, then, what are the goals and objectives of discipling and discipline? The honor of Christ is the first and foremost goal, just as it is in everything we do. The second goal is the welfare of the church. There are times when the old leaven has to be purged out, or the whole church will be affected adversely by it. Thirdly, the reclamation of the offender is also in view. We'll talk more about this third objective as we go along.

Now discipline is the right and privilege of every believer, and we must never look upon it as anything less. It is not only a right but also a privilege. Jesus Christ set up discipline in His church. When churches refuse to exercise discipline, they take away a God-given right. They rob their congregations of a precious privilege without which they cannot do. Every congregation must have discipline if its members are to learn, to grow, to be what Jesus Christ wants them to be. Without discipline, a church is chaotic, and the lives of its members suffer.

And so I want to warn you that discipline is not optional. It's mandatory. We will see this in the passages we shall consider later. But let me note one more fact first. Not only is church discipline a right and a privilege, it is a mark of the true church. It provides the only way you can tell the church from the world. If a church allows people who deny Jesus Christ by their words or actions to remain in the congregation, it refuses to draw the line between the world and itself and cannot—at that point at least—claim to be a true church of Christ. The world looks at that congregation and says, "It's no different from a country club." And it really isn't. Together with the preaching of the gospel, the right administration of the sacraments, and unity with other believers, church discipline is a sign or evidence of the true church. Even if you have all the other marks but do not have church discipline, you will destroy your congregation, because there's no way of distinguishing it from the world.

The Function and Process of Christian Discipline

Those are some of the preliminary facts that you must understand about discipline and discipling before you can appreciate how discipline works. Now we must turn to the function of church discipline. We should start our study of discipline in Galatians 5:23. Among the fruits of the Spirit we read about *egkrateia*. This Greek term is usually translated 'self-control' or 'self-discipline.' Discipline is the Spirit's work or fruit. The Holy Spirit is concerned about producing discipline in His church. His concern is not only for love and peace and patience and kindness and goodness and faith and meekness; He's also in the business of producing self-discipline in us. That's where discipline begins and where it ought to continue to grow—in the individual.

All other discipline aims at producing self-discipline, but not in the sense that we are able to produce it, so that it is of ourselves, apart from the Spirit and apart from His Word. Rather, it is *self*-discipline, discipline in the sense that one is matured in the things of God by those teachings which have been implanted in his life and have grown so fruitful that they cause from within a disciplined, structured kind of life. Then those outside influences that the Spirit uses—elders, deacons, friends, parents, and others—can be relaxed. That's what self-discipline is; it's a result of the Spirit working in us through the ministry of His Word. It's the Spirit's fruit.

But there are times when self-discipline is not exercised. Either it hasn't been developed, or one is frustrated in his attempts, or he refuses to exercise it in a certain situation because he likes the sin in which he's involved, at least momentarily. That is what Paul goes on to talk about in Galatians 6:

> *"Brothers, even if a person is caught in some trespass, you who have the Spirit should restore him in a spirit of meekness, watching out for*

yourselves so you won't be tempted too. Bear one another's burdens and so fulfill Christ's law."

If a Christian can't, won't, or doesn't know how to exercise self-discipline in a given situation, consequently falls into sin, becomes entrapped, and does not extricate himself from that sin, it becomes the duty of every Christian who discovers this fact to get involved and exercise informal discipline. Note: at this first stage, discipline normally would be informal. Of course, the sin could be so wide open and the person's rebellion so arrogant that discipline might have to be started at a more formal stage by the church elders. But usually it will be informal at the beginning.

Consider, for example, a husband and wife whose marriage does not seem as good as it ought to be. They're not filing for divorce; he's not running out of the house and getting drunk every night or staying away from home and drinking up his paycheck; and she isn't running around with other men. There is nothing like that, but you have detected problems: nasty words now and then are exchanged between them; you often sense coldness; the kids tell you about other difficulties; word comes back that things are not what they ought to be. In one way or another, you discover the growing rift, so you must go and, in an informal way, offer help.

There may be a communication problem. The communication dilemma demonstrates why a third party is necessary and why counseling may be necessary. The communication dilemma is this: communication is needed to solve problems, including a communication problem! What do you do when someone is in a dilemma in which communication is needed, but the problem itself is a breakdown in communication? When the lines have been snipped, somebody else must grab both ends of the wires and hold them together so that the parties involved can start talking again. Informal discipline often will do the job.

Informal discipline may not be enough, however, when schismatic tendencies are present. According to Titus 3:10, after you have confronted a person nouthetically once or twice (as it says in the original Greek), you are to get rid of that person quickly. Some of our churches do not allow for a quick excommunication of schismatic people; the process they require takes too long. Paul says if the person is still acting schismatically after two admonitions, excommunicate him. There is reason for haste: if you wait too long he'll split your church. If he's really schismatic, he must be dealt with quickly.

Let's talk now about the ordinary process of discipline that is described in Matthew 18:15 and the verses following. Consider, for example, two brothers with whom we see discipline proceeding much more slowly through its various stages. These two brothers have a problem. Let's say they have a dust-up and part in a huff; they are both huffing, but one of them is puffing as well. Since the first has only been huffing, by now he has calmed down and realizes, "Well, I've got to do something about this difficulty. Bill is still puffing, although I'm over my huffing. So, I guess I'd better talk with him and get this thing straightened out. I know we've got to be reconciled." So Joe goes out to talk to Bill. He says, "You know when we had that talk a while ago, I …"

"I sure do know about that talk!"

"Well, Bill, I came over to try to get things straightened out …"

"No way are we going to get it squared away! Not after what you said to me!"

"Well, now Bill, wait a minute. I didn't say all that much."

"Oh yeah? It seems to me every time you want to get things straightened out, you come excusing yourself. Get out of here—fast!" And Bill slams the door.

It seems that Bill is even more upset now. Should Joe go and get one or two others, as Matthew 18:16 says? No, not yet; it's still too early. Bill is still puffing and huffing. Joe ought to take another shot or two at it, perhaps waiting a day or two for Bill to calm down. In most cases, reconciliation will then take place. But, what if it doesn't? Let's see.

"Hello, Bill."

"Yes, I'm here. What did you come back for? I told you to get out; I don't want to see you anymore!"

"Well, I thought maybe you would have calmed down a little bit by today, so that …"

"Calmed down! After what you said to me you're coming over here again?"

"Well, now, wait a minute, Bill. Wait a minute; wait, wait, WAIT!" Bang! Bill slams the door.

Two days later Joe says, "Well, I'll make one more try, but this time I'll call before I go. Maybe having a little time to calm himself down before I arrive will help."

So Joe calls Bill. "Hello, Bill, this is J …" (Click!) Bill won't even talk to Joe. That is bad news! "If he will not hear you, then take one or two others and go see him" (Matthew 18:16).

(Knock, knock) "Pastor, I need your help. Would you come along with one of the elders or the deacons?"

"Sure Joe. I'm glad you came." So all three arrive at Bill's house.

"What are you all doing here?"

"Well, Joe has a problem, Bill."

"Yes, I know he's got a problem. He is a problem!"

"We've come to resolve that problem. May we come in?"

"Well, I don't see any need for that."

"Yes, there is a need; we want to straighten this matter out. You know you should straighten things out. Jesus Christ says so; it's He who won't let this matter rest. You and Joe must be reconciled; there is no other option."

"Well, I could be reconciled with most people, certainly with you, Pastor, and with Elder So-and-So, but that guy? Never! Do you know what he said to me?"

"We'll find that out in the course of our conversation I'm sure, but right now that's not the point. The point is that no matter what he said, if he's willing to repent and seek your forgiveness, you've got to grant it. That's what the Bible teaches (Luke 17:3ff)."

"I might be able to forgive somebody something, but not him that!" And so it goes until finally every attempt has been made, once, twice, three times, or more. Usually, few situations go this far without reconciliation being affected. But some do. Suppose this one does. The door is slammed in the face of the pastor and the elder and 'click' goes the telephone. In the next verse of Matthew 18, we read what to do: "if he will not heed you." (The original meaning is that he 'ignores' you. The only other use of this word is in Mark 5, where we read, "they ignored the

Lord Jesus.") If he ignores all entreaties and turns down and disregards every offer of help, then Christ says, "tell it to the church." The operative idea that appears in Matthew 18:15f is not hearing, for at each point, what moves discipline to the next stage is the refusal to hear.

Now we have to think about this matter. How is telling the church done, and what does that involve? Here's where I want to spend a little more time, because I don't think enough has been said about this in other places.

Certainly, telling it to the church means first telling the pastor (if he doesn't already know) and those in authority. The elders of the church, representing the church, should then sit down with Bill, talk to him about his behavior, and try to persuade him to obey Jesus Christ. And they must speak with the authority He has given them. You see, at first it was a private matter, involving one-on-one, informal discipline in which his Christian brother confronted him after self-discipline failed. Then, as the problem moved into the second stage, it was still only semi-formal when the pastor and the elder went and talked with the two parties. Since it could not be settled at those lower levels, it has now become a formal matter and must be officially told to the church.

Now the church gets involved. The elders' exercising their authority as men who have rule over Joe is the first way the church gets involved in stage three. The elders attempt to persuade Bill from the Word of God and warn him of the danger of not listening to what Christ has to say. If he does repent, of course, at any one of these stages, the process quietly ceases right there and everybody rejoices. (I will cover what happens then later on.) But let's suppose, for the sake of the argument, that Bill refuses to acknowledge their authority, does not heed their words and remains in his unreconciled condition. In such situations, Joe's status must be told to the church at large.

You may wonder about that, and I want to go into it just a bit more deeply. First, look at 2 Thessalonians 3. In verse 14, Paul writes, "Whoever doesn't obey what we've said ..." There Paul is speaking as an elder, as a church authority along with others (in this case he is also speaking as an apostle, and you can't get more authority than that!). It is Paul and the others with him saying to the local congregation, "Whoever doesn't obey what we say in this letter, mark that person." It is evident that they first made an attempt that failed. Now they call on the members of the congregation for help. Like Paul, the officers of the church in our example address the whole congregation and instruct them about their obligations toward Bill. The congregation needs to know about Bill's refusal in order to obey the elders according to the authority of Christ invested in them. They are told not to "mix with him." The congregation needs to know his condition so that by obeying the command not to mix with Bill, they can cause him to "become ashamed of himself." In other words, hopefully, this action will bring him to repentance.

Paul continues, "Don't regard him as an enemy, but rather counsel him (there's our word again: νουθετεω) as a brother." It is important to note that during the third stage of discipline, Bill still must be considered a "brother." And the whole church here is called upon to become Bill's counselors.

When Paul says, "Don't mix with him" (the word means 'mingle or mix'), what he's saying is, "You cannot have an ordinary relationship with him while he continues to reject Christ's authority." He means that when Bill says, "Hey, Tom, let's go out and have a round of golf", Tom has to say to him, "You know, Bill, I'd love to play golf with you, but things just aren't straight between you and Joe. If I went out and played golf with you as though everything were all right, I'd be condoning what's going on, and I wouldn't be helping you. I'll be glad to sit down with you, Bill, and talk to you about what you ought to do in regard to Joe. If you want me to spend some time doing that, I'll be glad to, but until the matter is straightened out, things aren't right between us either. This is not only a problem between you and Joe; it's a matter of refusing to relate yourself to another part of the body in the proper way, and I'm a part of that body."

Consider a second example. Mary is rebelling against church discipline rightly exercised and should be treated in the same way. When she asks Mildred, "How would you like to go shopping?", Mildred should reply, "No, Mary, I'm so sorry. I can't. Things aren't right between you and Suzy. I'd love to talk to you about the problem so we can get on a normal basis again, but you have broken fellowship with us. There's something wrong with the body. You are tearing it apart; until you stop and those wounds are healed, the whole body will suffer. We're all concerned. It's not just Susie that you're having problems with. The whole body is suffering; you are making us all hurt." When you hit your thumb with a hammer, the whole body is affected; everything you do is affected by the pain. You try to put on your coat—ow! You start clapping at the opera—ouch! The whole body is affected when one part is in trouble. And so, after the leadership has failed in its attempt to bring about submission to Christ, the congregation must be informed so that the whole body may admonish or counsel the offender as a brother or sister. Tell it to the Church! We don't often do things like that, but we ought to. Christ said so.

In 1 Corinthians 5, there is more information that cannot be treated in detail here, but at least must be mentioned. It is interesting to discover in this chapter that one can mingle with an unbeliever but can not mix with the so-called brother who is unrepentant. Why? Because one expects dogs to bark and cats to meow, but he doesn't expect dogs to meow or cats to bark. Fornication, lying, and other sinful ways of life are normal for unbelievers, but not normal for believers. Yet, when we fail to exercise church discipline, we treat the unrepentant as though it were normal for him to rebel against Christ and as if that is of no consequence to us. There's not much sense appealing to an unbeliever to obey Christ; he can't, and therefore we need to talk to him about the gospel. So we help a believer who is under formal discipline when we don't mix with him. We admonish him in order to help him, recognizing that he has broken fellowship.

In 1 Corinthians 5 Paul says," Don't even eat with him." What does that mean? It means fellowship. Eating was the sign of fellowship; when the brethren met together, they sat down and ate. We can't have normal fellowship with a so-called brother who is rebelling against the authority of Jesus Christ rightfully exercised by the church. That is what Paul says we must acknowledge by our actions.

Unless you tell the members of the church these things and carefully instruct them, as Paul did in his letters, few people will know what to do. The rest will have only a partial idea or not even the faintest idea about how to treat Bill. Then the help offered by the congregation as a whole would be weak, confusing, and ineffective, if there is any help at all.

If careful teaching is not given, there will be some members who think Bill and Mary are being persecuted. Then they are likely to begin commiserating with them and defending them; the first thing you know, you've got a split in your church. You may have thought you were going to avoid division by not telling the church and not following Jesus' directions. Not on your life! It is only when all involved understand both the goals and the process of church discipline, as well as their part in reclaiming a brother or sister, that you avoid such division.

Of course, if Bill won't even hear the church and ignores the help of all the brothers and sisters, then Christ says let him be "as a heathen and tax collector." That means treat him as though he were a heathen and a tax collector—excommunicate him. The heathen and tax collector were outside the body, not a part of it; you have to treat Bill as an unbeliever. That doesn't say that you are calling him an unbeliever—there's a great deal of difference between these two things. But neither must you call him a believer or treat him as one. Earlier when Paul says, "Admonish him as a brother," he is saying to treat him on the basis that he is a believer. But here Paul is saying, "Treat him on the basis that he isn't." What you're making in both instances is a functional judgment, i.e., a judgment about how you will function in relation to Bill and how you will treat him.

You must have some relationship with him, so this functional judgment, or relational judgment, determines how you, as a member of the church, and how the church as a whole will relate to him now that he is out of the church. You do not relate to him as a believer, even though in his heart he really may be one who is in rebellion and who eventually will repent when he's handed over to Satan for the destruction of the flesh in order that his spirit may be saved in the day of Jesus Christ (1 Corinthians 5:5). You do not know his heart. All you can deal with is what he says and how he acts. Both his words and actions are like those of an unbeliever who refuses to submit to the authority of Christ. He acts like an unbeliever, so you must treat him as one.

Even after Bill is excommunicated, you still are to think of his welfare and to try to win him. You hope that if he is a believer in rebellion, excommunication will bring repentance. But you have to treat him as though he were an unbeliever because he has treated himself as though he were one. He has denied Christ, denied the church, denied the authority of the Lord, denied the teaching of the Word, denied everything down the line. He is in a contumacious condition, and out he must go, because that's where he puts himself by his action. So if he puts himself out there as an unbeliever among unbelievers, that's how you have to treat him. You start evangelizing him, just as you would any unbeliever; you don't ignore him.

Now remember that you haven't made a judgment about Bill's heart; you can't judge hearts. Only God knows what is really in his heart. That is God's business. It says in 1 Samuel 16:7, "Man looks on the outward appearance, but God looks on the heart." So God makes the heart judgment. Yet you and I have to make a functional judgment as ministers in the church of Christ. We have to tell our people, "Okay, we now must evangelize Bill as an unbeliever."

So we judge the tree by its fruit. Even the Lord, in the final judgment, judges by fruit. Have you noticed that in the judgment scene in Matthew 25, judgment is made on the basis of works? Judgment about whether a person is saved is made on the basis of fruit. Salvation is by faith, but judgment is by fruit. In the Bible, judgment is always made on the basis of fruit, which is the evidence of salvation by faith. Justification takes place by faith, but judgment is made on the basis of fruit. That's the only basis on which you and I can work.

But God's discipline continues. Suppose Bill ultimately comes to realize his sin. It's tough out there in that world. Bill didn't realize how bad it would be without the fellowship of the brethren, having removed himself from the preaching of the Word and been buffeted about by Satan, with no encouragement from the church. God tells you to turn him over to Satan to let him have a go at him. Hopefully, if Bill is a believer, he will be brought to his senses. Sure enough, let's say that he comes to himself, as the prodigal son did in the far country. In the far country—that's exactly where he is. Well, then, what happens? Bill comes back repentant. Now what happens? Do you just ignore that? Do you just receive him quietly? No. You told his sin to the church and how to treat him; now you've got to tell the church something else. The church has to be informed of Bill's repentance.

At this point, it is essential to read 2 Corinthians 2:6, where Paul refers to "the punishment." By the way, the church exercises the right of disciplinary punishment; discipline is not merely administrative. It is Jesus Christ punishing the individual through this process of instruction. A part of the instructional process, we saw, is punishment; that's how children are trained. The word Paul uses for punishment is επιτιμια, which means a restriction on one's rights as a citizen. And by excommunication, that is just what you've done: taken away one's rights of citizenship in Christ's church. The "punishment that the majority inflicted" upon the person in Corinth had been sufficient, Paul says; but now, as then, some people may want it to continue.

Some would say, "Let's wait and see if he really means what he says. Let's see if this repentance is genuine. We'll wait and see. We should wait a while because this sin was really gross. Even if we restore him, we'd better not let Bill do much for at least three years. We may let him serve at the men's breakfast if he gets up early enough, but he should do a little penance first."

What do you think of that? It is all wrong: "the punishment the majority has inflicted is sufficient." So, instead of going on with it, you should rather forgive and comfort him so that he won't be overwhelmed by too much pain. Therefore, says Paul, "reaffirm your love" to him.

Three things are done to restore Bill at this point. These three things are essential and involve the whole church. Not only must the members be told that Bill has repented, but also they must be instructed in their duties of restoration. First they must forgive him (verse 7). To forgive means you can't keep bringing up the past. When God forgives, His forgiveness comes in the form of a promise: "Your sins and your iniquities will I remember against you no more" (Isaiah 43:25). Forgiveness is a promise not to bring up the matter again. Don't exhume the bones periodically and beat Bill over the head with them. Bury them and forget where you buried them. Forgive him.

The next term in 2 Corinthians 2:7, παρακαλεω, is an interesting word. Sometimes it means to comfort, sometimes to urge, sometimes to act as an advocate. It is a broad word. One of the reasons we didn't choose it for "to counsel" is because it's so broad. It includes counseling, but it also includes a lot of other things. It could even mean picking up a man's suitcase and carrying it for him if he couldn't. Whatever help he needs, you give him—that's the idea. Perhaps it is best translated to assist or to help.

A man in Bill's situation is going to need help. He's going to need help to reestablish friendships, help to reestablish himself in the body, help and encouragement not to fall back into the same sin. You're going to have to help him set up radical amputation to structure against the sin in the future. You're going to have to do all sorts of things to help this man. And every member of the body ought to be alert to give whatever help is needed to assist him in the restoration process.

Thirdly, Paul says that the church must reaffirm its love for Bill. That word reaffirm is not just a warm word that means," We love you and it's nice to have you back, Bill. "It's κυροω, which is a very specialized term referring to a formal readmission of someone into a body. It is a legal term. Just as Bill was formally excommunicated, removed from the body, kept from the Lord's table, and deprived of all the rights and privileges of God's covenant people, so too he must now be reinstated formally and officially into all that he had before. He's not to be considered a second-class citizen, and he does not need to undergo a period of penance. He must be declared a part of the body as much as anyone else. The closest thing to it in the case of the prodigal son was that great banquet, the robe, the ring, and the fat calf; there was a declaration by the father that his son was restored, and all the signs of restoration were present.

This restoration, then, involves a declaration by the body. In fact, the declaration ought to be recorded in the elders' Book of Minutes so that there will be some standing word that this matter has been dealt with satisfactorily before God and the church of Jesus Christ and is now closed. This notation should be made for Bill's protection as well as for the welfare of the church so that if, in the days to come, somebody brings up this matter again, those concerned can say, "That matter was dealt with. If you don't believe me, you will find the fact in the Minutes." A formal declaration that Bill is restored is the way to finalize the restoration in a good and solid manner.

So, in summarizing the whole of Christian discipline, consider the following diagram. You will note that each stage broadens to include a larger number of persons.

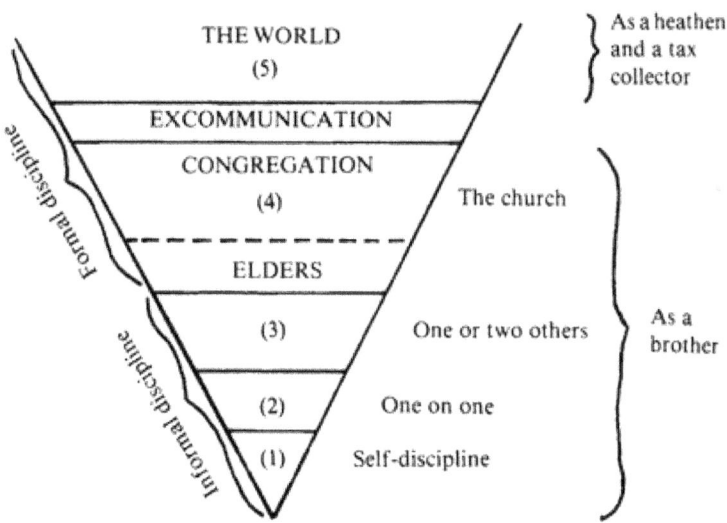

Now I want to emphasize one more thing: you must recognize and respect church discipline. I don't mean just in your local church, but also in other churches. It really discourages me when a church finally gets the courage to discipline someone lovingly, for the right purposes, in the right way, only to find that all these efforts are undercut by another congregation. Too often, when a church excommunicates someone, he runs across the street to a church where the minister, one who preaches the gospel (of course not as well as you do, but one who preaches the gospel) and his people say, "Oh, it's so nice to have you. Welcome!" What a horrible tragedy!

What can you do about that? I have a suggestion-a concrete, practical suggestion: get together with the pastor of every Bible-believing church in your community and discuss this matter. You can't agree on everything, but one thing you ought to be able to agree on is the recognition of one another's discipline. Talk about the whole process of church discipline. Work it out in practical terms and then say, "Here are the steps that we all agree to take when someone runs from a church." Your aim is to develop a common method of handling the church-hopper. When he comes to your church and you see him, you say to yourself, "He may be hopping." He's there a couple of weeks and pretty soon, when you are talking to him at the door, you ask, "Are you new here in town?" He says, "Oh, no." "Are you a Christian?" "Yeah, I'm a Christian." "Well, where have you been going to church?" "Oh, I used to go over there, you know." "Did you change your doctrine?" "Oh, no, things are just so much nicer over here in your church, and the preaching is so much better." "Well, thank you, but on the other hand, why did you leave? The pastor is a faithful shepherd of Jesus Christ. He preaches the Word. I know he doesn't have all his i's dotted and t's crossed the way I do, but he preaches the Word. Why is it that you're not over there with your shepherd? You're his sheep."

He answers, "Well, you know, young people are so much kinder than they are. They were sort of rough on me. I had a little trouble getting along with them. I didn't like all that was going on. So I thought I'd come over here." "Oh, you had problems over there?" "Yeah, I had a few problems." "With the pastor?" "No, with a couple of deacons." "Well, I'd be happy to help you get that matter straightened out so that you can return to the flock where you belong." "Oh, no, I'm not interested in that. I'd like to stay here." "But you haven't straightened that matter out. Now, if they really thought you ought to come over here because some point of your doctrine has changed radically, or something like that, we could work that out between the two churches, but you're leaving on the wrong basis. You must not leave because you've had a problem with somebody. You have to get that problem resolved. You have to be reconciled with that person."

"Oh, no, I'm not going to do that. Thanks for your offer, Pastor, but I don't think I'll see you again." He then runs to a third church down the street, and they say, "Nice to see you here. Whose church are you from?" And he says, "———." "Oh, have you had a problem over there?" "Yeah." "Well, we'll gladly go back with you and help get it resolved." "Hey! What's going on around here?"

The first thing you know, the church-hopper is in trouble. The only places left to run are to the liberal churches in town, and he can't do that.

That's the way it ought to be. But you may say, "Our whole church growth has come from taking in such people." Then there's something wrong with you and your church. Let me tell you, you don't do anybody a favor, least of all yourself and your church, when you take a Jonah on board.

I had gone to a new church as its pastor and hadn't been there two weeks before I received a phone call from a pastor in a nearby community. He said, "Do you know Mr. and Mrs. So-and-So?" I said, "I don't even know the names of all of my elders well yet. I just arrived on the scene." And he said, "Well, they tell me they used to be members up there in your church. It seems that something a bit strange went on up there." I said, "I don't know, but I'll find out." So I talked to the elders and they said, "Oh, Mr. and Mrs. So-and-So? We worked long and hard with them for about a year. In fact, we worked too long and too hard. They were divisive people. We should have been done with them a lot sooner. They tried to split this church. In the end, they actually did lead a couple of people off. We finally found it necessary to excommunicate them." Here was a church that did its job.

So I got on the phone, called that pastor and said, "Look out. Those people are excommunicated. If they repent and become reconciled to our church and yet want to go to your church, we can work that out. But first, they should come back here and deal with their problems before they go anywhere else. They have been excommunicated. They can't join your church. You'd better watch out for them." He thanked me, and I didn't hear any more about it. Several months later I was in a meeting and I met this same pastor. I said, "Whatever happened to Mr. & Mrs. So-and-So?" He said, "Them? Oh." I said, "What do you mean, 'oh?'" "We took them in anyway, and they just walked off with several of our families!"

You don't get any bargains when you welcome somebody who is running from his responsibilities. That's one reason so many churches split. They've taken in people on the wrong basis. I want to urge you to start respecting each other's discipline. Even if you can't agree with everything done or taught in another church, if there is faithful preaching of the Word, then respect the discipline of that church.

Discipline is the means to discipleship, because there can't be any real learning or teaching apart from the proper structure. Discipline is the means of creating, maintaining, and restoring those structures that lead to the building of strong disciples of the Lord Jesus Christ. You can't afford to be without it.

www.ingramcontent.com/pod-product-compliance
Lightning Source LLC
Chambersburg PA
CBHW071309110426
42743CB00042B/1237